VINCENTE MINNELLI
and the Film Musical

VINCENTE MINNELLI
and the Film Musical

Joseph Andrew Casper

SOUTH BRUNSWICK AND NEW YORK: A. S. BARNES AND COMPANY
LONDON: THOMAS YOSELOFF LTD

A. S. Barnes and Co., Inc.
Cranbury, New Jersey 08512

Thomas Yoseloff Ltd
Magdalen House
136-148 Tooley Street
London SE1 2TT, England

Library of Congress Cataloging in Publication Data

Casper, Joseph Andrew.
Vincente Minnelli and the film musical.

Bibliography: p.
1. Moving-pictures, Musical—History and criticism.
2. Minnelli, Vincente. I. Title.
ML2075.C37   782.8′1′0924 [B]   75-20614
ISBN 0-498-01784-2

PRINTED IN THE UNITED STATES OF AMERICA

Each one has a guardian angel who watches over us . . .
  (Mother Superior to Yolanda, *Yolanda and the Thief*)

This book is dedicated to mine . . .
  Irwin R. Blacker

CONTENTS

PREFACE

One of the intriguing ironies that contributes to this best and worst of times in American film is the ever-increasing, unselfconscious interest and study of the Hollywood film, its products, and its craftsmen, despite the ever-quickening disintegration of same. The precedents set by our transatlantic cousins are encouraging. Demythologization, which turns out to praise, and not bury, Caesar, while suppressing once and for all that most condescending of queries, "can anything good come from Hollywood?", is pleasantly surprising. The security of nostalgia, the sympathy for the dying, and, no doubt, a resentment of the current cinemobile available-light, garbled-soundtrack school of filmmaking have also contributed to this devotion to the Hollywood film. This study is part of that devotion.

Specifically, this work is a study of Vincente Minnelli, a major American director, commercially and critically acclaimed, whose career of more than twenty-five years comprises thirteen musicals and numerous musical sequences,[1] eleven melodramas and one episode from a tripartite melodramatic film,[2] and eight comedies.[3] That he has contributed to the development of the film musical is an accepted fact. The precise nature of his contribution and the exact methods entailed, however, are less certain. No definitive American or English study has been devoted to Minnelli's work, let alone to the above aspects of it. Frenchman Francois Truchaud's *Minnelli* is the only attempt to bridge this gap in film history. This study is another attempt.

More specifically, this study is concerned with Minnelli's musicals. The film musical, since it contains, and often attempts to unite all the elements that Aristotle deduces in his *Poetics* as constituting the full and genuine poetic experience, simultaneously and at their most intense points, thereby taxing the resources of the medium, has the theoretical potential to be the most highly developed genre of the fiction film. The musical is also one of the most commercial film genres. After tabulating the boxoffice plusses and minusses (since it can be one of the most commercially disastrous), the musical still comes out in the black. As well, the musical is an indigenous American genre.

In spite of the first fact and because of the second (anything popular runs the risk of being berated, patronized, even eventually condemned) and third (the "indigenously American" smacks of being naive and second-rate), this genre is considered among artists, aestheticians, and audience to be the least inherently respectable, the least inherently valuable form. Many people, when they make, review, or attend musicals, feel they are slumming. In Sturges' *Sullivan's Travels*

(1941), the girl at the owl wagon tells comedy director John L. Sullivan: "I don't care for musicals. They hurt my ears." Tom Jones, lyricist of *The Fantasticks* and *I Do I Do,* in an article, "For People Who Hate Musicals" in the *New York Times* stated:

> The musical-haters whom I encounter are generally quite intelligent people. They tend to be, in fact, what one might call the 'intelligentsia' (critics, teachers, creative people, etc.). They dislike musicals because they find them frivolous. They point out that a great many of the big musical shows are hollow, gaudy, nervous shams . . .[4]

Librettist and lyricist Arthur Laurents in an article, "Look, Girls, There's the Man with Our Tap Shoes!" in the *New York Times Magazine* wrote:

> The musical is most deplored . . . because many think it never has been and never will be anything but trivial (and there are many who want it to stay that way) . . . What I do ask for is more respect for musical theatre from all people who work in it. More respect should produce more artistry and in the end, that is what makes any theatre form less trivial. That and content.[5]

By unraveling the musical's most sophisticated aesthetic in Minnelli's work and by discussing its significance in one's life, this volume attempts a farewell to this snobbism.

ACKNOWLEDGMENTS

This book, like a Minnelli musical, is a community effort. I would like to acknowledge and thank the members of this community: The Maryland Province of the Society of Jesus for encouragement and support; Dr. Bernard Kantor, Chairman of USC's Cinema Department, Professors Irwin Blacker, Arthur Knight, Allan Casebier, and playwright Anthony P. Scully for their suggestions in the preparation of the text; MGM's Daniel Melnick, producer Howard W. Koch, Film Incorporated's Walter Calmette, and Dr. Robert Knutson of USC's Special Collections for the use of films and photographs; caricaturist John Manning for the cover design; photographer Joseph Fornal for portraits; Gerald Lee Patton for typing; Mario Beguiristain and Nolan Miller for research; and, of course, Vincente Minnelli for conversation, materials, and inspiration.

VINCENTE MINNELLI
and the Film Musical

1
TRADITIONS: MINNELLI

VARIETY AND VAUDEVILLE

If the time of Vincente Minnelli's birth is up for grabs, the place is not. He was born in a trunk in Chicago.

His Italian father Vincente, orchestrator and pianist, his French mother Nina Lebeau (Mina Gennel on stage), directress and leading lady, his uncle the manager, a cast of ten, two carloads of equipment, and a thousand-seat tent comprised *The Minnelli Brothers Big Dramatic Company* that played one-week stands in the Midwest. Their fare consisted of suburbanized versions of Broadway hit melodramas followed by a concert of songs, dances, comic routines and skits, juggling, and magic acts. Theirs was one of the numerous types of variety entertainments, along with the olios of the minstrels, boat shows, specialty shows, medicine shows, circus concerts, dime museums or store shows with the "professor" out front, and the blue-specialties that played almost every street corner, vacant lot or field, slab or honky-tonk, tavern, hall, or stage of America in the late 1800s and early 1900s.

By the age of three, Vincente appeared as Little Willie in *East Lynn* and went on to act in such pieces as *The Little Minister, The Golden Giant Mine,* and *Uncle Tom's Cabin*. The boy was also a critic-in-residence, observing that "eyebrows were too black" or that there was "not enough red"[1] and the company's most enthralled patron, as his father recalled to a reviewer.

Through the tactics of Edward Franklin Albee, Benjamin Franklin Kelly, and Frederick Francis Proctor, these forms of variety and acts proper to them become streamlined into a commodity known as "vaudeville". Circuits were mapped out and theatres erected. The policy of continuous, as opposed to two-a-day, performances went into effect. The format was regimented and the acts standardized. This lucrative industry, along with the increasing popularity of another form of mechanized entertainment, the movies, put an end to the Minnelli travelling troupe.

Stranded in Delaware-on-Ohio, what else could the eight-year-old former actor, critic, and theatre-devotee do but enroll in St. Mary's grammar school? During these brief years of academia, he secured a job as an apprentice to the local signpainter. One weekend, the owner of the local picture house commissioned the painter to redo his canvas curtain. Since the boss kept Saturday and Sunday sacred, the assignment fell into the fourteen-year-old assistant's lap. Early Monday morning, the design of the thirty-foot drop curtain was completed.

A graduate of Willis High at sixteen, Minnelli migrated to Chicago and worked as a window dresser at Marshall Field's and then as a theatrical photographer's assistant at the Stone Art Gallery. An exhibition of Whistler's oils and etchings, the first paintings he had even seen, inspired him to be a painter. He devoured books on Whistler and on painting in general. Returning from the theatre, which he had habituated since his arrival in the Windy City, he began making crayon sketches of scenes that most excited him.

On the merit of these sketches, Frank Cambria, art director of the Balaban and Katz theatre chain, employed the precocious youngster as costumier and, eventually, set designer and stage manager at the palatial Chicago Theatre which featured a stage show and a movie. Here, Minnelli received credit for his first stage production, *Birdland Fantasy*. When the organization took over the New York Paramount, Minnelli did too.

REVUE

During his five-year stint at the Paramount, Minnelli was engaged to design a three hundred foot curtain for the 1931 edition of Earl Carroll's *Vanities* and costumes with Charles LeMaire for subsequent editions. *Vanities* was a type of musical entertainment known as a revue, a series of unrelated acts—songs, dances, comic sketches, acrobatics, production numbers, tableaus—whose main ingredients of personality, cheesecake, pageantry (lavish sets and costumes, phenomenal stage-effects, supernumeraries galore), and topical satire were crystallized and perfected by Florenz Ziegfeld's *Follies* in the first decade of the twentieth century.

When Minnelli arrived, this form had already seen the three periods of Ziegfeld's work, Messers Shubert's *Passing Show Revues* (1911–1925), which aped Ziegfeld's *Follies*, John Murray Anderson's *Greenwich Village Follies* (1919–1928), with its distinctive avant-garde, ultra-sophisticated tone, Irving Berlin and Sam Harris' *Music Box Revues* (1921–1924), which concentrated upon glorifying Broadway songs within a set frame, the *Grand Street Follies* of 1922-1927,

and the *Garrick Gaieties* of 1925–1926, a new kind of revue—simple, intimate, smart, and highly critical of the status quo. The *George White Scandals* (1919–1939), noted for their scores by the Gershwins and Brown, DeSylva and Henderson were still in vogue.

Carroll's *Vanities* (1923–1932) was an attempt to outdo Ziegfeld, especially in the female pulchritude department. Ziegfeld's "glorifying the American girl" became Carroll's "through these portals pass the most beautiful girls in the world." Robert Baral in his *Revue: The Great Broadway Period*, remarked that Carroll was

the potentate of the living curtain motif . . . He went overboard with seasonal floods of girls posed against plume curtains, hanging gardens, gates of roses, swings, ladders, bejeweled ruffles, chandeliers, horns of plenty, the prehistoric, the futuristic, bottles, veils, glass scimitars, spunglass, mosaic glass, friezes of metal, bars of gold, revolving flowers, subterranean fog, more feathers and virgins wrapped in cellophane . . . He built his platforms, pedestals, and stairways much more economically out of large hollow cubes that could receive colored lights and create eye-filling splashes.[2]

With a turn of the cubes, a new stage was set.

Besides the series-revues, in which one man actually produced a show stamped with his personality, there were some individual revues. Most of these, certainly the better ones, used a slight framework or structure—a subject, a theme, or a persona upon which to fling its frippery.

In 1932, about to depart for Paris to paint, Minnelli was cajoled by Grace Moore to do the sets and costumes for her *DuBarry*, a fustian

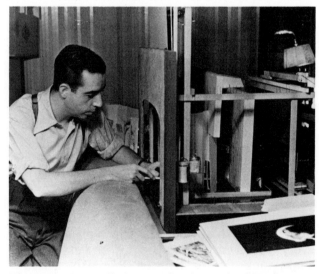

The young Minnelli designs for the Radio City theatres.

16

Viennese operetta with the music of Carl Millocher. This endeavor to revive old world operetta, which along with its naturalized child, the American operetta of Victor Herbert, Rudolph Friml, and Sigmund Romberg, had monopolized the American musical stage from the last quarter of the nineteenth century to the first quarter of the twentieth, was ill-timed and embarrassing. Every cent, however, of the $75,000 shelled out for the decor and fabrics showed.

The Radio City theatres, the Roxy and the recently erected Music Hall, beckoned the following year. With the "e" rightfully restored to his first name at the advice of a numerologist, Vincente designed costumes for a family of about forty roxyettes, thirty-six ballet girls, sixty singers, scores of extras, and guest artists who came and went with each weekly show. In less than six months, he assumed the responsibilities of art director of the Music Hall. On the world's largest stage, which boasted interlocking platforms, elevators, and a lighting system that rivalled the heavens, the young Minnelli supervised, designed, and lit these mini-revues that shared the bill with movies. No holdovers being the house policy, the wonder-worker spun a miracle each week. His own production, *Coast to Coast*, the ballet *El Amor Brujo*, and his *Scheherazade*, with

six scenes and a dozen costume changes for a company of around two hundred singers and dancers, were landmark entertainments.

Minnelli, while at the Music Hall, was lured by the Shuberts to direct their revue *At Home Abroad* (1935), with book and score by Howard Dietz and Arthur Schwartz, dances by Gene Snyder and Harry Losee, and personalities Beatrice Lillie, Ethel Waters, Herb Williams, Eleanor Powell, Reginald Gardiner, and Paul Haakan. This critically acclaimed and commercially successful revue at the Winter Garden showed

what an American, wearied of his own country, might hope to enjoy should he make his home abroad. The curtain rises on a darkened stage. A man asleep in a huge bed is in the throes of a nightmare. He is tortured by fantastic visions of much-publicized celebrities of the day amusingly shown by cleverly manipulated marionettes. When the man awakens he promptly determines to escape from them all by going abroad.[3]

Steamboat Whistle, staged in a heartwarming West Indian wharf setting, *Death In The Afternoon Ballet*, depicting a bullfighter dressing to meet his death in the bullring, and the finale, *Pomp and Peculiar Circumstances*, set against a swirling baroque gold lamé perspective, dazzled the audi-

A sketch for the "Death in the Afternoon Ballet," At Home Abroad.

17

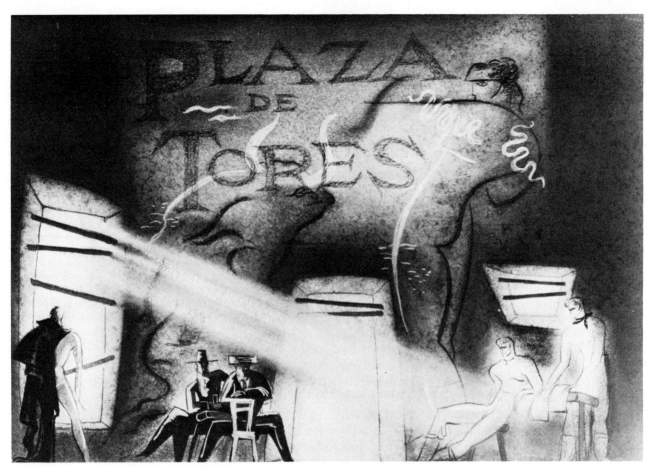

One of the surrealistic designs, Ziegfeld Follies of 1936.

ence. With this revue, Minnelli emerged as one of the top stagers on Broadway. The *New Yorker* acclaimed him as a "prodigy."[4]

Even after Ziegfeld's death in 1932, revivals of the *Follies* continued—*Ziegfeld Follies* of 1933, 1936, 1943, the MGM film musical of 1945, 1956, and 1957 with two editions, the straw hat edition of 1960, and the Australian version of 1960. Minnelli concocted two of them—the 1936 version and the film musical.

For the 1936 edition, staged by John Murray Anderson, scored by Vernon Duke and Ira Gershwin, written by David Freedman and Moss Hart, choreographed by Robert Alton and George Balanchine, the white-haired boy did the sets and costumes. The cast included Fannie Brice, Bob Hope, Gertrude Niesen, Hugh O'Connell, Harriet Hoctor, Eve Arden, Judy Canova, the Nicholas Brothers, Edgar Bergen, and Josephine Baker. George Balanchine, a former Díaghiliev protégé with the Russian Ballet turned headmaster of the New York City Ballet, and designer Minnelli introduced surrealist choreography which in-

trigued all and puzzled not a few. "Night Flight" was a dream in which the dancer hovered like a released spirit over an airplane's grim shadow. "Words Without Music" had living shadows on an apple green ramp against a lavender background. The first act finale, with its cellophane pillars and chorus with masks of cellophane topping multi-colored costumes, was ravishing. Of Minnelli's contribution, reviewer Brooks Atkinson wrote, "Without being in the least sensational, he has managed this season to reanimate the art of scenic display and costumery . . . The *Follies* that comes off his drawing board is a civilized institution."[5]

"A new Minnelli production meant excitement on Broadway—his name went above the show's title . . ." reported Baral. They "were a high mark of the thirties and brought considerable class and distinction to the Winter Garden."[6] In 1937, Minnelli conceived, staged, and designed *The Show Is On* about show business. Although every minnesinger on Broadway contributed to the score—Dietz and Schwartz, Rodgers and Hart,

A sketch for Josephine Baker's impersonation of a French soprano, Ziegfeld Follies of 1936.

the brothers Gershwin, Duke and Fetter—the show boasted no single song hit. David Freedman and Moss Hart scripted. The cast included Beatrice Lillie, Bert Lahr, Reginald Gardiner, Mitzi Mayfair, Paul Haakan, and Charles Walters. The ballets, *Casanova* and *The Tragedian*, were highlights.

In an interview with Mabel Greene for the *New York Sun*, Minnelli stated that he believed in the more intimate revue and favored the adaption of dramatic technique to musical shows. "The public wants the satirical twist and an intelligent idea as well as sophisticated, punchy melodies."[7] This point was expanded for an out-of-town newspaper column:

> The public expects to see beautiful girls, but today they must do much more than wear their clothes well . . . The shows of 1936 are in a very different tempo and move at a far more rapid pace than did the famous Ziegfeld revues. You ask me what the public wants today? They want drama in every scene, even if the act is only whoopee. Ziegfeld had excellent writers, the best available talent and the loveliest girls anywhere. But these aren't enough for today. Tastes are changing all the time, and now there must be excitement in every scene—a story value in every sketch . . . There must be more to intrigue the patron than just first-rate dancing, amusing comedy and beautiful girls. And I call that something dramatic value.[8]

Minnelli revealed his method to Hugh Troy for his article, "Never Had A Lesson" in *Esquire:*

> The first and most important problem for the designer is to work out a point of view for the show, to set a style for it. All the fantasy, satire, and color running riot in a revue must stem from some common idea or it will lack unity . . . *At Home Abroad* which has essentially a travelogue theme was conceived as a flat design like a map, filling in the spaces with clear colors . . . The *Follies* was

done in the spirit of fashion photography as epitomized by Cecil Beaton, with its quality of diffusion and unexpected, clear light . . . For *The Show Is On* . . . built around the history of show business in America, the costumes and sets were given the arresting appeal of a theatrical bill poster.[9]

For Norris Houghton's essay, "The Designer Sets The Stage" in *Theatre Arts Monthly*, Minnelli detailed his method which consisted first in establishing the idea of production that is the basis of the entire show ("the revue audience has grown to demand a show that has some definite idea behind it; there must be continuity"); then, working out a synopsis of the show, devising a skeleton outline of the form in which it is to be constructed, that is, a tentative plan for the type of music, dances, or sketches that will be required to put across the idea; next, developing their position and shape in the pattern of the whole revue; finally, turning various collaborators loose on their respective jobs of creating a book, music, choreography while he himself designs ("the time has passed when revue scenery needed only to be handsome to be successful; now the designer must produce something which will complement the material").

The designs are developed in large-scale color sketches which contain people and an indication of light sources and quality. Rough mechanical drawings and models are constructed to clarify movement. Details for the scene painter, complete mechanical drawings for construction, a ground plan for setting, and a hanging plot and storing plan of the stage are then laid out ("such a designer is faced with the task of creating twenty or thirty settings which will follow each other at four or five minute intervals with complete precision and without intermission").[10]

Minnelli not only worked in the theatrical revue, he developed it. A middle-aged, adipose, sluggish, and gilded woman, silly but winsome, became a light, intelligent, beautiful, and charming young lady.

MUSICAL COMEDY AND THE MOVIES

The belief in the importance of dramatic value and of a teleological thrust made Minnelli's leap easy, graceful, and inevitable to the theatrical musical comedy or book show, that twenties upstart which deposed operetta as queen and was soon to depose revue as princess of the American musical stage. The parvenu was clearly foreshadowed a decade earlier in the guise of George M. Cohan.

Cohan combined the most irresistible elements of native American musical entertainments, made them even more democratic and national, and gave them a lightning pace: "Speed! Speed! And lots of it. That's the idea of the thing. Perpetual motion." Irving Berlin solidified the type of song in musical comedy. The show tune was somewhere between light opera and the popular song. He also confirmed its American spirit. Composer Jerome Kern, along with producer Elizabeth Marbury, librettists and lyricists Guy Bolton, P. G. Wodehouse, and Schyler Green, in their Princess Theatre Shows of 1915–1918, cut the tonnage, yardage, and cast of thousands. They chose instead, to concentrate on good texts with contemporary plots, characters, settings, and novel points of view, sharp humor based on the texts' situations and characters, and related songs and dances. What they came up with were coherent musical comedies. Kern's *Showboat* (1929), with Oscar Hammerstein II as librettist and lyricist and Ziegfeld as producer, was Janus-faced, nostalgically looking back at where musical comedy had been, while dauntlessly looking forward to where the genre was going. The Gershwins' contributions to the genre lay in the quality of their scores. Showing little obeisance to formula, cliché, or conventional procedure, the scores reverberated with fresh, surprising harmonies, rhythms, tempos, lyrics, and rhymes. The Brown, DeSylva, and Henderson efforts displayed knockabout fun and witty satire. Porter achieved the closest integration of lyric and music in musical comedy yet. Along with his librettists, Cole brought wit, chic, a tinge of cynicism and iconoclasm, sexual liberation, and brashness to this world. Kern and company's successors were Rodgers, Hart, and Herbert Fields. Lyrics were married to the melodies. Scores, choreography, and design all had something to do with plot, characters, and settings. New subjects were tried, and the possibilities of dance were further explored.

The theatrical musical comedy was evolving steadily when the sorcerer supervised, directed, and designed the Shuberts' *Hooray For What!* in 1937. Howard Lindsay and Russell Crouse's book told the story of a zany clown, portrayed by Ed Wynn, called upon to save the world from ruin by employing laughing gas. Harold Arlen and E. Y. Harburg did the music, Robert Alton and Agnes de Mille, the dances, and Raoul Pene du Bois, the costumes.

Although the musical was a substantial success, Minnelli headed for Hollywood that same year with a lucrative forty-week, three-picture contract from the president of Paramount and his own musical script entitled *Times Square*. His eight months at the studio of doing nothing practical catapulted him back across the continent and made him anxious to essay another musical.

The credits for Max Gordon's *Very Warm For May* (1939) read like a page from *Who's Who*—book and lyrics by Oscar Hammerstein II, who co-directed with Hassard Short, music by Jerome Kern, choreography by Albertina Rasch and Harry Losee, sets and costumes by Minnelli, with Jack Whiting and Eve Arden. It all had to do with the ingenuity of the heroine extricating herself and her father from the meshes of a not very wicked gang of gamblers, the highbrow ambitions of a summertime barn theatre, and, naturally, love.

A second offer from Hollywood came from Arthur Freed, lyricist *(Broadway Melody of 1929)* and producer of musicals at MGM *(Babes In Arms,* 1939, *Wizard of Oz,* 1939). The failure of *Very Warm For May* almost obliterated the memory of the sterile Paramount venture. Minnelli's acceptance was his road to Damascus. Only once in the late sixties was he to return to the stage as director of David Merrick's ill-fated *Mata Hari*.

A two-year apprenticeship followed in diverse studio duties—script reader, script-adviser, writer, designer, and then director of special musical sequences that included Judy Garland's solo numbers in Busby Berkeley's *Babes On Broadway* (1941) and Lena Horne's scenes in Norman McLeod's *Panama Hattie* (1942).

From the tent's sawdust aisle, its flickering gaslit torches, rough board platform, and big top to the Winter Garden's plushy upholstered and chandeliered auditorium, squares of amber, blue, red, and green spots, and cavernous stage, Minnelli created make-believe from reality. And now, inside the cement sound stage, under the cross-hatching of electric lights, amid a peripatetic camera and microphone, Merlin once again was to unleash his magic of sounds, figures, textures, shapes, colors, designs, movements, tempos, and rhythms harmonizing in a dramatic whole. This time, however, he was to perform as never before in a film genre that desperately needed his wizardry.

2

TRADITIONS: THE FILM MUSICAL

BEGINNINGS

Being the eighth and very latest in art's progeny, film has the distinct advantage of leaning upon, borrowing, taking over, and even transcending the vast experience of its brothers and sisters. In its green years, this rich, spoiled child frolicked with the stage more than with any other sibling. Everything from "the magic rhythms of Bill Shakespeare's immortal verse to the magic rhythms of Bill Robinson's immortal feet" was tried. Like Minnelli, film grew up with the proscenium arch, greasepaint, and the crowd.

If film's timely birth was the occasion for its property of appropriation, its very nature was the cause. Film was joined at the hip with theatre. Dramatic structure, enactment, set design, lighting, and costumes also were up film's sleeves.

Life being continuous rather than discrete, the origin of most things or events is murky. So, too, is the film musical. The turn of the century witnessed those one minute French audiovisual recordings of the vaudeville routines of Little Rich and Vestry Tilley and of Enrico Caruso's opera arias. George Méliès' *Cinderella* (1900) touted ballets and marches accompanied by live music. The *Film d'Art Series* of 1907–1912 included ballet with live music as part of its repertory. Lee De Forest's short Phonofilm experiments in the early twenties reproduced the vaudeville acts of Eddie Cantor, Phil Baker, Weber and Fields, and others, as did the Vitaphone shorts of 1926. The short that followed Vitaphone's *Don Juan* featured the New York Philharmonic Orchestra of 107 men, opera stars Giovanni Martinelli, Anna Case, Marion Talley, the Metropolitan Opera Company Chorus, violin solos by Harbel Bauer, Efrem Zimbalist, Mischa Elman, and the Spanish dancing troupe, the Cansinos—variety gone hoity-toity. Then there was Warner Brothers' feature-length Vit-

21

aphone film, *The Jazz Singer*, in 1927, the first to employ sound, which was always around, with an image to boost a sagging box office.

The Jazz Singer, based on Samson Raphaelson's play, was a series of silent vignettes interlaced with songs. It could be considered a type of variety. Sometimes rip-roaring or gushy melodramas were leavened by musical numbers sprinkled throughout the performance.

Rabbi Rabinowitz and his wife wait for their boy Jakie (Al Jolson) to chant "*Kol Nidre.*" Fifteen-year-old Jakie is discovered singing in a saloon ("Frivolous Sal") and, consequently, ousted from home. Years later, Jakie, with his name bobbed to "Robin", entertains in a London restaurant ("Dirty Hands, Dirty Face", "Toot, Toot, Tootsie") and meets Mary (May McAvoy) who gets notice of a role in a Broadway show. At the train station, Jakie also receives a telegram about the show. Returning home ("Blue Skies"), he is once more rejected by his father: "Leave my house, I never want to see you again, you jazz singer." *The April Follies,* Jakie and Mary's show, rehearses. While the dying Rabbi worries, "Who is to sing 'Kol Nidre' tomorrow on the Day of Atonement?," the show's cast frets about their opening tomorrow: "The show is weak; it's up to the jazz singer to put it over." Mama visits to tell Jakie about his father's condition and after the dress rehearsal concludes: "That's not my boy anymore. He belongs to the whole world." Jakie is reconciled to his father: "Son, I love you", and chants "*Kol Nidre*" as his expiring father listens through the bedroom window. A title then proclaims that the "season passes, time heals, the show goes on," as does his romance with Mary and his love for mom ("Mammy").

The episodes were almost held together by Jolson's plastic face, his peripatetic eyes and limbs, his heartfelt voice. The show motif was pronounced and the romance slightly realized. Liszt, as background music, rendered the scenes between the son and his parents even more affecting. The film even proclaimed a proletariat metaphysics of music: "Jazz is misunderstood prayer . . . You taught me that music is the voice of God." Spectacle and dance were nil. Nor did the medium make the genre feel at home. The picture was primarily a demonstration of sound. Jolson's strutting of his stuff came second.

With *The Jazz Singer* and the overflow of the tills, Hollywood was convinced that the most successful way, technically and financially, to fill the soundtrack was with screen adaptations of stage operettas, revues, and musical comedies or originals written directly for the screen. During 1927–30, certainly every third picture was a musical.

The Hollywood hills were alive with the sounds of Vienna—Johann Strauss II, Franz Lehar, Oscar Straus—and of Vienna domesticated—Herbert, Friml, Romberg. Original operettas included Oscar Straus' *Married in Hollywood* (1929), Romberg's *Viennese Nights* (1930), and *Children of Dreams* (1931).

The screen revues were mostly original since this format provided one of the best advertisements for a particular studio and its star personalities under contract. *Hollywood Revue* (1929) and *March of Time* (1930) were, on one level, musicals about MGM while *Paramount on Parade* (1930) and *The Big Broadcast* (1931) ballyhooed Paramount. Fox's foray into this field was entitled *Movietone Follies* (1930). Warners' made *Show of Shows* (1930). Universal produced *King of Jazz* (1930).

The musical comedies of Cohan, Berlin, Kern, Brown, DeSylva and Henderson, Youmans and others were adapted. Brown, DeSylva, and Henderson wrote a musical for the romantic team of Janet Gaynor and Charles Farrell, *Sunnyside Up* (1929), and the first science-fiction film musical, *Just Imagine* (1930), both directed by David Butler. Arthur Freed and Nacio Herb Brown collaborated on an original entitled *The Broadway Melody* (1929), directed by Harry Beaumont. Rodgers and Hart, for Lewis Milestone's *Hallelujah I'm A Bum* (1933), wrote sixty percent of the dialogue in rhyming couplets to make transition between talk and music smoother. The score even bore some relation to dramatic action and character.

The adaptations, on the whole, were nothing more than literal translations, the photographing of a stage show by a camera set up fifth row center or on the edge of the proscenium. The microphone recorded every sound. Songs and dances started and stopped without flowing from and into the dialogue and preceding and subsequent movements. As a result, they seemed separate from the texture of the film, almost like specialties inserted into the drama. No rethinking or refeeling by the medium was done. All the energy, after all, went into the thorny business of recording sound and synching it with the image. The originals did not fare that much better. *The Broadway Melody*, however, did set the pattern of the backstage musical, an offshoot of the original film musical comedy, to be crystallized later in the decade by Busby Berkeley at Warners.

The plethora of product plus the dullness and impersonality that results when one medium re-

Hank (Charles King) and the line in the first of the back-stage musicals, The Broadway Melody.

sists another produced the musical limbo of 1930–1933. The apathy, even hostility, to this genre on the part of the public was so intense that many pictures, shot as musicals, had their musical sequences edited out before release, a procedure which did not say very much for the thematic value of the numbers. Only musicals which starred Eddie Cantor and Maurice Chevalier had a chance.

A diligent search for the reasons behind the success of the Cantor musicals ends only at the doorstep of Eddie's personality. As for the Chevalier musicals, the answer is, quite simply, director Ernst Lubitsch.

ERNST LUBITSCH

Besides his costume spectacles, intimate dramas, and satirical comedies, Lubitsch made musicals, which constituted the genre's first significant development. *The Love Parade* (1929), *Monte Carlo* (1930), *The Smiling Lieutenant* (1931), *One Hour With You* (1932), and *The Merry Widow* (1934), a cross between old-world operetta and new-world musical comedy, introduced a new type of film musical and attempted a unification of elements through music.

Lubitsch took an ambivalent attitude to the operetta. He loved his royalty and aristocrats in spite of—but even more, because of—their amorous, professional, and cultural poses, their sentimentality, their frivolity, their mythical (Sylvania, Segovia) and romantic (Monte Carlo, Vienna,

23

Paris) milieus, and the splendiforous trappings of their life style. He enjoyed the sweet-and-light complications and sweeter–and–lighter climaxes of the plots of their lives. But Lubitsch had a sense of humor and saw the point of it all, revealed that point, and thereby tempered his affection by suavely debunking them. Parallel editing equated the behavior of the aristocrats with that of the commoners. Images and sounds undermined pretensions. Queen Louisa's swoon after Count Alfred's first kiss is deflated as she bangs her elbow on the lowest keys of the piano which emits a blood-curdling sound (*The Love Parade*). Count Rudolph comments on the opera being performed, a comment applicable to the film itself and every Lubitsch musical, ''It's a silly story only possible to music'' (*Monte Carlo*). With extravagant sets and costumes, and a gigantic cast (''Dream Lover'' from *The Love Parade*), Lubitsch was able to elicit still more satire. His warm acceptance, coupled with an urbane mockery that bore no trace of the reformist's fervor, is a characteristic attitude of musical comedy.

Lubitsch's technique of the elimination of interval in the story's continuity was also that of musical comedy where the concern in construction is only with the story's essentials. This, along with his famous ''touch,'' which, in its broadest sense, meant ''going from the general to the particular, suddenly condensing into one swift, deft moment the crystallization of a scene or even an entire theme,''[1] besides achieving a definite air of sophistication, endowed the pieces with a sprightly, jaunty tempo, a tempo that is musical comedy's.

As for the players, Jeanette MacDonald was operetta, while Maurice Chevalier was music hall or vaudeville, a forerunner of musical comedy. She had to be brought down a peg. He had to be brought up one or two.

Nowhere was this middle kingdom more apparent than in the films' scores. In *The Love Parade*, Clifford Grey's pointed lyrics met Victor Schertizinger's overripe melodies. Richard Whiting, Frank Harling, and Leo Robin of *Monte Carlo* had one foot in Tin Pan Alley, the other in an Austrian meadow. Grey and Oscar Straus duetted for *The Smiling Lieutenant*. Whiting and Robin almost collided with Straus in *One Hour With You*. In *The Merry Widow*, Franz Lehar was adapted and arranged by Herbert Stothart and updated by Lorenz Hart and Gus Kahn.

Lubitsch also developed the genre by striving to create pieces informed by music, a contribution dependent upon his inventive use of sound.

Songs often advanced the plot or developed character. Patter songs (speaking coupled with singing) were frequent. Music was a transition device between incidents. ''Always'', from *Monte Carlo,* does not terminate when the Countess and Count finish singing but carries the duo through the doors toward the apartment's entrance, through a dissolve of them in a car where they pantomime talk, then through a cut to a long shot of the Count getting out and taking the driver's seat, and finally through the dissolve of the car approaching the casino. Music commented on a situation as narrator or omniscient observer (the clock tower in *Monte Carlo*). Music accompanied gesture and facial expression of the players to convey ideas or feelings (the slow, ominous strains underlining Queen Louisa's reading of Count Alfred's confidential report under his very nose and her storming out of the room, and the tripping, bubbly music accenting her hurried toilette at the boudoir in *The Love Parade*). Music played under passages to create mood.

The transitions from dialogue into song and out again were smooth. In ''Give Me a Moment Please,'' from *Monte Carlo*, a telephone conversation turns into a song on the phone off the hook, his voice over her image and vice versa. Vera hangs up in the midst of Rudolph's song, continues the song in bed, stops to turn off the light, and hums a few bars to put herself to sleep. In *One Hour With You*, Lubitsch experimented with rhymed dialogue that framed each song. This novelty, however, had a curiously ironic effect. Instead of making the transitions smoother, as intended, this technique made one aware of the desire to make the transitions smoother. A device to get one into the film actually threw one out of it.

Prince Danilo (Maurice Chevalier) is courted by girls, girls, girls in The Merry Widow.

Music dictated the cutting. *Monte Carlo*'s "Blue Horizon" sequence, for example, was a rhythmic mosaic of a racing train, whirring train wheels, a stack shooting smoke, flying rails, a huffing front engine, the waving and singing peasants of the passing countryside, and the Countess chanting from the train window and in the compartment seat.

Despite the imagination of this sequence, and most other sequences in Lubitsch's work, it remained this side of the tracks. The Countess sings most of the freewheeling, expansive number locked in a medium shot and then in an extreme medium shot in the compartment's seat. The direction of the heroine did not involve her bodily response to the music. The camera did not feel the song's pace and rhythm. Besides that, there was no movement within the frame as the Countess sings to suggest the movement of the train and thus confirm the exhilaration of the music. Music did not influence the art direction in his films.

These shortcomings probably had something to do with the absence of dance in his films. Except for the maid and valet's brief routine in the park, "Let's Be Common," and on the kitchen table, "The Queen Is Always Right," from *The Love Parade* or the ball in *The Merry Widow*, what usually occurs in Lubitsch is movement accompanied by music.

Lubitsch did not go far enough in musically shaping his pieces. Also, his musicals, especially the first two, were demonstrations and justifications of the marriage of the image and the track. That is probably why music, an element of the soundtrack, was seized upon as the structuring device. Lubitsch's panache was also on parade, thus making one very much aware of his craft and talent. This, also, undermined their effect. Art can never be self-conscious.

ROUBEN MAMOULIAN

Rouben Mamoulian, with a halo of A's from his work in opera and the theatrical musical comedy, as well as drama, followed the Lubitsch tradition, but carried the whole thing off with more dexterity and polish in *Love Me Tonight* (1932) and in *The Gay Desperado* (1936) and hinted at the genre's future in *High, Wide, and Handsome* (1937).

Love Me Tonight was, at once a spoof of operetta, Lubitsch's style, the film musical, and the sound film. In this ingratiating tale of a male Cinderella, Lubitsch's darlings, Maurice and Jeanette, parody themselves.

Absurdly grand moments dot the film, especially Jeanette warbling "Lover" while horseback riding deep within the woods against a full studio orchestra or racing on horseback through the fields to stop the train carrying her lover away, and when that fails, defiantly straddling the tracks to bring the fierce locomotive to a halt. As for the Rodgers and Hart score, it was the wittiest one in a film musical thus far.

The songs' relationship to the drama was more tenacious and their technical inlay smoother. "The Song of Paree," a plot and character exposition as well as a transition device, takes Maurice from dressing in his bedroom, through his walk to work, and to his changing clothes in the tailor shop. The conversation between the porcine customer and the tailor underlined by the melody of "Isn't It Romantic?" shades off into doggerel which works and then becomes the lyrics of the song which, eventually, takes one from the common worker Maurice in the tailor shop to Princess Jeanette on her palace balcony, thereby counterpointing and juxtaposing two different life styles and enunciating the love-as-leveler motif. Rhymed dialogue between Jeanette and her doctor boomerangs as a transition device to "A Woman Needs Something Like That" but the song does advance the plot. "The Son of a Gun Is Nothing But a Tailor," a patter song, brings the shocking revelation to all the characters in their respective settings—the Duke, the Vicomte, Valentine, the footman, the butler, the valet, the chambermaid, the laundress.

Integration was also helped by "having the unlikeliest actors sing in their own voices"[2] and having the characters sing snatches of a song without any musical accompaniment.

Mamoulian orchestrated sound effects or natural sounds to approximate music. The opening sequence, a reprise of his own production of *Porgy* in 1927, is a symphony of urban sounds from the waking Parisian streets and households that quicken in quantity, tempo, and volume—a pealing church bell, the unpacking of a worker's tools, the picking of an ax, a bum's snore, brushes scraping the dirty streets, smoke rising from the stacks, a clock's alarm, a baby's cry, scissors being grinded, shutters being pulled up, a blanket being shaken, two cobblers hammering away at shoes, rugs being beaten, the chugging of automobile motors, the honk of horns, the screech of brakes, people buzzing along the sidewalk, and a phonograph blaring from a window. Mamoulian often used sound effects as part of the musical score.

Music dictated the cutting. The camera, at times, was musicalized. In many passages, music accompanied action—Maurice's arrival at the palace and entry into various rooms, the hunt in fast, normal, and slow motion, and Jeanette's pursuit of Maurice. An approximation of choreography but no dance.

The Gay Desperado, with its desert romance, its Mexican bandit inspired to reassemble his outlaw band after seeing an American gangster film, and its mixture of Verdi and south-of-the-border folk was less successful than his previous musical, yet imaginative and charming.

High, Wide and Handsome's romantic wooing, marriage, and reconciliation were played against the struggle of farmers in Western Pennsylvania to get their oil to the refinery through their pipe lines, thereby eschewing the cutthroat machinations of the train companies. The fair to middling Kern-Hammerstein score was beautifully inlaid. The jamboree's square dancing with its music colored by horses neighing and the wedding polka were photographed and cut to music. The pipeline montage was an arresting combination of natural sounds and music. Unlike his other two efforts, this piece, which was a musical comedy, exuded warmth and sentiment—the crumbling marriage of Sally (Irene Dunne) and Peter (Randolph Scott), the farmers' drive to beat the railroaders, Mollie (Dorothy Lamour), the shanty-beat woman, hounded out of town by the righteous. With more aplomb than ever before, Mamoulian did not have to remind one of his technical virtuosity.

It was ironic that Mamoulian, who made the first color film in the new three-color technicolor process, *Becky Sharp* (1935), did not employ it for the latter two musicals.

Minnelli's tribute to Mamoulian was recorded by John Kobal in his *Gotta Sing Gotta Dance: A Pictorial History of Film Musicals*—"When I arrived in Hollywood . . . I would often look at Mamoulian's *Love Me Tonight*, as it was such a perfect example of how to make a musical."[3]

BUSBY BERKELEY

In those salad days of sound, Hollywood, believing the New York stage knew all about the uses of sound, turned to it for redemption. Sam Goldwyn's salvation came in the form of Busby Berkeley, a bright Broadway dance director, who displayed some imagination and verve in the dance sequences and production numbers he directed for Eddie Cantor's stage-to-film transcriptions, *Whoopee* (1930), *Palmy Days* (1931), *The Kid From Spain* (1932), *Roman Scandals* (1933).

His apprenticeship over, Berkeley was nabbed by Warner Brothers at the suggestion of studio manager Darryl F. Zanuck. Here, Berkeley solidified a new form of film musical comedy, the backstage musical, which contained another significant development of the genre and made it, once again, the apple of the public's eye.

In these Warners musicals, *Forty-Second Street, Footlight Parade, Gold Diggers of '33* (1933), *Dames, Wonder Bar, Fashions of '34* (1934), *Gold Diggers of '35, Stars Over Broadway, In Caliente* (1935), *Hollywood Hotel, Gold Diggers of '37, Varsity Show, The Singing Marine* (1937), *Gold Diggers in Paris, Garden of the Moon* (1938), as well as in his subsequent work at other studios, especially MGM, Berkeley shuttled back and forth as director of production numbers and director of the entire film.

The plot of a Berkeley musical inevitably revolved around putting on a show, always on the edge of disaster, always facing the most appalling obstacles, for the "swellest" reason in the world. The show must go on in *Forty-Second Street* and *Gold Diggers of '33* to provide jobs during the Depression. *Footlight Parade*'s concern is to stage prologue shows with talking pics, again as a boon to unemployment. In *Gold Diggers of '35*, a revue is conceived at the Hotel Wentworth for the milk fund. To revive the drooping spirits of their vaudevillian folks, to prevent their houses from being mortgaged, and to evade the state work school, *Babes In Arms* (1939) produce a mini-musical. In *Strike Up the Band* (1940), the kids give a concert to pay off the school debt. A minstrel show to send the city kids to the country and prevent rickets is what puts *Babes On Broadway* (1941). *The Gang's All Here* (1943) stages its show in Westchester County to sell war bonds. To hold the team and circus intact and bring entertainment to millions is the motive for the shows in *Take Me Out to the Ball Game* (1949) and *Jumbo* (1967) respectively.

Berkeley could not care less about the story line. William Murray, in his article, "The Return of Busby Berkeley" in the *New York Times Magazine*, quoted Berkeley: "I did my numbers and the director did the story . . . Sometimes I'd even forget who was directing . . . No one ever knew exactly what would finally emerge from such a collaboration until the day of the first screening."[4]

Although these production numbers were dramatically motivated, arising as auditions or, more frequently, as opening night presentations, their style was so preposterous, florid, and exciting that they were purple passages in a text of humdrum prose. In these patches, Berkeley's unique contribution to the film musical was to be found.

There are three types of movement in film—movement within the frame, movement of the camera, and movement created through editing. Oddly enough, Berkeley's production numbers contained very little dancing, and therefore, very little movement within the frame. When there was movement, it was of the basic, simple kind—bending, nodding, or turning a head, lifting an arm, kicking a leg, walking or marching. "As for the dance routines themselves, I left the teaching of actual steps to underlings . . . Hell, I don't know the first five positions of dancing."[5]

Berkeley played with the second and third types of film movement and the element of spectacle (decor, costume, and cast). By exploring the technical possibilities of the camera and editing, the camera's spectrum of movements, image sizes, angles, and the splicer's ability to juxtapose images according to lines, movements, shapes, figures, colors, textures and according to a distinct interval of time, he created a montage that had tempo, rhythm, and melody which was then related to the music and sound effects. "I soon realized that in the theatre your eyes can go any place you want, but in pictures the only way I could entertain an audience was through the single eye of the camera."[6]

What resulted was an exhilarating and vastly entertaining musical montage, associated but unrelated to the rest of the picture; in fact, a world sufficient unto itself. The sequence's abstract quality was underscored by the infinite repetition of subjects within the frame.

The Berkeley musical montage or production number, the better ones characterized by an inherent dramatic structure ("Remember My Forgotten Man" from *Gold Diggers of '33*,

An infinite number of Berkeley babes rehearse, among them Mickey Rooney and Judy Garland from Babes On Broadway.

27

"Shanghai Lil" from *Footlight Parade*, "Honeymoon Hotel" and "Lullaby of Broadway" from *Gold Diggers of '35*), burst the proscenium arch which plagued many film musicals then and now, musicalized the camera and editing, and made spectacle expressive. "But with that single eye I could go anywhere I wanted to. You couldn't get any of my sets onto a legit stage but I didn't care about that. To be entertaining and spectacular, that's what I cared about."[7]

Someone once estimated that each minute of a Berkeley production number cost $10,000. A number ran from seven to ten minutes. Each film comprised three or four numbers. This was a staggering bit of multiplication for the Depression.

During Minnelli's training at Metro, Berkeley was one of the top musical directors in residence, having immigrated to Culver City to direct the Garland-Rooney romps. Their paths crossed and, in fact, Minnelli directed Garland's solos in Berkeley's *Babes On Broadway*. Concerning Berkeley's work, Minnelli was silent save for one remark: "Busby Berkeley's large-scale numbers never moved me."[8]

FRED ASTAIRE AND GINGER ROGERS

Side by side with the Berkeley musicals at Warners, another type of musical happened at RKO, the Fred Astaire-Ginger Rogers vehicles, which also helped to revive the genre. *Flying Down to Rio* (1933), *The Gay Divorcée, Roberta* (1934), *Top Hat, Follow the Fleet* (1935), *Swing Time* (1936), *Shall We Dance* (1937), *Carefree* (1938), and *The Story of Vernon and Irene Castle* (1939) were showcases for these two personalities and their prodigious talents. Although *Rio* was not planned as such, it did eventuate that way.

The undistinguished plots evolved from the on-again, off-again, sparring relationship between suave, eloquent, cajoling, ambidextrous Fred and feisty, blunt, but in the end, malleable Ginger. When Fred and Ginger reflected the bright side of the romantic moon, the films contained another romance, a "serious" one—Gene Raymond and Dolores del Rio in *Flying Down to Rio,* Randolph Scott and Irene Dunne in *Roberta*, Scott and Harriet Hilliard in *Follow the Fleet*. The intended contrast resulted in downright schizophrenia for the latter duo and their scenes were wooden and dull. When Fred and Ginger played it straight, the plot was injected with the comic relief of Edward Everett Horton, Eric Blore, Eric Rhodes, Franklyn Pangborn, Alice Brady, Helen Broderick,

and Edna May Oliver. Most of the films contained a putting-on-the-show subplot which climaxed with a pseudo-Berkeley extravaganza. The direction of these vehicles (Mark Sandrich being at the helm of five of them) was usually listless and pedestrian.

Besides Fred and Ginger's personalities, these musicals contributed two additional items to the genre's development. Almost all the major American popular composers wrote scores for these works—Vincent Youmans, Gus Kahn, and Edward Eliscu for *Rio*, Cole Porter for *Divorcée*, Jerome Kern, Otto Harbach, Dorothy Fields, and Jimmy McHugh for *Roberta* and *Swing Time*, Irving Berlin for *Hat, Fleet, Carefree*, the Gershwins for *Dance*. Standard pre-World War I songs interlaced the last film suggested by the Castles' life. The songs were tailored more for their personalities than for the plots. Melodies and rhythms had to be such that they could sing, but more importantly dance to. The scores themselves (not as a function of the whole) were the best in film musicals up to that time. Composers of this stature added prestige to the new genre.

This cycle's most noteworthy contribution lay in its revelation of the dance's dramatic possibilities. Many of the dance numbers were motivated by audition, rehearsal, or performance and as such, reproduced a display of remarkable terpsichorean talent. Quite a few numbers did more than that. These numbers were an overflow of feeling on the characters' part and as such, dramatized their meeting ("No Strings" from *Top Hat*), their getting acquainted ("Isn't This a Lovely Day to Be Caught in the Rain?" from *Top Hat*), their budding trust and love ("Night and Day" from *The Gay Divorcée*), and some like "Cheek to Cheek" from *Top Hat* expressed seduction and acquiescence. In "Too Hot to Handle" from *Roberta*, the dance supplanted dialogue as the couple conversed with each other through steps. Fred suggested a proposal or some kind of engagement. Ginger repeatedly refused. Then Fred hinted at something indelicate or, perhaps made a proposition. Ginger slapped his face. These numbers were romantic dramas, microcosms of their far from steady relationship, revelatory of character and mood.

The technical inlay of these *pas de deux* was smooth. After all, Fred and Ginger walked with the same grace as they danced. The technical handling was a function of the dance and their talent. The numbers were composed in long shot to frame their expressive bodies and mostly in one take to preserve the continuity of the dance. Camera movement was dictated by the dancers'

The Barkleys (Astaire and Rogers) perform, The Barkleys of Broadway.

movement. It moved only to keep the dancers within frame. Cutting was spare and as invisible as possible. Cutaways during the dance were eschewed. Decor never distracted from the dance and costumes emphasized it. Of course, these dramatic numbers did not shake themselves entirely free of the recording-of-a-performance trapping.

At the decade's finish, Rogers turned to light comedy and drama while Astaire continued in musicals, freelancing at Columbia (*You'll Never Get Rich*, 1941; *You Were Never Lovelier*, 1942), Paramount (*Holiday Inn*, 1942; *Blue Skies*, 1946) and at MGM (*Broadway Melody of 1940*) where he joined forces with Minnelli and encored with Rogers in Charles Walters' *The Barkleys of Broadway* in 1949.

The Astaire-Rogers vehicles, musicals tailored after a star, musicals in which all the elements and the filmic expression of them were geared to showing off a star's personality and musical talents, were so lucrative that each studio jumped on the bandwagon by grooming a musical star and adapting films to his or her specifications. Paramount grinded out Bing Crosby vehicles (*We're Not Dressing*, 1934; *Mississippi*, 1935; *The Big Broadcast of 1936*; *Pennies From Heaven*, *Anything Goes*, 1936, whose plot and score were so altered that it bore little, if any, resemblance to Porter's dazzling Broadway show) and continued to do so for the next quarter of a century. Zanuck at Fox supervised the Shirley Temple creampuffs (*Stand Up and Cheer*, 1934 to *The Bluebird*, 1940), Sonja Henie's ice capades (from *Thin Ice*, 1937 to *The Countess of Monte Cristo*, 1946), Alice Faye efforts (from *George White's Scandals*, 1934 to *Four Jills in a Jeep*, 1944) and the subsequent Betty Grable (from *Down Argentine Way*, 1940 to *The Farmer Takes a Wife*, 1952) and June Haver (from *Irish Eyes Are Smiling*, 1944 to *The Girl Next Door*, 1952) starrers. MGM blazoned Eleanor Powell (*Broadway Melody of '36, '38, '40*; *Born to Dance*, 1936; *Rosalie*, 1937) and babes Rooney and Garland (from *Thoroughbreds Don't Cry*, 1937 to *Girl Crazy*, 1943). Universal trumpeted forth Deanna Durbin (from *Three Smart Girls* and *One Hundred Men and a Girl*, 1937 to *Can't Help Singing*, 1945) and young Frank Sinatra (*Higher and Higher*, *Step Lively*, 1943); while Columbia flaunted Rita Hayworth (from *Music in My Heart*, 1940 to *Pal Joey*, 1957).

THE MUSICAL BIOGRAPHY: THE GREAT ZIEGFELD

In 1936, MGM produced *The Great Ziegfeld* and

The revival of the operetta in the thirties, Jeanette MacDonald and Nelson Eddy, New Moon.

popularized a new type of film musical, the musical biography. Structured by a clodhopping and inaccurate chronology of a famous, usually American, composer, singer, dancer, or producer of musical shows, written very romantically—slicking up the high points, toning down the low—boasting an endless amount of stagily-mounted production or rehearsal numbers or creative sessions where the 'work of art' seemed to materialize on the spot, over-long but briskly-paced, heavy on sentiment and period flavor, with the romantic motif sharing time with that of name, fame, and fortune, the musical biography alternated between personality revues (*Rhapsody in Blue*, 1945: Gershwin; *Night and Day*, 1946: Porter; *Till the Clouds Roll By*, 1946: Jerome Kern; *Words and Music*, 1948: Rodgers and Hart; *Three Little Words*, 1950: Kalmar and Ruby; *I'll See You In My Dreams*, 1952: Gus Kahn; *The I Don't Care Girl*, 1953: Eva Tanguay; *The Best Things In Life Are Free*, 1956: Brown, DeSylva, and Henderson), and fairly engrossing dramas interrupted by musical sequences (*The Great Waltz*, 1939: Strauss II; *Yankee Doodle Dandy*, 1940: Cohan; *Swanee River*, 1940: Stephen Foster; *With A Song In My Heart*, 1952: Jane Froman; *Five Pennies*, 1959: Red Nichols). This musical type had its heyday in the forties through mid-fifties.

A scene from the The Great Ziegfeld.

JEANETTE MACDONALD AND NELSON EDDY

The mammoth Berkeley backstage musicals, the intimate Astaire-Rogers and subsequent star-vehicles, and the extravagant musical biographies were not the only fare that lifted the genre out of the doldrums of public indifference. At MGM, the unexpected success of Lubitsch's *The Merry Widow* (1934) led to the teaming of film soprano Jeanette MacDonald and Nelson Eddy, a concert-stage singer, in a series of operettas, adapted and original, that resuscitated this type of film musical.

Bright, coquettish Jeanette and stolid, monotoned Nelson courted, fell in love, kissed and embraced, usually married and lived happily ever after but occasionally were separated, all to lush, romantic operetta airs. Every so often, they had time off for good behavior. Jeanette consorted with Alan Jones in *The Firefly* (1937); Nelson with Rise Stevens in *The Chocolate Soldier* (1941). But it was their teaming in *Naughty Marietta, Rose Marie* (1935), *Maytime* (1937), *Girl of the Golden West, Sweethearts* (1938), *Bitter Sweet,* and *New Moon* (1940) that kept the coin rolling in. Their one attempt at musical comedy, Rodgers and Hart's *I Married an Angel* (1942), was a bust and disbanded the entente.

In operetta, the music, especially the always hummable melodies, surpassed, even eclipsed, the other elements. Spectacle came off second best. In these film versions, the score was intact but handled in traffic cop fashion by technicians W. S. Van Dyke or Robert Z. Leonard. The songs were recorded in static medium shots. Little or no care was employed in their technical inlay. As the box office momentum grew, the studio shelled out more money for spectacle (*Bitter Sweet* was photographed in color) which was poured over the pieces rather than directed into them. The settings were picturesque places of the distant past—the colony of Louis, the French King, the Canadian Northwest, Utah and Maryland on the verge of statehood, the artists' district in golden Vienna. Dancing was part of the setting or background. The plots, elaborate but shallow affairs, made the wait between those "unforgettable" melodies interminable. Comic relief in the guise of Henry Morgan and Elsa Lancaster, Una O'Connor and Alan Mowbray helped the time to pass, however.

It would be easier for a camel to pass through the eye of a needle than to discuss the contribution of these innocuous film-operettas. Douglas McVay, in his book, *The Musical Film,*[9] completely ignores the series.

Foxy blondes Betty Grable and June Haver as The Dolly Sisters.

The romance-motif: Esther (Judy Garland) delays John (Tom Drake) as her sister Rose (Lucille Bremer) encourages her to bed, Meet Me in St. Louis.

OFFSPRING OF THE FILM MUSICAL

In addition to the film operettas, revues, musical comedies, adapted and original, and the off-shoots of musical comedy, the backstage musicals, the star-vehicles, and the musical biographies, comedies and dramatic films contained musical sequences—Mae West's seductions, the Marx Brothers surreal visual and aural flights, the Crosby-Hope-Lamour road series, Danny Kaye romps, Vidor's *Hallelujah,* Mamoulian's *Applause,* and most of the Von Sternberg-Dietrich collaborations. Gene Autry and Roy Rogers' westerns sported songs and folk dancing. Musical passages graced Disney's cartoons—*Silly Symphonies, Snow White and the Seven Dwarfs, Pinnochio, Dumbo, Fantasia, Bambi,* and Max and Dave Fleischer's animated version of *Gulliver's Travels.* In the *Silly Symphonies* and *Fantasia,* unlike the other Disney efforts where action took precedence over the music, a particular theme was chosen and then drawings were added to it. None of these groups of films, however, apply for film-musical status.

1927 to 1942 comprises fifteen years of fits and starts, glimmers, intimation, and hopes. But there were no masterpieces of the genre, no amalgam of theme and technique, content and craft.

32

3
DRAMA

PRINCIPLES

Viewing *Cabin in the Sky* (1942) with the tradition of the film musical sharply in focus, one immediately senses that, in spite of some musical stuffing, one is in the presence of something different. That difference is augmented if Andrew Stone's black musical of the same year, *Stormy Weather,* Fox's answer to Metro's *Cabin,* is unspooled before or afterwards. Minnelli's second feature, *I Dood It* (1943), fairly undermines this sense. Reprise rather than revelation, this film is the divine Keaton's *Spite Marriage* (1929), directed by Edward Sedgwick, brought down to earth by Red Skelton with the musical sequences, excepting those of Hazel Scott and Lena Horne, shot by another director and inserted where the plot begins to sputter and run down. Even some of the dramatic sequences bear a signature other than Minnelli's. With *Meet Me in St. Louis* (1944), and subsequent Minnelli musicals, however, no longer is it a matter of an inkling but of knowledge. One realizes one is in the presence of something special, something previously unseen and unheard of in this genre.

What immediately distinguishes the Minnelli musical from the genre's first sixteen years is the director's attitude toward his materials and his handling of them. With Kobal, Minnelli expatiated on this point: "When I arrived in Hollywood, I didn't look down on musicals as so many people who were doing them did, treating them as a romp, a slapstick, nothing to be taken seriously."[1] During a speech in San Francisco, recorded in Albert Johnson's article, "The Films of Vincente Minnelli, Part I," the director stated that "the search for an appropriate style is as valid for musicals as it is for drama."[2] Minnelli's serious attitude toward the genre is the key unlocking his style and aesthetic.

This seriousness is manifested essentially in three ways. Minnelli knows that the film musical can and should be like Joseph's coat of many colors—a matter of drama, enactment, spectacle, music, and dance. Each of his musicals contains all these elements that "create a little magic."[3]

Furthermore, this "magic" arises not from the display of these elements as in a parade where one follows another, but in their coalescence. The elements' integration, one with another as well as with the whole, is called for. Minnelli permits neither the assimilation of elements as in grand opera, most forms of light opera, and film adaptations of these where almost everything is drowned out by the music, nor their appendage as in variety, vaudeville, theatrical and film revues, or most star-vehicles.

Minnelli achieves this particular integration in two ways. Each of the elements to be integrated is more or less equal. Each is able to hold its own. Condescension or subservience is out of the question. The elements resemble partners in a friendship. Also, each of the elements is complementary to every other element as well as to the whole. The quality of his pieces is directly proportional to the unity achieved among the elements. A definite teleological thrust, indispensable for any work of art, informs a Minnelli musical.

But integration does not stop there, since the film musical, according to this maestro, is not a photographed recording of an organized whole on a stage but an expression of this whole through photography, editing, and sound track.

Minnelli commented on this concept of the total musical to Kobal: "I'm only interested in musical stories in which one can achieve a complete integration of dancing, singing, sound, and vision."[4] During an interview with Charles Higham and Joel Greenberg, Minnelli was more specific:

Of course, I had problems with the MGM art department, I had to revolutionize them initially. They were shocked at a lot of things I wanted to do. At the beginning it was rather a strain, but they saw everything my way in the end. Their methods were staid and old-fashioned and they weren't integrated enough; and I liked to feel that numbers should be given as much importance as dramatic sequences, that they should be woven into the story completely in a way they hadn't been hitherto. I worked very closely with the art directors . . . I worked with the writers on the scripts in detail . . . And I worked very closely with the dance directors.[5]

Film is a collaborative art, especially when the film is a Minnelli musical. The filmic translation of the reciprocity of the musical's elements demands more collaborators than most film genres and, moreover, it asks the utmost from them. The talent of producer, scenarist, player, art director, set decorator, photographer, editor, costumer, composer, lyricist, arranger, sound recorder, and choreographer is stretched to the breaking point.

To raise a salvo to Arthur Freed, the producer of all of Minnelli's musicals except *I Dood It* (Jack Cummings) and *On A Clear Day You Can See Forever* (Howard W. Koch and Alan J. Lerner), is appropriate here at the start of this exploration since he was responsible for the start of the movie musical phase of Minnelli's career. Minnelli referred to Freed as "a marvelous showman" with a wonderful flair for getting people together and allowing them to create. "He wasn't creatively involved himself; we'd talk over everything with him in the broadest terms."[6]

If integration of the elements is the road taken, a principle of integration is necessary. For Minnelli, it is the drama, still another testament of his earnestness. The drama is the fundamental structuring element because, after all, it is a drama, not a clothes tree upon which to hang spectacle, music, and dance in their Sunday best, and not a striking of attitudes, something that has to be gotten through for convention's sake. His musical dramas operate from a set of principles—beginning, middle, and end—a coherent plot with a conflict expressed through incidents so selected and so ordered that they look both ways (to what precedes and to what follows), that they build to a climax and erupt in a resolution or denouement, as well as expressed through sharply limned characters so that a need is created in the audience to see and hear, think and feel the conflict through, so that there is entertainment. Thus, the drama determines the movement of the piece both objectively, in filmic time and space, and subjectively, within the audience's mind and heart. The audience sticks with the situation in a Minnelli musical. The characters have enough life to connect with. The audience cares. A Minnelli musical is not sterile at its core; something is going on inside it.

"A musical must have its own importance and reason"[7] wrote Minnelli in his article, "The Rise and Fall of the Musical Film." In Digby Diehl's article, "Directors Go to Their Movies: Vincente Minnelli and *Gigi*," Minnelli was expansive:

You can see how worried I am about content. I worry a great deal about the characters—what they're thinking, what their lives are like, what their point of view is . . . The important thing is the situation, and that is played seriously . . . If you want to do a musical, it requires just as much plot and preparation as *Hamlet*. You have to make it seem as though it could have happened.[8]

In an interview with Charles Bitsch and Jean Domarchi, Minnelli remarked that he always collaborates with his scenarists.[9] "From the first, that which interests me is the literary content of the film,"[10] he averred to Jean Domarchi and Jean Douchet. In an interview conducted by Ernesto Serebrinsky and Oscar Garaycochea, the director stated, "Nearly always I have the opportunity of working with the writer more or less from the

The production-motif: another creation of the poet (Howard Keel)—mesmerizing the Wazir's court, Kismet.

beginning. In cases where the script has not been completed, I generally work with the writer for at least five or six weeks."[11]

In addition, the drama is "the force that through the green fuse drives" the flower since every other element takes its basic cue and hue from the drama.

> Scene dictates style.[12] The style is always dictated by what's in the screenplay; you shouldn't have to worry about it . . . it has all to come out of the material.[13]

Minnelli's film debut coincided with Curly bounding over the backyard fence to serenade Aunt Eller about the "beautiful mornin'." Rodgers and Hammerstein's *Oklahoma*! was considered the first theatrical musical to achieve perfectly the elements' integration or at least an integration tighter than the Kern musicals and the Rodgers and Hart pieces. Of course, there were precursors. But dates and names are convenient, even necessary, for those who remember and record, so lyric-theatre historians seized upon 1943 and *Oklahoma*!

Both Lubitsch and Mamoulian attempted the integrated film musical. "Attempt" is by no means a begrudging description since all the elements were not whirled out. Moreover, their employment of music as the structuring device was not strong and pervasive enough to hold the pieces together. Their films were also textbooks for sound, a flirtation with—not love of—the genre, and a grandstanding of their own expertise.

DRAMATIC TYPE

Before inspecting each of the elements and its

35

functions, some propaedeutic remarks about the species of drama used in the musical are in order.

More often than not, the question of the film musical's dramatic type would be answered by "comedy." The musical comes along tossing many comic favors and one kind has "comedy" as a surname. Operetta cuts to clowns and comic performers every now and then to prevent the audience's deafness and diabetes. Topical satire is an ingredient of the revue, certainly in the sketches with its doggerel drama. Comics people backstages: the millionaire and dowager wife, the bumbling stage manager, the quipping chorines. Comics are foils for the stars in their vehicles when the stars do not handle the comedy themselves. Funny buddies keep the "genius" from taking himself too seriously. The question of dramatic type *seems* to be extremely clear-cut. For to say that the musical's drama is comedy misses the mark.

Where there's life, there's mud, cries comedy. Comedy deals with man's dark side, his shabby actions, his baser motives. Arisfotle and Kerr (and everyone in between) concur. Man's coming apart, his splintering, and his journey from home is grist for comedy's mill. It is a lament of man's contingencies. Comedy's reaction to the underside of man is laughter. Its point of view is from the high (what man should be) to the low (what man is), from the outside looking in. In comedy, the audience keeps its distance and, consequently, its power.

Tragedy, on the other hand, exclaims where there's life, there's sky. Despite—and more importantly, because of—the shattering and splattering, man must pull himself together, man must go home again, to his own self he must be true. Tragedy deals with man's bright side, his reputable actions, his nobler virtues. It is a paean to man's freedom. Tragedy's attitude to the overside of man is pity and compassion. Its point of view is from the low to the high, from the inside looking out. In tragedy, the audience, being made to slip into the character's shoes, runs the risk of vulnerability.

The answer lies in the realm of melodrama, but a distinct brand of melodrama, one peculiar to the musical. In Thrall, Hibbard, and Holman's *Handbook to Literature*, "melodrama" was defined as:

A play based on a romantic plot and developed sensationally, with little regard for convincing motivation and with a constant appeal to the emotions of the audience. The object is to keep the audience thrilled by the awakening, no matter how, of strong feelings of pity or horror or joy. Poetic justice is superficially secured, the charac-

ters (who are either good or very bad) being rewarded or punished according to their needs . . . The term literally means 'a play with music,' and at one time it was applied to the opera in a broad sense. Melodrama came into widespread use in England in the nineteenth century as a device to circumvent the Licensing Act which restricted 'legitimate' plays to the Patent Theatres but which allowed musical entertainments in other theatres. The use of songs, recitative, and incidental music disguised the dramatic nature of popular stage pieces, and they came to be known as melodrama. The first English melodrama is believed to have been Thomas Holcroft's *A Tale of Mystery* (1802). These melodramas usually exhibited the deplorable characteristics already listed, and finally, the term by extension was applied to these characteristics independent of the presence or absence of music.[14]

Motifs—Romance, usually that unspoiled, stirring stage of courting and engagement between a young man and woman, makes the musical world go round. Most of its energy is spent in getting the girl or boy—the chase rather than the fulfillment. Variations occur. Sometimes the romance is between older people; sometimes within marriage and the concern here is with the prelapsarian state of grace to be regained. Romance constitutes the musical's plot. Lovers, usually young, are the chief protagonists. The conflict involves the overcoming of the obstacles to the romance—external ones like a third party, society, or class and/or internal ones like prejudice or ambition. The climax occurs when the obstacle is about to be definitively defeated. Happy endings are the rule. Even in the exception, some compensatory item ends the piece on an upbeat.

In the screen revue, the backstage musical, and in some star vehicles where the concern is primarily with parading the star's personality and musical talents, romance is not dead center but off center. Here the primary concern is with putting on the show or strutting the star's stuff. The protagonist is the show—cast, crew, angels, press—or the musical star. The conflict involves jumping hoops to keep the show on the boards or devising means to maintain the star in the spotlight. The plot climaxes with the show's knockout production number or the star doing his or her thing incandescently.

In the musical biographies, the romance is slightly circumferential. The immediate concern is with attaining name, fame, and fortune, with an air of Calvinistic predestination about it: "this God-given talent will find an audience." Often name is equated with fame and fortune. The composer, lyricist, vocalist, dancer-protagonist climbs. Regression constitutes crises or complications which comprise the conflict. The ultimate progression is climax.

All motifs—romance, production, name, fame, and fortune—involve the dimension of transformation in one or both of the lovers, in the show or star, in the nobody who becomes a somebody. This inner moment of transformation, either the cause or more usually the effect of the struggle, enriches the plot and conflict, while making the climax a bit more thrilling.

Pursuit of a mate, putting on the show, or strutting one's stuff, and the rags-to-riches climb are images of drive, movement, and energy. Since achievement is always attained, they are also images of success and crystallizations of the American Dream.

These patterns criss-cross each other through the Minnelli tapestry. Petunia Jackson strives to get her husband, Little Joe, back on the straight and narrow which involves, among other things, a surcease of his infatuation for sultry Georgia Brown (*Cabin in the Sky*). Pants-presser Joseph Livingston Reynolds is daffy over musical-comedy star Constance Towers and unwittingly woos and wins her (*I Dood It*). In almost every room of the Smith residence, romance is in the air—the oldest daughter Rose and Warren Sheffield; Esther, the next oldest, and John Truett; brother Lon and Easterner Lucille Ballard; and the Mr. and Mrs. (*Meet Me in St. Louis*). Her "guardian angel" is everything that heiress Yolanda Acquaviva wants or almost wants. When the angel tumbles *from* the altar into none other than Johnny Parkson Riggs, a two-bit swindler on the lam, she rushes him *to* the altar (*Yolanda and the Thief*). In "This Heart of Mine", from *Ziegfeld Follies,* a rich, titled young lady waltzes with a petty crook, falls prey to his charm and he to hers, discloses to him her knowledge of his appropriation, and wins him over. Similarity of plot, character, cast, composer, and lyricist make this sequence a microcosm of *Yolanda*. "Limehouse Blues" from the same film depicts the infatuation of an emaciated Chinese menial for a comely Eurasian career woman. Serafin pursues Manuela home and retrieves her from her husband-to-be—on her wedding day no less (*The Pirate*). Jerry strolls down the steps hand in hand with Lise into the Parisian night after his sponsor-mistress Milo is left at the ball and her warder-fiancé in the car (*An American in Paris*). Insecurity becomes trust and antipathy tenderness between hoofer Tony Hunter and prima ballerina Gabrielle Gerard who will "run together forever" (*The Band Wagon*). *Brigadoon*'s Fiona Campbell so enchants Madison Avenue executive Tommy Albright that he

finds himself capable of loving once again and returns to reclaim that love. Only love permits his reentry. Two romances whirl from *Kismet*'s legerdemain—the poet and Lalume, the Wazir's wife of wives, the Caliph and Marsinah, the poet's daughter. In the twinkling of an eye, *Gigi*'s "sparkle" turns to "fire," her "warmth" becomes "desire" within Gaston amid a milieu of amatory intrigues—Honoré Lachaille and his current butterfly, Liane d'Exelmans and her skating instructor, and to a certain degree, Madame Alvarez, Gigi's grandmother, and Honoré. Ella Peterson is "in love with Plaza O, double four, double three" who is darkly handsome Jeffrey Moss. When Ella materializes, Jeff's flashy brunette evaporates (*Bells Are Ringing*). Daisy's three lifetimes are equally romantic. Passion for Adonis Robert Tentrees ends her marriage with nebbish Lord Percy Moorepark. Her priggish fiancé is ditched for her liberated stepbrother Tad. With Dr. Marc Chabot, with whom she is enamored, she will live in sweet domesticity. Although Melinda is the object of Chabot's professional and amatory pursuit, he returns to his wife (*On a Clear Day You Can See Forever*).

Transformation is in store for Minnelli's lovers, the effect of romance. The hottest scamp in town converts by ordering the sweepstake ticket and the "two calamity cubes" burned. The unassuming, maladroit tailor turns into a dominant, ingenious hero who uncovers the Nazi spy-ring in time to foil its arson plot. Rose and Esther Smith, engaged to be married, hint of womanhood, Lon of manhood while the head of the house nixes the move. Johnny undergoes metanoia. He confesses his intended theft to Yolanda, forsakes his career of crime, and settles down to connubial bliss. The crook departs with the lady. The coolie and his mysterious beauty are metamorphosed into the inhabitants of an Oriental paradise for a little while. Superego strangled, Manuela has found herself. The troupe's ravishing soubrette co-stars with the dashing matinee idol and will travel and play the world's capitals. Milo may be the occasion of Jerry's renewed determination and drive to have an exhibit, but Lise is its cause. Tony Hunter's self-wallowing "I'll go my way by myself" becomes part of the group's celebrative "No death like you get in *Macbeth*/No ordeal like the end of *Camille*." Gaby sloughs off her pomposity and her self-consciousness. Tommy Albright renounces Madison Avenue, his bitch fiancé, and *angst*. The beggar poet rests content with Lalume. His last tale, a departure from the rambunctiousness of the others, softly states that neither princes nor savants, only lovers know the riddle of life.

The transformation of Gigi *(Leslie Caron) and Gaston (Louis Jourdan) meets the approval of Honoré (Maurice Chevalier).*

Gone is Lalume's boredom, Marsinah's hunger and worry, and the Caliph's wide-eyed questing. Gigi grows into a woman, not a female, and playboy Gaston supplants proposition with proposal. Through Jeff, Ella accepts her masks and the goodness behind these poses. Daisy is cured of cigarettes, Warren, and neurotic insecurities. Chabot's fascination for Melinda brings mystery back into his life.

The production pattern—that of putting on the show—appears in the Minnelli melodrama, interpenetrates the romance, and involves a subsequent transformation of chaos to order. The pattern is sometimes literal, sometimes metaphorical. *I Dood It, Ziegfeld Follies, The Pirate,* and *The Band Wagon* are concerned explicitly with putting on the show, while the other musicals contain metaphorical extensions of this pattern. On the radio show and at the USO Benefit,

Constance Towers' new show is plugged. The producer is on the lookout for prospective angels. The money finally comes from the blue collar worker who proffers his reward from capturing the spies. The film's finale features a Brobdingnagian production number from the new show.

"Couldn't there be a new follies? . . . What I wouldn't give to open a new follies . . ." is the momentum behind the crayon and sketch pad's materialization in Ziggy's hand and the subsequent creation of another extravaganza combining his legendary showmanship with prestigious MGM stars which constitute the rest of the film. Since each sequence parades a star's personality and talent, the film also contains the production pattern's second aspect.

In Port Sebastian, the troupe of travelling thespians play a one-night stand, advertised by the wharf parade and previewed by Serafin's stroll.

And in Manuela's hometown, on and off the stage, the show goes on, no matter the star's impending execution. Simultaneous with Serafin's courting Manuela is his attempt to enlist her in the dramatic company. His love for her varies directly with his estimation of her as a performer. After her hypnosis, he exclaims: "They're cheering for you, your singing and dancing. You set them on fire." He is quite unable to fathom her marriage to Don Pedro in the light of her stage success: "Are you planning to get married?" When his protestations of love go unheeded, he matter-of-factly declares: "You know it isn't essential to love me to be in the troupe. It helps but it isn't essential . . . All I ask from you is to appear with us just once . . . Sing one song . . . just to know what a thrill it is." Throughout the film, Manuela figuratively puts on a show—a dramatic reading, a procession, a seduction, and a trance.

The Band Wagon dissects the mechanics of a musical show—casting, rehearsing, opening, and revamping..

Little Joe undergoes the rituals of Bible-reading, whereby its principles are appropriated and enacted in one's life, of confession of sins, and of worship consisting of psalm-singing, swaying, and hand-clapping in order to be saved. With its similar liturgy of enactment, confession, song, and dance, affecting *catharsis* or purification, the Church is the theatre's counterpart. For the Smiths, it is not so much putting on the show as remaining in the Midwest to attend the fair or show. Esther is a perennial poseur; Tootie, a thoroughbred show off. To pilfer Yolanda's money, Johnny must put on the show of being an "angel," involving at times, actual sets, props and lighting. In Paris, the shows are the forthcoming exhibit of Jerry's painting, Adam's platonic concert, and Henri's American-importable revue. *Brigadoon* prepares for the wedding of Jean Campbell, Fiona's sister, and Charlie Dalrymple. The wedding itself is a production—the gathering of the clans, the procession, the exchange of vows, the merrymaking afterwards. The chase for Harry, Jean's former suitor, is another metaphorical extension. Each poiesis, the result of the poet's imaginative twists of situation, characters, and setting to his own advantage, is a show. The search for the Caliph's bride involves a presentation of the maidens and their wares at the Grand Ceremonial. Gigi is being sculptured by two fine artists of the Parisian demi-mondaine school, Aunt Alicia and Grandmother Alvarez. "This work of art" or piece of showmanship is to be purchased by Gaston. Ella puts on a "show" for each client. She is the exemplary cause in getting her Prince Charming to write the play, Larry Hastings to produce it, Blake Barton to act in it, and Dr. Kitchell to compose songs for the nudish cuties at the Pyramid Club. Daisy's chain-smoking cure and Chabot's exorcism of Melinda are accomplished by ritualistic hypnotic sessions requiring a distinct setting, the proper positioning of patient and doctor, and special lighting.

The name, fame and fortune pattern, with fortune not being solely monetary, occurs, interpenetrating the romance and production patterns and involving transformation. Minnelli, however, never makes the crass equation of name equals fame and fortune. At times this pattern approaches an identity crisis.

Little Joe is saved. Investment in Connie's hit show increases the pants-presser's monetary reward. The tuxedo he wears in the last shot is his own. The move to New York is not financially necessary for St. Louis, and, by implication, the Smith family is headed for "a boom that will make the world sway," typified by the fair. Johnny secures the fortune and the estate legitimately through love. September 25, 1946 beholds another successful Follies. The company has another player, "the divine Manuela", and a better show as the packed house attests to. If Lise comes, can recognition as a painter be far behind for Jerry? Tony regains star status. "The show is a hit and will run a long, long time." Tommy opts for spiritual riches. A beggar and his daughter's rags metamorphose into robes; famine into feast. As Gaston's wealthy wife, Gigi will no longer have to earn her living in the salons. Ella marries play-

The name-fame-fortune motif: Daisy (Barbra Streisand) and independently wealthy Tad (Jack Nicholson), On A Clear Day You Can See Forever.

39

wright Jeff, successful in his solo effort. Blake will become a star. Kitchell markets a song. Her orphanage blackmail and union with Moorepark attests to Daisy's adherence to her mother's dictum: "Never, never do anything except for money." Struggling Warren is shed for independently wealthy Tad. Future bliss with Chabot implies comfort and security. Chabot's "adventure" is underwritten by the university's benefactor.

In these motifs, Minnelli's musicals reflect the tradition. To say only this about the drama of a Minnelli musical, though, is to leave the greater part unsaid. For Minnelli's drama deals with something much more, something that connects, underscores, and enriches these motifs while subsuming them.

Minnelli's melodrama is primarily concerned with the motif of creation—the making, from reality or the state of the way things are, of a fantasy or a state of a different, alternative, new, even radical life style on the protagonist's part. This notion of fantasy is derived from Harvey Cox in his book, *The Feast of Fools: A Theological Essay on Festivity and Fantasy*, in which he defined fantasy as "the faculty for envisioning radically alternative life situations."[15]

This motif, first of all, involves a spectrum of feeling ranging from a restlessness or dissatisfaction with reality to an estrangement from reality, concomitant with the desire to alter the present situation.

Further, this motif involves choice on the protagonist's part, a choice conditioned, caused, and molded by his/her private, interior, and imaginative levels of being—remembrance, wish, hope, daydream, dream or its opposite nightmare, awe, wonder or belief in mystery, faith in God, vision, extrasensory perception, projection and pretense, be it theatrical or atheatrical. Felt pressures of experience send Minnelli's people deep within themselves where they touch the core of their being. Slight though this touch may be, it nevertheless energizes the reshaping of their lives.

Lastly, the two spheres are presented oppositely. Dialectic rather than juxtaposition is Minnelli's method. That is, the worlds are not presented matter-of-factly, they are interpreted and evaluated. Reality versus fantasy, the central conflict of the film, comes down to the impersonal vying with the personal, the objective with the subjective, the functional with the essential, the realistic with the idealistic, the classical with the romantic, the prosaic with the poetic, and the Apollinian with the Dionysian. Fantasy's triumph culminates the story.

This motif, experienced vaguely if at all in previous film musicals, is an explicit presence in Minnelli's work. Although imaging movement, energy, drive, and success, this motif is not primarily denotative of Yankee mythology. But more of this later.

Since the dimension of transformation is also involved, since romance, production, name, fame, and fortune are some of the specific embodiments of the fantasy, this motif unites the other motifs, heightens them, but most importantly, realistically grounds or motivates them. Consequently, the traditional motifs are not as shallow, crude, and eminently forgettable as before.

Cabin in the Sky's story is built from Negro folklore. The foreword rolling over the painted clouds after the credits declaims:

> Throughout the ages, powerful and inspiring thoughts have been preserved and handed down by the medium of the legend, the fable, and the fantasy. The folklore of America has origins in all lines, all races, all colors. This story of faith and devotion springs from that source and seeks to capture those values.

Cabin depicts the survival of archaic beliefs and mores among the rural Negroes in the South—their anthropomorphic concept of God and Satan, the practice and power of prayer and other religious ritual, the belief in divine providence, the soul's existence, and the afterlife. Furthermore, it presents these elements as valuable. This tone is partly responsible for the egalitarian treatment of the blacks in the film, in no way chic at the time. Minnelli is neither irreverent nor patronizing nor sanctimonious (segregation in reverse) toward the material. In the temporary complete script, for example, Little Joe works as an elevator operator in a white man's hotel. In the final version, Joe is a trucker at the mill—a small but telling change by Minnelli.

The film is a product of nostalgia and memory on the director's part, as all folklore is. Though made and released during the war, at a time when America attempted to mend its tattered beliefs and polish its tarnished traditions, the entire piece functions then as now as a fantasy, a world at variance with the secular and scientific one. Like *Cabin*, many of Minnelli's musicals as a whole (*St. Louis, Follies, Yolanda, Brigadoon, Kismet*) function as fantasies, counterpointing the world lighted on the screen with that in the darkness.

Within the film itself, the motif of creation is present. Reality finds *homo viator* in trouble. The good that Little Joe wants to do, he does not. The bad he does not want to do, he does. The Paradise

Cafe wins out over the church service he is supposed to attend with Petunia. The sweepstake ticket and dice are not destroyed but stashed away in the bureau drawer. This reality frames Little Joe's nightmare that turns into dream during his delirious recovery from Domino Johnson's bullet wound received in the cafe. The nightmare commences with Lucifer Jr. and company's arrival to claim his soul at his death. The nightmare shades into a dream when the good angel, having received "the powerful prayer of Petunia," appears to tell Joe that on account of Petunia, the Lord gives him leave to stay on this earth for six months more. If he whitewashes his soul in that time, he makes the grade with heaven. If not, Lucifer Sr. gets permanent control. The continuing dream includes his recovery from the gunshot wound, his awakening faith, the security of a job at the mill, personifications of his interior thoughts about good and evil,

and finally, despite Petunia's slight misunderstanding and his own even slighter waywardness with Georgia, the books' balance permitting him to climb heaven's stairs with Petunia. His new life ends with his ascent, or rather only begins, for with his descent to grovelling underneath the bed sheets, Little Joe begins his metanoia, urged by his nightmare-dream. The laurel of Little Joe's fantasy must not be placed on his pate alone. Petunia's faith and the Lord have something to do with it.

The level of faith in the Lord, expressed and fed in private prayer and liturgy, an extraordinary level of living, is one which Petunia straddles within the frame as well as within Joe's dream. Petunia chants "Li'l Black Sheep" with her congregation. Her glassy eyes and tear-streaked cheeks bargain with God for Joe's life: "Joe won't give you any more trouble if you will let him live."

The nightmare begins as Petunia (Ethel Waters) is told of Little Joe's mortal wound by the doctor, Cabin in the Sky.

The nightmare ends with the balancing of Little Joe's
(Eddie 'Rochester' Anderson) books on the stairway,
Cabin in the Sky.

"Happiness Is Just a Thing Called Joe," delivered on her knees, is both a prayer of gratitude and joy for an answered petition and a romantic protestation. When beating Jim Henry and Dude at their own game, she rolls her eyes skyward: "Please forgive me for backsliding. But sometimes you got to get the devil with a pitchfork." At the picnic, she tells Joe of the Lord's providence and obliges with "Cabin in the Sky," a mellifluous profession of faith. A miracle climaxes the festivity. Joe's cane breaks and he walks unaided. Piqued at Joe, she questions God: "Lord, why do You let me love him so much that he hurts me so bad?" During the cafe brawl, Petunia prays: "Do something, Lord. Send down Your wrath and destroy this wicked place." Another answer to her prayer, this time in the form of a tornado that pummels the cafe to pieces. Like the film as a whole and Little

Joe, Petunia also embodies the motif of creation, hers elicited and nourished by faith in the Lord.

The contrast between Joe Reynolds' prosaic world centering around the Park Savoy Valet Service and his poetic world shaped by hope, dream, projection, and pretense centering around Gotham stages, informs *I Dood It*. The contrast, though, is not as sharp as it can or should be since the film omits scenes of the hero at work.

The opening sequence articulately delineates this contrast. Tuxedoed (he dons the habiliments of wealthy customers) Joe is shown in a space and time apart from the radio audience he is amongst. While the audience swings to Jimmy Dorsey's "One O'Clock Jump" and then storms the proscenium, Joe remains still and transfixed, eyes glued to the wings opposite where Connie awaits her cue. After kissing the star at a USO benefit,

Poetry within prose: musical star Connie (Eleanor Powell), the apple of the pants-presser Joe's (Red Skelton) eye, I Dood It.

Joe floats down the street in a trance, oblivious of the people who must step aside to prevent his crashing into them. On the wall of his room is a conglomeration of clichéd theatrical poses of the actress, a shrine at which he worships. His vestments in this scene—top hat, starched shirt, vest, tie, and alas, underwear—encapsulate the conflict. During a performance of *Dixie Lou*, he projects himself in the melodrama's every part in order to co-star with Connie. The audience's applause at the curtain forces him to take a bow. At the club he pretends to be "the owner of gold mines" and Connie's fiancé in conformation with her game of revenge. Joe, however, is unaware it is a game. To avoid detection from his employer, he pretends to be a waiter. Arriving at Connie's suite to marry her, a gambit in her scheme, Joe announces: "This is the moment I often stayed awake dreaming about." When his fantasy topples, Joe begins the restoration by placing a vase of roses before Connie's altar. Turning on the gas jets which, unbeknownst to him, happened to be shut off after business hours, Joe, recalling Connie's words of the previous night, "Just go to sleep," does exactly that and dreams of her, all satin, silvery, and slithery in an exotic Hawaiian setting. The dream revitalizes his fantasy. Returning to Connie, he is plummeted on stage playing the villain in *Dixie Lou* vis-à-vis her and then backstage becomes a hero under her approving guise. The final sequence finds Joe again taking bows in the front row of the audience after the performance of Connie's new and appropriately titled show *Star Eyes*. Fiancé of the musical star,

angel of her hit show, tuxedo-owner—this is the consummation of a pants-presser's fantasy.

The structure of *Meet Me in St. Louis*—four faded seasonal photographs of the Smith house on Kensington Avenue, St. Louis, circa 1900—relates that the film is a memory and establishes the awesome and nostalgic tone of the entire piece.

Moving into Kensington Avenue and this world as each photograph fills with color, blows up, and comes alive, the film sets itself up as a contrast with one's own world. This vanished, almost mythic past is a fantasy burgeoning from the seeds of remembrance and counterpointing present reality. Here is a world of a family that spans all ages from the tot Tootie to Gramps, of homemade ketchup, corned-beef-and-cabbage nights, and chocolates in lavender tin boxes topped with a pink satin bow. Young ladies heat water on the kitchen stove to clean their tresses. Pictures of butterfly wings grace the walls. An ice wagon hobbles down the street. "Clang, clang, clang [goes] the trolley." The measure has three beats. Rituals, like grace before meals, bon voyage parties where a female trumpeter performs a solo and the "welch rabbit is ginger peachy," Halloween, Christmas, and of course, the commemoration of the Louisiana Purchase are kept. Boys do not like girls with the bloom rubbed off. When a lad in New York telephones a girl in St. Louis, the urgency and financial expenditure are expected to indicate nothing less than a proposal. A girl is in love with the boy next door. The family's happiness takes precedence over financial gain.

Within the film itself, the venture from reality to fantasy is undertaken. In mid-summer, the Smiths anticipate (a form of hope), project, and envision the fair, still seven months away, and their city which will be transformed because of the fair. Esther and John are part of an outing to the fairgrounds in late summer. On Christmas Eve, Mr. Smith makes extravagant predictions about the future of the city. With the Smiths' springtime visit to the fair, their expectation is rewarded, their vision comes true. St. Louis is transformed.

Esther's reality of being a high school senior with "too much bloom" leaves something to be desired and that something is John Truett. "The Boy Next Door" and "Over the Bannister Leaning" are daydreams and picturesque poses. These pretenses are much more professionally crafted than that wispy, half-baked pose on the porch's wooden rail with a rose almost kissing her cheek opposite John smoking his pipe on the lawn. With John's proposal, elicited by her, Esther's reality is transcended.

The mythic past: Lon (H. H. Daniels, Jr.) samples Katie's (Marjorie Main) homemade ketchup with his mother (Mary Astor) overseeing, Meet Me in St. Louis.

Esther (Judy Garland) and Rose (Lucille Bremer) pose on their porch before the boy next door, Meet Me In St. Louis.

Tootie imagines all the time—her doll with the four fatal diseases, and the entire trick-or-treat sequence from Mr. Bankoff's murder to John's assault. With her, it is not a question of making but of sustaining a fantasy.

"You and I" of Mr. and Mrs. Smith is a wedding-day reminiscence. The song's lyrics paraphrase the wedding vows. The tune approximates Wagner's *Lohengrin*. Their duet transports them (they are oblivious to their family's intrusion during this memento) to a state different from the one they inhabit in the film's opening two-thirds where he barks and she submits, where her feelings are overlooked in his decision to move to New York. For the rest of the film, they exist in a new way, eloquently imaged in their ardent, tender kiss and embrace, her uncontrollable tears of joy, and his soft hushes on Christmas Eve. The

fantasy of their first days together is renewed.

The mythical, "out-of-the-way place" of Patria with its equally mythical transpirings constitute the modern fairy tale or fantasy, *Yolanda and the Thief*. It is spun, as all fairy tales are, from the realm of wish. The film opens with the schoolmaster conducting a geography lesson to second graders:

This is a land which you can see is warmed by the sun and cooled by the benevolent wind. Here life is pleasant, because people are good. It is a fact that jails are empty and the churches are filled. Over us is the Patria sky, which is the color of heaven; and around us are the fields of flowers, and the cool streams, full of friendly fish . . .

Girls grow up in convent schools. Processions accompany homecomings. A guardian angel

Yolanda (Lucille Bremer), about to leave the convent school, is assured by the mother superior that she has a guardian angel, Yolanda and the Thief.

45

walks the earth and arranges his ward's life in answer to her prayer. "I want you to be the husband of Yolanda," prescribes the angel to the young man on the train leaving Patria. The mere mortal deems the whole thing quite impossible. Indignation elicits the angel's "I just made a flood, broke a bridge, and had a train go back and you have the nerve to sit there and tell me that something is impossible?"

The management of the Acquaviva funds, land, and enterprises is thrust upon Yolanda, fresh from a convent school. Her fantasy of a guardian angel to help, protect, even to love her in this real burden of coming of age is expressed in prayer and ignited by faith in God. In the sunken garden before the statue, she kneels: "Dear guardian angel, come to my aid. Tell me what to do. Help me." When the "angel" telephones her, she wonders: "Is this the earth I really occupy/ Or am I really living in the sky?/ Oh where, oh where am I?" She makes her devotion before the "angel" in the hotel lobby. Again in the garden, she confesses her love and yearns for a reply. Her prayer is fulfilled and her fantasy runneth over, with a helper, protector, lover, and four children.

Johnny, along with his old crony Victor, plans to purloin the Acquaviva dough. But the reality of being a crook weighs heavily on him. His projection as to the identification of the three men opposite him on the train attempts to assuage his guilt. All three, to him, seek the spoils. The fashion plate reading a newspaper, strictly a dilettante type, is Casanova in a rented suit. The monocled man with the mink eyebrows has a scheme for building a bridge with the lady's money from which he will hurl her. The last, a charming man, well-groomed and intelligent, is the most dangerous of all since he has an honest face. Johnny's pretense of being the "angel" sends shivers of remorse through him. After Yolanda's devotion, his countenance crinkles with worry. His nightmare energizes his guilt and affection for the girl. Johnny's substratum has laid the foundation for the fantasy that is to be erected by the guardian angel at Yolanda's faithful behest.

Like Tootie, Aunt Armarilla lives continually in an abstraction, a world concocted by her own projection, at variance with the way things are. At her niece's arrival, her descriptions of the servants have no reality content whatsoever. This Patrician indulges her passion of sliding down the bannister in imitation of a peasant boy. Yolanda's signing over the bonds to Johnny is interpreted as a declaration of marriage. Johnny's confession note is "one of the nicest love letters" she has ever read. She utters not a peep about his intended nefariousness.

Johnny (Fred Astaire) purloins Yolanda's (Lucille Bremer) money, Yolanda and the Thief.

Ziegfeld Follies plunges one through pink swirling clouds and transports one over Shakespeare's Globe, P. T. Barnum's circus tent, and a Ziegfeld theatre which dissolves to a pink and white apartment floating in a starry blue sky where Ziggy enjoys another heavenly day. This brief space odyssey deposits one in a realm of fantasy—heaven.

Within this fantasy, old man Ziggy toys "with the memories of yesterday," the era of his Follies and his present situation yields to a previous one—spiffy folk flock to the Jardin de Paris. Mrs. Astor alights from her carriage pulled by her famous horse. Diamond Jim Brady assists a blonde down his transport's steps. Inside the theatre, Anna Held and the Hour Glass Girls kick up their heels, Marilyn Miller pirouettes, Fanny Brice romps as an Indian, Will Rogers philosophizes while twirling a lasso, and Eddie Cantor warbles: "If You Knew Susie Like I Know Susie . . ." The applause is intense. Then, a succession of marquees twinkle with the titles of Ziggy's shows. This memory dissolves into the present reality, which eventually veers off into projection and vision. On a marble balcony, Ziggy, with brightening eyes focused downward, considers: "What I wouldn't give to open a new

The memories of yesterday, Ziegfeld Follies.

Follies! There are great personalities down there to choose from.'' Asking for a crayon and paper which immediately transpire in his hands, he starts to design a new Follies:

> How would I open? . . . Let's see. Well, maybe with a beautiful pink number, with a beautiful pink and white blue-eyed girl. And maybe to introduce the whole thing, who would be better than my old friend, Fred Astaire—a great star, yes . . .

A top-to-bottom screen wipe, and Fred "Bring[s] on the Beautiful Girls" and Ziggy's new Follies materializes, which transforms the reality of "just another heavenly day" into one of glamor, frolic, and elation. The individual acts' titles and casts are introduced on a sketch book, an image recalling the pad in the showman's hand.

"This Heart of Mine" and "Limehouse Blues" contain in miniature the creation motif. The

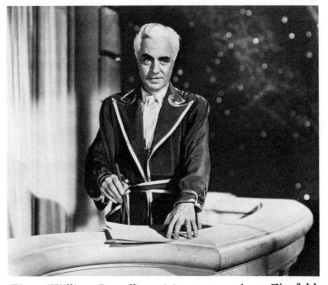

Ziggy (William Powell) envisions a new show, Ziegfeld Follies.

47

thronged red ballroom opens out mysteriously to a blue fairy garden, empty save for white wintry trees and love seat—a visual encapsulation of the opening of the thief's spirit by a daydream which eventually encourages his submission: "This heart of mine/ Was doing very well/ The world was fine/ As far as I could tell/ And then quite suddenly I met you/ And dreamed of gay amours . . ." Moments before his death, the lowly servant envisions himself and his Eurasian in celestial bliss. The fantasy triumphs since he departs his wretched Limehouse life with this dream in his heart and the lady by his side. Fortunately, his expiring eyes witness neither the lady's release of the blood-stained fan nor her departure with the lecherous Oriental businessman.

The other sequences, although they do not contain the motif's full movement, do contain stages of it. "Bring on the Beautiful Girls" is a merry-go-round of fantastic females. "Water Bal-let" suggests the reality-fantasy duality as the swimmer performs above and then below the water. "Number Please" spills into nightmare as a man in a hotel lobby is unable to get a call through to a neighborhood cigar store. "Pay the Two Dollars" is a nightmare in which expectoration in a subway and an intransigent lawyer lead to a jail term, expenses totaling $463,663.63, ruined health, the loss of a business, a divorce, and finally, a first-degree murder pardoned in the nick of time. The skit concludes with the Sisyphian suggestion that the whole process is about to begin again. "A Sweepstake Ticket" is Montie and Norma's wish come true. "When Television Comes" verges on nightmare as the advertiser-announcer becomes inebriated on the product. "A Great Lady Has an Interview" describes a star's pretense. "The Babbit and the Bromide" is a time-and-space trip from youth and middle-age on earth to senior citizens in heaven. The finale is a

Norma (Fanny Brice) and Montie (Hume Cronyn) attempt to retrieve the winning ticket from their landlord in the skit, "A Sweepstake Ticket," Ziegfeld Follies.

48

projection of "Beauty" in moonlight and at sunrise.

Closing the illustrated history of *The Pirate* and pressing it to her bosom, Manuela's imagination burns as she addresses him from her balcony:

Macoco, where are you now? . . . They'll never hang you. On the moving waters of the Caribbean he darts about like a dragonfly . . . glittering . . . uncaptureable. He's magnificent, ruthless, romantic. If he saw the woman he wanted, he would take her and carry her off on his ship. He'd treat her like a queen.

To Casilda's chiding: "I don't want anyone swooping down on me like a chicken hawk. I want a good steady man with a plantation, not too big, not too small," Manuela proves indomitable: "Casilda, I wish you were a little more spiritual. Don't you ever dream of a man who will come and take you out of this village . . . this little saucer in the hills?" Aunt Inez flutters in full of excitement at her portentous news. A marriage has been arranged between her orphaned, penniless niece and Don Pedro, the portly, pompous, pitiful mayor who espouses the values of home and hearth. The first dozen shots reveal the conflict between fantasy nourished by wish, hope, daydream and pretense, and reality informing the entire piece.

After the material remunerations of the match have been detailed, Manuela, beside a map of the Caribbean, importunes her aunt to travel to Port Sebastian and meet the ship transporting her trousseau from Paris: "I'd so love to see the Caribbean. It holds a special fascination for me. It means adventure, romance. And I shall never have any . . . I'll make him a good wife . . . I realize there is a practical world and a dream world. And I shall never mix them."

On Port Sebastian's seawall, the pious, repressed, and betrothed damsel encounters the Caribbean with eyelids closed and nostrils inhaling the

Manuela (Judy Garland) arrives in the fabled Port Sebastian with Aunt Inez (Gladys Cooper), The Pirate.

salty air as Serafin, a dramatic troupe's leading player, encounters her: "I see you find your romance in daydreams. I know that underneath that prim exterior there are depths of emotion, romantic longings, unfulfilled dreams." At their second encounter under the performing tent, Serafin with the help of "that new and sensational science of animal magnetism taught by the great Mesmer himself" unlocks her inner sanctum.

Back home on her wedding morn, Manuela doubts her future happiness. Aunt Inez tells her that she "can make anything come true by wishing for it." Manuela begins to mold another fantasy from memory and wish. Retrieving her picture hat, limp and soggy from the salt water on the sea-walk, she caresses it dearly and laughs exuberantly. It is her first laugh in the film. Then, music of the strolling players comes up in the distance and suddenly, Manuela's countenance blushes incredulously. Her fantasy of wild, extravagant, romantic Serafin and the acting company begins to take shape.

Cognizant of Manuela's infatuation with Macoco and discovering that Don Pedro is the real Macoco, Serafin pretends to be the bold-faced buccaneer, thereby uniting her two fantasies. Manuela's marriage to Don Pedro is off. He, Macoco/Serafin, is to marry her in ten minutes or the town will be burned. In the courtyard, the folk cower before him while above, Manuela daydreams of his dauntless derring-do.

While she awaits her husband-to-be, one of the players lets the cat out of the bag: "This is what you dreamed of, isn't it? and Manuela revenges herself. A pummelled room later, she succumbs to Serafin and the sock and buskins's aura of magic.

Serafin (Gene Kelly) as Macoco ravishes Manuela (Judy Garland) on her wedding day, The Pirate.

The reality-fantasy conflict is played out by another set of images. Serafin is a "master juggler, conjurer, dancer, singer of songs," who, along with his troupe, stages entertainments, creating a world of romance and adventure, thrills and titillation, gaiety and pleasure: "Ladies and gentlemen, come tonight to see the magic of our art." With a talent for pretense, Serafin is a master of fantasies. His performances, both on and offstage—his appetizingly antic advertisements on the wharf, square, and sea-walk, his role-playing as Macoco, his death by picture frame scene, his execution, the *sturm und drang* menage à trois, and his mischevious auguste—are fantasies, the creation of another world to woo Manuela and Don Pedro, thus bolstering the troupe, while astonishing and delighting an audience.

Although reluctant to admit it at first, Manuela is a born actress also. A raised platform and proscenium arch are no necessities for her to create another world to relieve and counteract her own, and other's, estimations of her humdrum existence. On the balcony, in the presence of her girlfriends, she histrionically recites Macoco's history. (Once again, the hocus-pocus of art, this time literature and painting). With unveiled knee and calf on the shoulder of a sailor before her on all fours in the tent, she becomes a Dietrich-like femme fatale. In her mind's eye, she plays a ravaged virgin. Before the villagers, she enacts the sacrificial victim with lowered eyes, stolid dignity, black veil, and mahogany dress. Before Serafin, an audience of one, she pretends to be a vehement censor of the acting profession and seductress. Before the court, she attempts the role of the stock heroine of Victorian melodrama rather successfully. Finally, she triumphs as a riotously happy auguste before countless enthralled spectators.

As such, the principals play on two levels in the film, both embodying the creation theme. They are Serafin and Manuela as well as eternal troupers.

An American in Paris commences with three consecutive interior monologues over accompanying images. Each, the expression of wish and hope, assails the narrators' present state of affairs. Jerry Mulligan avows that he stayed on in Paris after the war to paint because "for a painter, the mecca of the world for study, for inspiration, and for living is here on this star called Paris . . ." During his introduction, the camera, after roving through painterly Parisian sights, stops at an apartment window through which a young couple kiss. Two impressive paintings adorn the wall. It is an image of Jerry's desires—romance and fame. "That's not me," Jerry wistfully butts in as the

*Serafin (Gene Kelly) and Manuela (Judy Garland) as
augustes in their entertainment, "Be A Clown," The
Pirate.*

*Jerry (Gene Kelly) is besieged by the French children
—the only fame he warrants, An American in Paris.*

image cuts and the camera tracks through the window of a two-by-four garret to find Jerry alone in bed with unfinished canvases strewn everywhere.

Adam Cook begins: "I am a concert pianist. That's a pretentious way of saying I am unemployed at the moment . . . I'm here on scholarship . . ." The camera frames a man placing a parakeet, after bussing it, into a cage. The image denotes the placid contentment Adam seeks. "That's not me", Adam groans, "he's too happy." The felicitous image contrasts with that of neurotic, hypochondriac Adam, who abruptly interrupts his piano practice by rifling a pack of cigarettes, rummaging for an ash tray and matches, and putting drops in his eyes and nose.

Henri Baurel is a famous French music-hall star. As the camera dollies toward a mirror on a street pole, a youthful handsome face appears, a reflection of how Henri wants to look. "That's not me. I'm not that young," Henri corrects as he approaches the vacated mirror to fix his tie. "Let's just say I am old enough to know what to do with my young feelings."

As the picture proceeds, each one's psychic pressure weighs so heavily upon him that wish and hope become daydream and vision. Henri's Utopian abstract concerns Lise, the neophyte he is engaged to. The mirror that images Henri conversing with Adam about Lise dissolves to the girl in a congeries of situations depicting the opalescent facets of her personality; Adam's persistent taunts unsuccessfully attempt to temper his idealization.

Adam's pipedream occurs at the film's center. His slouchily smoking in bed dissolves to him performing *Concerto in F* not only as a solo pianist but as every member of the symphony orchestra—violinists, xylophonist, drummer, cymbalist—as well as conducting and applauding "Bravo" from a box seat. Back in his flat, he rises from the bed and unwraps a white linen napkin from a bottle of coke plunged in the ice of a silver magnum—a detail epitomizing the reality-fantasy dynamic.

The film's concluding section "An American in Paris Ballet," is Jerry's recapitulation of his innermost needs—Lise and painting. At its conclusion, Lise returns. One half of Jerry's fantasy is achieved; the other, presumed.

The romantics' courtship is presented as a private sphere blotting out other people, even the lovers' past. "Can't we have our own special world and not talk about anything that happens when we're apart?" Lise, like Jerry, embodies fully the creation motif. (Adam's hopes are left up in the air; Henri's flounder.) The reality of being

Henri's affianced ward becomes the fantasy of being Jerry's lover, ignited by the daydream of "Our Love Is Here to Stay."

Throughout the film, Jerry is seen painting as well as role-playing, both of which create a world abstracted from the ordinary, the one urged on by vision, the other by pretense. Café Muguette, the Left Bank, the Parisian child, the Place de la Concorde, and Lise are all transformed by his canvas, paints, and brushes. Before bemused patrons, Jerry turns the cafe into a scene from Viennese valse-opera with "By Strauss." He is a chain of American inventions during a French lesson for the neighborhood kids—"I Got Rhythm"; he's a drunk, inebriated with love, with Adam—"Tra-la-la-la"; and a harlequin for Milo at the ball. Henri's "I'll Build a Stairway to Paradise," through show-biz magnetism, also fashions a mini-universe.

The Band Wagon is haunted by memory. At the Bolwinkle Galleries in Los Angeles, "Tony Hunter's personal effects as used in his starring roles" are being auctioned—top hat, white gloves, and cane. Hunter, "perhaps the greatest singing and dancing star the films have ever known," is not dead, only *passé*. But then, to be *passé* in Hollywood is even worse than death. Takers are nil when the auctioneer starts the bidding at five dollars and reduces it to two, fifty cents, anything. Reality turns its back upon memory-fantasy.

On the Twentieth Century which brings Hunter to Broadway for a show, and hopefully, to regain the spotlight, tension is rife. Two businessmen comment on a magazine photo of Tony advertising cigarettes: "He was good twelve or fifteen years ago but columnists say he is all washed up." Tony, within earshot, concurs: "He's all washed up . . . hasn't made a picture in three years." The royal carpet treatment, presumed for himself, turns out, in fact, to be for the famous, contemporary silver screen star, Ava Gardner.

Friends Les and Lillie Marton, composer and librettist-lyricist of musical shows, attempt to revive the good old days as they race into Grand Central with Hunter fan-club paraphernalia, a brouhaha worthy of twenty-two people (no one else in the thronged terminal recognizes Tony), and a show to reinstate him in the public's graces.

As the trio saunters along Forty-Second Street between Eighth Avenue and Broadway, the conflict is again sharply focused. Being informed that Jeffrey Cordova will produce and direct the show, Tony's face wrinkles into a question mark: "But he doesn't direct musicals." Lillie, however, sets Tony straight: "No, but what's the difference? He's theatre. He can do anything.

Jerry, through painting, creates a world within a world,
An American in Paris.

He's a new kind of theatre man, Tony. The theatre's changed, you know. Lots of things have changed.'' Lillie's bold observation as well as the environs' riff-raff and honky-tonks, reducing the avenue to a Coney Island midway, push Tony's perplexity to horror. Tony achingly wonders what happened:

> There's the New Amsterdam Theatre. Remember? Fifteen years ago, I was starring there in *Flying Banners* . . . The Sam Harris Theatre . . . Look across the street—the Selwyn. That's where Noel Coward and Gertie were playing in *Private Lives*.

Backstage at *Oedipus Rex*, Cordova's secretary rattles off the usual, ''Hello, Mr. Hunter; I admire your work,'' while devoting all his attention to cueing the gaffer. Cordova himself mistakes Tony for an errand boy: ''Order me a corned beef sandwich—lean, no fat, no gristle, sans pickle, creme soda.''

With Cordova joining the fray, the conflict deepens. Now Tony's memory-fantasy must fly in the face of his present dethronement as well as Cordova's projection-fantasy which consists of the remaking of the Martons' ''light and intimate show'' to showcase Tony's personality and talent into his own image and likeness, ''a modern version of Faust . . . a modern musical morality play with meaning and stature.'' Tony flatly refuses: ''I know what I can do. I'm going to stick to it.'' Cordova applies the bait:

> That's the trouble, Tony. You've stuck to it and you're stuck with it . . . But let's face some brutal facts. Times have changed and you haven't changed with them . . . You've gone stale, Tony . . . We're going to make you explode on the theatre scene like a skyrocket. Not just a trademark with the taps and top hat and tails, but a great artist at the peak of his powers—the new Tony Hunter, Tony Hunter, 1953.

53

At a rehearsal, Tony (Fred Astaire) tries to bring out the "meaning and stature" of the text, intimidated by co-star Gabrielle (Cyd Charisse) and goaded by director Cordova (Jack Buchanan), The Band Wagon.

Tony accepts, and is pitted against the young, tall ballerina Gabrielle Gerard, who refers to Tony as "an historical character," her fiancé-choreographer (Tony has not done ballet since he was a kid), and a Stanislavsky acting type. In the midst of rehearsals, Tony stomps out: "I am not Nijinsky, I am not Marlon Brando. I'm Mrs. Hunter's little boy, Tony, an entertainer. I've entertained millions of people in my time but I am not entertained by this little ballerina's snide insinuations that I'm a no talent bum!"

Gaby's apology causes Tony to take stock: "Look, we're from different worlds . . . two eras and yet the two of us are supposed to dance together, work together." He suggests they find out. In a secluded area of moonlit Central Park, Tony leads Gaby in a *pas-de-deux*—the first steps in the achievement of his fantasy.

Cordova's disastrous rehearsal, The Band Wagon.

On the sidelines, Jeffrey's projection-fantasy playfully winds down. The smoking effects rehearsal is a mine disaster. The show's scenery, more than Yellowstone National Park, becomes a Frankenstein. A coughing jag, brought on by the spectacular explosions, interrupts the principals' number, "You and the Night and the Music." The show bombs in New Haven.

The rest of the film deals with Tony's revamping. The devil's costume is burned. The lights are turned up full. "It's going to have laughs and entertainment . . . remember entertainment, Jeffrey?" Paul quits. Tony choreographs. A hit show and the memory of Tony Hunter is alive and well, and living on Broadway.

As in *The Pirate*, the reality-fantasy melody is played in another key. The entertainments created are fantasies within reality, a world within a world with its own order, logic, and rules. One of Jeffrey's pep talks is devoted to this very notion.

Well, there it is, folks, the work light . . . For the next four weeks, this will be our sun, our moon, our stars. These four walls will be our universe, our private world. We enter with naught but a dream but when we leave, we'll have a show.

The razz-ma-tazz "That's Entertainment" sequence encapsulates this motif: "The world is a stage/ The stage is a world" where weakling Les puts Lillie on his shoulders and balances Tony and Jeffrey on each hip, where a squeaky noise substitutes for voices, where a hand becomes a

gun, where Les carries both the beginning and end of the same ladder, where Jeffrey's cigarette is lit mysteriously, where three people materialize on the spot. The number summarizes Minnelli's vision.

Brigadoon is a fantasy springing from faith in God as the dominie Mr. Lundie explains to the two lost and weary hunters:

Two hundred years ago, the highlands of Scotland were plagued with witches, wicked sorcerers who were takin' the Scottish fold away from the teachings of God and puttin' the devil in their souls. (Reality.) Now here in Brigadoon we had an old minister of the kirk named Mr. Forsythe. A good man he was. So he began to wonder if there wasna somethin' he could do to protect the fold of his parish, not only from them, but from all the evils that might come to Brigadoon from the outside world after he died . . . Then one day he came to me an' told me he had decided to ask God for a miracle . . . He went out to a hill beyond Brigadoon and made his prayer to God . . . Brigadoon would vanish but not always. It would return just as it was for one day every hundred years.

The Manhattan bar sequence, Tommy and Jeff's world and one's own, sharpens the fantasy-reality antithesis. This antithesis also is stated in terms of the two intruding New Yorkers on vacation. Tommy is a popular metaphysician; Jeff a diehard pragmatist. Tommy's "there's something about this forest that gives me the feeling of being in a cathedral" elicits a disgruntled snort from Jeff: "I can understand, you know, anything that's real to me, like things I can touch, taste, hear, see, smell, and swallow." "What about things you don't understand?" asks Tommy. "I dismiss them," scoffs Jeff. Tommy's unstable relationship with Jane makes him question his ability to love. Nevertheless, he is open to Fiona. To the shepherdess complaining that there are "not enough lads in Brigadoon," Jeff comments on the institution of marriage: "I don't believe in marriage. I've seen too many happy love affairs broken up by it," and scurries away. Tommy, alive with wonder, wants to stay a little longer. Jeff, bugged by mystery, urges a prompt departure. During the schoolmaster's etiological narration, Tommy's eyes are aglow with reverence and awe. Perturbed, Jeff squints with disbelief. In Manhattan, although Jeff is as malcontent with modern, urban life as Tommy, he confronts the situation with the facile, short-lived strategem of nasty, cynical remarks. This is the extent of Jeff's creativity. Tommy counters reality with memory: "So many things remind me of her. When I'm with people and they might say one little word that

A summary of Minnelli's vision: Cordova (Jack Buchanan) with Lillie (Nanette Fabray) and Les (Oscar Levant) remind Tony (Fred Astaire) the "world is a stage/The stage is a world . . ." in "That's Entertainment," The Band Wagon.

Fiona (Cyd Charisse) brings Tommy (Gene Kelly) and Jeff (Van Johnson) to Mr. Lundie (Barry Jones) for the explanation of Brigadoon's *existence.*

opens the door to a memory for me and suddenly I don't hear them any more.'' During a conversation with Jane, her ''I saw a wonderful place rather interesting, Colonial and right on top of a high, beautiful hill . . .'' dissolves to Fiona singing ''Heather on the Hill.'' Jane's ''You certainly wouldn't keep me waiting'' triggers off Fiona's ''Waitin' for My Dearie'' and Tommy's closed eyelids. Rising suddenly, Tommy shouts to Jane that the engagement is kaput. In an attempt to smoothe things over, Jane suggests they ''go home.'' The remark ignites the villagers' volatile ''I'll Go Home With Bonnie Jean.'' Spurred on by these souvenirs, Tommy returns to Brigadoon. This is the extent of his creativity. Jeff demands a reason. Tommy is impatient: ''Never mind what for! I know it isn't here, but I want to see where it

was . . . Who cares if it doesn't make sense.'' Deep within the woods, Jeff confesses to Tommy that he must work hard to convince himself that Brigadoon happened at all. For Tommy, Brigadoon is more real to him than ever before, in fact, most real: ''That's the big difference between us. Sometimes the things you believe in become more real to you than things you can explain or understand.'' The mist scurries. A light cuts the grayness in two. Lundie's voice fills the silence: ''Tommy, lad, ye really did come back.'' Tommy runs down the hill into Fiona's arms while Jeff waves goodbye. Tommy's awe, belief in mystery, and memory have realized his fantasy.

Fiona's fantasy of her ideal man is nourished by daydream and a soupçon of extrasensory perception. Fiona shares her daydream with her girl-

Back in Manhattan with his fiancée (Elaine Stewart),
Tommy (Gene Kelly) remembers only Brigadoon.

friends as they prepare for her sister's wedding: "I hold a dream an' there's no compromisin' . . . For ye see, I believe that there's a laddie weary and wanderin' free/ Who's waitin' for his dearie, me." Right she is, for the previous sequence depicted Tommy, physically and psychologically depleted. Tommy's arrival and return consummates Fiona's fantasy.

Lundie also possesses extrasensory perception. He confides to Tommy his dream:

> For me 'tis like bein' carried in shadowy arms to some far-off cloud an' there I float till mornin'. And yet sometimes I think I hear strange voices. They say words I can't remember. But they're voices filled with fearful longin' an' after they seem to be callin' me back. I have a feelin' I'm hearing the outside world. There must be lots of folk out there who'd like a Brigadoon.

And right he is, as Tommy's return awakening Lundie from sleep, confirms.

Kismet is an Arabian Nights fairy tale set in fabled Bagdad of the fourteenth century. Night prayers are chanted atop minarets. Houses are inlaid with gold. Merchants display rare silks and jewels in the marketplace. Lovers stroll in perfumed gardens where only peacocks and birds of paradise can espy them, leaves of mulberry trees whisper and nightingales sing at noon. A wicked and corrupt Wazir meets his just deserts. A father finds his long-lost son. A beggar becomes Emir;

Lalume (Dolores Gray) witnesses the poet's (Howard Keel) right hand being chopped off, Kismet.

the beggar's daughter, the Caliph's wife.

Within the fantasy itself, reality clashes with fantasy and is defeated. A poet's creative imagination informs the film's core, by which he not only selects and orders words into verse, thereby making fantasy from reality, but also transforms the usual sour situations of life into unusually sweet ones. The buffets of fate, at his touch, become benefits. He refuses to let life happen to him: "Why should I sigh that my lot is my lot/ That I can't make it anything more/ When this is a lie, an excuse, for a fool to snore/ . . . I walk with my eye upon a star. . ."

Empty coffers send the poet to the temple steps where he stands in for Haj the beggar to receive coins. Mistakenly seized by the guards of the desert chieftain Jawan for being Haj, who cursed the chieftain fifteen years ago (the chieftain's son was stolen from him), and sentenced to be blinded, the poet, feigning priesthood, uncurses the curse for the small sum of one hundred gold pieces. The money purchases shelter, victuals, and garments for himself and his daughter. Since his purse has the markings of Jawan-the-brigand, whom the

police are pursuing in the robbery of the house of Achmed, the poet, pilloried, is dragged to the Wazir's palace. The cutting of his right hand is ordered but he narrates a tale of his hand, a series of examples detailing how the right hand is a requisite for his trade: "When you tell a story/ Amorous or gory/ You can tell it best/ If you gesticulate." During the delay caused by the poet's tale, the guards have seized the real Jawan and doom is averted. Jawan recognizes the Wazir as his son because of a similar amulet. Impressed by the poet's power (his prayer over Jawan had come true), the Wazir enlists his help in preventing the Caliph's marriage to a girl of his own choosing since it will dash his financial scheme. The wedding procession transpiring, the poet is sentenced to be skewered but escapes over the parapet's side by having the courtroom writhe in the frenzies of mysticism from his vivid personification of mighty fate. Aborting his daughter's meeting with the gardener, he calms her distressed spirits with a story of "The Olive Tree," his philosophy of life. With the Caliph's marriage averted which he, in an oblique way, was responsible for, the poet resumes the Wazir's favor. He is made Emir; his daughter is brought to the palace. The Caliph sees her, his mysterious beloved, in the Wazir's harem and assumes that she is one of his wives. The Wazir permits this presumption and drugs the girl for a wedding with him. The poet, discovering his daughter to be the Caliph's enamored and victim of the Wazir's perfidy, devises an entertainment— a knife trick by which he attempts to drown the Wazir: "Note the blade with nothing written upon it. I throw it into the pool. When fetched from the water, this magic blade will be inscribed with the name of our Caliph's bride-to-be. I shall need an assistant." With the Wazir as retriever, the poet submerges him in the water while recounting the Wazir's "story of grief, of weird and unnatural sins, evil beyond all belief" to the court. For the attempted murder of the Wazir, the poet adjudges himself—condemnation with the Wazir's wife to the significantly titled "Oasis of Delightful Imaginings."

Marsinah is a creature of faith, daydream, and memory. After rising from sleep and shaking the coffers, she prays to Allah for food and money. She fancies the house near the pomegranate grove as being hers some day. She tiptoes through "Baubles, Bangles and Beads" as if not to awaken herself. The moonlight rendezvous smashed, she lives in the memory of her amoroso—"This Is My Beloved." Finally, fantasy comes full circle, partly through the poet's efforts.

The Caliph walks the alleyways incognito with

The poet (Howard Keel) escapes over the parapet's side after mesmerizing the court, Kismet.

The Wazir (Sebastian Cabot) feasts his eyes on Marsinah (Ann Blyth), Kismet.

his poet-laureate "to learn the ways of the people, to stimulate local storytellers, and to introduce a romantic notion into the dry business of government." This pretense leads to Marsinah, with whom he poses as a gardener. When his true love fails to appear, memory bolsters the tattered fantasy eventually patched by the poet.

Lalume envies the bard: "Every moment an adventure, a life totally without monotony." Since her so-called marriage, reality consists "of waking each morning with the chart of her day staring down from the ceiling, the path of every hour already mapped and the map of every hour the same." The poet stirs the air about her: "Then came your eyes compelling me/ Telling me something wild/ On your lips lay adventure/ And lightning flashed when you smiled/ . . . Wake the fires that sleep in me." And she will be "bedeviled, bedazzled, bewildered, but not bored." The poet provides her with an alternative life style she passionately yearns for.

Kismet, like *Ziegfeld Follies, The Pirate*, and *The Band Wagon*, is about the transforming power of art, its ability to create fantasy from reality before and within the spectator, its bewitchment.

The Caliph's (Vic Damone) memory: "This Is My Beloved" in the presence of his paternal poet-laureate (Monty Woolley), Kismet.

The poet's verses in the forms of prayers, curses, stories, and games soothe his audience, render it benevolent, clear its head of thoughts, and its heart of feelings that bode ill for the poet. "To a world too prone to be prosaic/ I bring my own panacea/ An iota of iambic and a little of trochaic/ Added to a small amount of onomatopoeia."

Gigi belongs to a long family tradition where the women do not marry at all or where "instead of getting married at once . . . it sometimes happens that they get married at last." Gigi's reality is one of do's and don'ts, unflagging inspections, lessons, and lectures, which eventually will launch her into society as a high-class demi-mondaine. How to eat ortolons ("bad table manners have broken up more households [not homes] than infidelity"), how to choose cigars, the classification of jewels, carry the day. "Love is a thing of beauty and like a work of art, it is created by artists. The greater the artist, the greater the art," her forebears profess.

This artificially imposed world irks Gigi. Gamboling in the Bois de Boulogne with her coevals is left reluctantly. Her tardiness for Alicia's lessons suggests repugnance. After the lesson, she mocks those Parisians, especially Alicia, who equate love with jewels and cigars and rob it of mystery and specialness. She is one with herself shadowboxing with Gaston, playing cards, and frolicking at Trouville.

When the possibility of being Gaston's mistress looms, Alicia demands "work . . . work . . . work . . . lessons . . . lessons . . . lessons": pouring and serving coffee, entering a room, "insinuating" oneself in a chair, "sipping" wine, choosing a wardrobe, all of which Gigi manages badly. Being Gaston's mistress is repulsive to her since it is part of a routine and she happens to be in love with him. Marriage is an all-consuming hope, as is the preservation of childlikeness. After all, she is a love-child, raised to be wordly wise from the very beginning of her life by two lonely women. She narrates all Gaston's affairs in an effort to embarrass him and excuses herself: "I don't have a world famous nature that won't do for [you]." She refuses to speak of her love. Her alternative, "Couldn't we go on as we are, only maybe seeing each other more often," elicits a confession of love from him. Shocked and bruised, she staunchly holds her ground: "You're in love with me and you want to drag me into a life that will make me suffer?"

Later, her agreement to the match compromises the fantasy: "I'd rather be miserable with you than without you." Before her Maxim debut, she prays that all go smoothly since this world is far from her

Aunt Alicia (Isabel Jeans) inspects Gigi's (Leslie Caron) complexion.

Aunt Alicia teaches Gigi bearing.

Gaston (Louis Jourdan) drags the woundup Gigi home.

heart. At Maxim's, she is a windup doll going through her paces, just as Liane and Gaston's other mistresses did previously—the entrance, the serving of coffee, the selection of cigars, the chit-chat. Gaston, realizing this, drags her home and finally asks for her hand.

Gaston, the socially approved, affluent French male of the time who will not marry, is extremely bored with the carousel of high finance, parties, and pleasure. In his drawing room, Gaston's insouciant ''I thought it would'' greets his lawyer's tidings that his railroad went up twelve points. The car salesman is befuddled when Gaston offhandedly remarks that it matters not at all which car he delivers. His parents are tedious. When Uncle Honoré inquires about his absence at the Embassy last night, Gaston replies: ''the thought of another Embassy dinner bores me.''

Trees, the same green every spring, the Eiffel Tower, incessantly ninety-stories high, red-or-white wines, yes-or-no girls, and horse-racing are monotonous. ''It's the same dull world wherever you go/ Whatever place you are at/ The earth is round/ But everything on it is flat.'' Even his ruminations (a type of daydream) of his present mistress's infidelity do not excite him. Pouring wine down Liane's cleavage relieves the ennui momentarily. Honoré encourages him to spy on Liane to force her hand. Gaston reluctantly capitulates: ''All right, Uncle, but it's a bore.'' After the split, a montage pictures Gaston yawning at his restaurant party in spite of a curvaceous blonde's sultry looks and a lady-on-a-horse performance in the background, uncomfortably sneezing with the victor on the Battle-of-the-Flowers float during a parade, and asleep on a

Gaston is bored despite Honoré's (Maurice Chevalier) ardor, Gigi.

couch behind a screen where on the other side, his masquerade ball is in full progress.

These images counterpoint Gaston escaping to Madame Alvarez's, where he serenely sips camomile tea, prepares string beans, plays cards where the matter of logic ("I know what I have and I know how many you have drawn") is pushed aside by Gigi's king seemingly pulled out of nowhere, and celebrates in high anticipation of a weekend at Trouville, where he capers in the ocean, clowns at tennis, rides a mule on the beach—images of domesticity and childlikeness, a world that Gaston, unbeknownst to himself, also hopes for, a world denied him.

After some weeks in Monte Carlo, he returns to Alvarez's apartment to find Gigi altered—upswept hair, a white lace dress—a wearisome carbon copy. His fantasy shudders. But he decides to chance it since he has fallen in love with her. The Maxim outing, this time around with Gigi, dwindles down to the same dull thing. His marriage offer unearths his dark hope.

Both Alicia and Grandmother Alvarez live in a memory world. Both fashion Gigi along their own highly arbitrary aesthetic lines. Alicia refuses to allow real time and space to ravage her. She is quite remarkable looking for her age. She never leaves her luxurious quarters, fraught with mementoes of her former triumphs. Her ideals and her patterns of propriety are the same as ever before. Her first-class jewels are relics.

Love for Honoré still quivers in Madame Alvarez. When Gaston visits, she comments on his clothing: "What beautiful material. And I adore plaid. Just the thing Honoré would wear—a bit more conservative perhaps." At his second visit, subtlety is forsaken: "How is Honoré these days?" In Trouville, her nostalgic and slightly sardonic look counters Honoré's attempt to slip a note to Simone, through the window of her beach house. She longingly watches Honoré passing behind spectators at a tennis match in which Simone is playing. Her lips curl up slightly; the scene's familiarity elicits a smile. She catches his eye as he is about to follow Simone up the steps to her hotel suite. Honoré surrenders by joining Madame Alvarez at her *alfresco* table where she relives—to the last minute detail—her relationship with Honoré, especially those last days they spent together by the sea. Even his grossly inaccurate replay does not tarnish her token. As for Honoré, his ruminations of girls in the park, of Maxim's, of changes, have kept the world of youth still inhabitable and warm.

At the switchboard of Susanswerphone, a Manhattan answering service, Ella Peterson, becomes

Ella (Judy Holliday) as "all things to all men" at her switchboard . . .

"all things to all men" (*Bells Are Ringing*)— classy-voiced secretary for Mrs. Van Rensaller, Santa Claus warning Mrs. Mallet's Junior to eat his spinach, an authentic Parisian (her French being faultless) for Le Petite Bergère Restaurante, a matchmaker for No. 63 and No. 78, efficient nurse for Kitchell's dentist clinic. Sympathetic to Kitchell's Gershwin complex, she visits him as a patient in pain to give him the address of a club auditioning new song-writers. As a beatnik, compliments of a trash collector's accouterments, she strolls into Mike's seedy cafe where client Blake "Brando" Barton hangs out: "Larry Hastings is sick of actors who won't wear suits and who sound as if they've got a mouth full of marbles." To get Jeffrey Moss on his feet in the morning, she is a protective "mom," a little old lady who does reveille in a high, squeaky soprano. Unable to relay the producer's message due to his unplugged phone, she descends upon Moss, who turns out to be "better than a dream," as Mellicent Scott, clairvoyant. Her encouragement is topped with a carton of coffee and a prune danish. "I'm psychic . . . I'm very intuitive. I get feelings about people . . . I know a lot about you just from listening to you talk. And I get visions." Her enthusiastic greeting of fellow pedestrians in the Broadway crosswalk inspires the apathetic crowd to delirious heights of camaraderie. She plays the Sutton Park circuit as a vaudevillian. At Hastings' penthouse bash, she simulates the sophisticates by taking the wind out of her *La Traviata*-sails and by "dropping names." Before the Corella gang, she becomes a tough secret agent working for the cops.

Ella's fantasy, a cross-breeding of hope, projection and pretense, wards off the impersonality and tedium of the secular city. "Oh I love it here. I used to be just a plain switchboard operator in a lingerie house. Pretty dull except for a little modeling on the side. But here it's all so personal." A confrontation with her employer hints at still another reason for Ella's skirting reality: "Why don't you help yourself?" A date with the employer's nephew, an olio of spilled drinks, broken wine glasses, stepped-on toes, a squashed cigarette, a bruised chin, bumped noggins, and a bustle that resembles baked alaska clinches this reason. Ella performs her ministries self-assuredly and with flying colors since she is neither their subject nor object. When it is a case of charity beginning at home, she is schlemiel and

. . . as a beatnik advising Blake "Brando" Barton (Frank Gorshin) about his image, Bells Are Ringing.

schlamazel for her self-acceptance and appreciation are bankrupt.

The fantasy flounders as she hastily departs the party and packs to leave the answering service:

Sorry Sue, I spent half my life tuning into other people's lives, playing all sorts of imaginary characters more real than my own life . . . Jeff fell in love with one of them and look where that's left me. But who is me? I don't know who I am.

To her rescue come her clients, convincing her that Ella is all these "characters;" the reality is the fantasy.

The opening sequence, in the style of a TV advertisement, is a demonstration of Susanswerphone as well as the film's dialectic. Reality (girls missing an important telephone call) counterpoints fantasy (girls receiving the call) because of their Susanswerphone subscription.

Daisy Gambol shuttles between the ordinary, real world and the fantastic world of extrasensory perception in *On a Clear Day You Can See Forever*. To avoid annoying the personnel director, which might prevent Warren from nailing the job with a life-time contract, this cigarette "addictive addict" undergoes therapy. Her courses in budget-making, domestic science, and child care are also Warren-inspired. Last year, she even took vocational guidance tests so Warren could know her better. But Warren's prescriptions do not end at cigarettes, courses, and tests. "A dress not too low, not too high . . . no opinion . . . and none of that kookiness," he warns her before the dinner party with his employer. Daisy's drive for conformity and repression of individuality is largely the result of Warren's brain-washing, as is her chain-smoking, her pushing of sliding doors, and bruising lamps, her hair fetish, her peripatetic arms, and her knock-kneed, pigeon-toed sitting position. The shrink finds her life "boring." To Tad, it is "impossible!"

Extrasensory-wise, Daisy talks to flowers and makes them grow "fast, I mean fast." Indirect regression is a common occurrence. She locates misplaced and forgotten items: "Are you looking for a paper with an address on it? The dictionary under X . . . The car keys? In your pocket." A feeling when the phone is about to ring or when someone is about to drop in or when people think about her (in which case, she drops in if she likes them) comes over her. Her alter-ego materializes across the room for a hot debate. When Chabot wants her back, his voice resounds wherever she happens to be—at Laura Bates Cooking School, at an intersection, at Bergdorf Goodman's, in her bedroom, in Central Park, and at Lincoln Center.

*. . . Ella (Judy Holliday) as Mellicent Scott keeps
Jeff's (Dean Martin) mind on his typewriter and off
Olga (Valerie Allen),* Bells Are Ringing.

Daisy also time-trips to a past and future existence as Melinda Wainwhisle Moorepark Tentrees
in England, 1790-1814, an orphan who becomes a
noblewoman (an inner reality-fantasy moment)
and as Laura Caswell in North Virginia, 2038.

But Daisy's graces embarrass her. At best they
are mere playthings. Chabot's lavish praise of
them finally encourages her to believe in this side
as the most valuable part of her being. Leaving his
office, she reiterates his dictum: "On a clear day
rise and look around you/ . . . How it will astound
you/ That the glow of your being outshines every
star/ You'll feel part of every mountain, sea, and
shore/ You can hear from far or near/ A world
you've never heard before." As the college grove
dissolves into a stratospheric dawn behind Daisy,
the light has been turned on in her eyes.

Science, logic, certitude, and answers constitute Chabot's realm. He has been making the
world safe for psychiatry by excising all the
mystery, wonder, and glory from it until Daisy
appears. At first he greets her with denial: "Rein-
carnation undermines Freud." Then attracted to
Daisy/Melinda, he is nonplussed, exasperated,
and chalks the whole thing up to his imagination. Faced with writing a letter of resignation or
denying that his press release about the case had
any mystical interpretation, he chooses the
former. On her rooftop, he excitedly proclaims to
Daisy: "We have a breathtaking adventure before
us." After Daisy's renewal of trust, he celebrates
this part of her (and perhaps the part of every one)
which has enlarged his humanity:

... *Warren (Larry Blyden) dictates to Daisy (Barbra Streisand), On A Clear Day You Can See Forever.*

... *Daisy's (Barbra Streisand) ESP includes hearing Chabot's voice from the policeman at a Manhattan intersection* ...

. . . and time-tripping to Regency England where the orphan (Barbra Streisand) who begs for soup . . .

. . . becomes a noblewoman (Barbra Streisand).

. . . Chabot (Yves Montand) blames Daisy's (Barbra Streisand) other worlds on her imagination, On A Clear Day You Can See Forever.

Why, Daisy, you're a bloody miracle/ Could anyone among us/ Have an inkling or a clue/ What wizardry and voodoo you can do/ And who would ever guess/ What powers you possess/ And who would not be stunned/ To see you prove/ There's more to us than surgeons can remove/ So much more than we ever knew/ So much more were we born to do/ Should you draw back the curtain/ This I am certain/ You'll be impressed with you.

By now the question arises as to how much of this was intended by Minnelli. Very much, this work proposes. For one thing, Minnelli does choose his scripts, excepting *I Dood It*, which was thrust upon him to doctor rather than direct. "A subject that interests . . . Just something that is exciting in itself regardless of whether it is modern or period or comedy or drama or musical"[16]—is his criterion in property selection.

Although the script is not essentially his creation, Minnelli collaborates with his writers— Joseph Schrank; Francis Goodrich and Albert Hackett; Charles Lederer and Luther Davis; Fred Finklehoffe and Irving Brecher, who provide two scripts; Betty Comden and Adolph Green, two; and Alan Jay Lerner, four. "I preplanned the films very carefully; I worked with the writers on the scripts in detail."[17] Despite different writers, the subject, theme, and vision have remained the same and are enunciated in all of the director's other works, the domestic melodramas and the rosy comedies.

Commenting on the critical thesis derived from his work: "Each person seems to preserve a dream . . . and forces himself to materialize his dream," Minnelli was hesitant at first: "Perhaps, but I never thought of it," but then continued:

In order to make a character come alive, you try to know what he loves, how he acts in daily life, you wish to know what is lacking to him, his dreams, his desires and his fantasies. If not, he is not a human being. Dreams play a capital role. It's the first thing a psychiatrist wants to know about a person.[18]

Minnelli wholeheartedly espoused the proposal of the principal motif as the conflict between a personal view of the world and the necessity of existing in it:

I think that is true. I find that it applies anywhere: that effort to reconcile the ideal or personal dream with reality or behaviorism in the real world is the eternal conflict. I think that is the essential or important thing in any medium, so naturally I always look for that.[19]

Thus, the textual analysis, the director's *ipsis verbis*, and other critical judgments, render critic Mark Shivas' remarks quite misleading:

Vincente Minnelli is concerned with the interpretation of someone else's story and will not employ it as a vehicle for his own views. He never writes his own scripts, contenting himself with the invention of a few lines for background and arty chit-chat. As Minnelli's films do not express any consistent viewpoint, it is difficult to write of his work en masse.[20]

Subplot—An inquiry into subplot retrogresses one momentarily to origins. Subplots were a necessity for the stage musical comedy since the main plot inherently precluded the kind of ambiguity and complexity of psychological, emotional, and intellectual exploration that in tragedy, comedy, and other forms of melodrama could sustain a single conflict for two and a half hours. Also, subplots provided the needed respite for the leading players, who, besides delivering lines, had to sing and perhaps dance.

Either the subplot involved another romance and transformation, another pair of lovers paralleling, or more likely contrasting with the main romance and being resolved in connection with it, thus underscoring it. Or the subplot concerned itself obliquely with the central romance, had a life of its own, was resolved side by side with the main plot and tinged with the dimension of transformation or it involved another area of the protagonist's achievement, thereby opening up the main plot.

The film musical comedy, adaptations, and, to a certain extent, the originals, followed this formula, even though dispensable, since the film's running time was an hour less and the players needed no time out. Consequently, the subplot

was reduced to such a ghost of its former self in adapted pieces or realized so slightly in the originals that it seemed an appendage. Or the subplot was translated whole in adaptations or realized so fully in the originals that the piece was bloated, interminable, and an infringement on the central action. Missing its intended effect, the subplot was an interruption, slowing down the pace and sometimes brewing confusion. Its inclusion was a clear instance of not thinking cinematically.

Excepting *I Dood It,* with its tacked-on German spy plot which has more to do with illuminating Hollywood's moral stance during the war than with plot and character, Minnelli's six originals contain no subplots. The creation motif encompasses while uniting the other motifs, providing the depth and breadth that subplot supplied. Minnelli's integration principle is at work again—motifs, one with another, and the musical-comedy melodrama with the film medium. The lack of subplot in Minnelli's originals is one of the reasons they fare better than the adaptations.

Something must be said about the plotting of *An American in Paris,* however, whose last quarter is uneven and disconcerting. Jerry's artistic life is not resolved. It is presumed. But then, what about Milo? Also, Adam is forgotten about. Referring to this point during a conversation with Minnelli caused him to recall a sequence excised before the film's release to shorten the running time, in which Milo makes overtures to Adam indicating that he is to be her next protégé. The inclusion of this sequence would have made the plotting smoother, a bit more substantial, and satisfying. Finally, there is the problem of the ballet at the end of the film which, as part of a whole, is too ambitious for its own good. It throws the entire film out of kilter.

As for the adaptations, Minnelli is not as fortunate. He and his writers more often prune than excise. *Cabin's* plotting is spare and direct. The overstuffing and inertia come from the specialty numbers. *Brigadoon's* subplot of Charley-Jean-Harry is controlled. "Come to Me, Bend to Me," a ballad with which Charley serenades Jean behind a closed door in observance of the old superstition preventing the bride and groom from seeing each other before the ceremony on their wedding day, is dropped. The situation of Meg, however, should have been eliminated completely, not merely her comic narrative regaling the wedding guests in "On My Mother's Wedding Day." Meg's encounter with Jeff comes off as no more than comic relief while her characterization of the highland nymph makes the soaring fantasy dip earthward. *Kismet's* subplot of Omar is cut, that of the Wazir reduced. The latter's character ballad, "Was I Wazir?" is dropped. A half-way route is taken with Sue and Otto in *Bells*. Their romantic duets are omitted but not the show-stopper. "A Simple Little System," which delays the central concern. *On a Clear Day's* plotting, albeit head and shoulders above the theatrical version, is still lumbering. Though pared down from the stage version, the exposition of the medical background approaches essay. The subplot of Kriakos, the wealthy Greek shipping magnate who finances the experiment, is excised. The character of Tad was written for the film to sharpen the theme, but many of his lines as well as his love ballad to Daisy were snipped before the film's release, rendering him as insubstantial as a shadow. The most admirable thing about the structuring is the complete revamping of Daisy's past life, the weakest part of the show. "I was responsible for that," Minnelli declared.

> Because the show was awful, because the thing that happened, what she went back to was a very pedestrian tale. She was a girl of the streets who married an artist. She was jealous when he had other people pose for him. Who cares about that? But I wanted her to come in on a moment of great drama, when she is on trial for her life. And you want to know why; so you keep coming back to it as you do to a detective story. And the thing would unravel as you would come back to it.[21]

The single point of view and the change of setting also help the plotting. On stage, a multiple point of view unfolds the tale—her parents, the servants, her suitor, her lover—and diminishes the story's intensity and concentration. And then, too, the Regency Period that Minnelli chose is visually more exciting and interesting than early eighteenth century.

Comedy—Subplots functioned in another way as well; they supplied the comedy that suffused the musical's melodrama. When the film musical comedy retained the subplot, if watered down or realized slightly, the comedy more often than not came down to comic skits, slapdash routines, or intermittent puns and jokes, falling from the blue with very little, if any, dramatic value. If the subplot was translated whole or realized in its entirety, the comedy seemed to be overstuffing or a bridge over the porous central action.

Eschewing the subplot in most of his works, Minnelli wrings his comedy from the central situation, the leading protagonists and the supporting players and bits who people this situation,

most of whom are limned as caricatures or grotesques.

Minnelli's melodrama is indiscriminate, as that of all musical comedy, embracing low comedy or farce with its chaos, commotion, and energy, its vulgarity and outrageousness, its playfulness and fun, its naïveté and simplicity, its primitive and rough physical beauty as well as high comedy or satire with its finesse, polish and acumen, its swift winks and slight nudges in the ribs. Satire in the Horatian, never Juvenalian, sense, with the moral implication of the betterment and improvement of humanity and human institutions there only unconsciously, is characteristic of musical comedy. Musical comedy catches the incongruously arrayed man out of the corner of its eye. It never turns its head to stare at him; it never fusses and fumes at him as the drama that is tragedy or comedy would. It sees—and what is more—accepts the discrepancies and kinks, finding them charming, laughable, and eminently forgiveable.

. . . Farce: Gigi *(Leslie Caron) is remade . . .*

The central situation in a Minnelli musical involves an irony. Although Minnelli handles this incongruity seriously, he touches, but never presses, the situation's comic dimensions. Since the discrepancy is embodied by the protagonists, they are the carriers of the comedy. At those points where the two worlds meet and sometimes collide, farce erupts. There is clumsiness and bumbling (Joseph Reynolds, Norma and Montie in "A Sweepstake Ticket," Adam, Gigi, Ella and the employer's nephew, Daisy), quarreling (Little Joe and Petunia, the caller and telephone operator in "Number Please," the client and his lawyer in "Pay the Two Dollars," Manuela and Serafin,

. . . and Manuela (Judy Garland) pummels Serafin (Gene Kelly) with anything she can get her hands on, The Pirate.

Tony and Gaby, Tommy and Jane, Daisy with Warren and Marc), fighting (Little Joe and Domino, Esther and John), boisterous (Connie, Manuela, Tony) or mischievous conduct (Tootie, Gigi, Gaston), boasting (Tootie, Serafin), conning (Lucifer Junior—the dark side of Little Joe, the thief in "This Heart of Mine," Johnny, orphan Melinda), hanky-panky (Johnny's attempted escape from Candle during the carnival, Jeff making room at a Manhattan bar, the Persian seer), masquerade (Joseph Reynolds, Johnny, Ella), buffoonery, knockabout, horseplay (Serafin and Manuela, Jerry, Tony), scolding (Petunia, Daisy), sneering (Lalume, Gaston), and mild seduction (Georgia, Petunia, Esther, Serafin, Jerry, Lalume, Melinda). Shrewishness, coarse jesting, leering, and drunkenness, also part of musical comedy's farce, have no place in Minnelli's world. Georgia's character is toned down considerably in the film version. *Kismet* does not show its leering face on the screen. The lascivious Hellrakers' sequence was written out of *On a Clear Day's* adaptation.

The target of satire in the Minnelli musical is "reality," the sphere the protagonists wish to transcend—the jitterbugging at the Paradise Cafe; the technological trappings intruding upon pastoral Patria; "that saucepan in the hills" with its repressive traditions and fuddy-duddy incumbents; the operetta tradition at variance with Adam's jazz; Broadway, its environs and its artists, especially the fomenters of the modish message-musical; the anxious, pell-mell, skindeep metropolis; the bored, dessicated French upper class; the silent, lonely New York crowds, the brittle penthouse party, the tacky, sensuous club; the pressures of urban living. The butts of the *Follies* skits comprise modern life—"Number Please" pillories telephone operators; "Pay the Two Dollars," lawyers; "When Television Comes," television commercials; "A Great Lady Has an Interview," movie queens and the press; and "The Babbitt and the Bromide," businessmen who conform unthinkingly to prevailing middle-class standards and the fatuity of conversations today.

Caricatures and grotesques occupy "reality." The caricatures include Lucifer Junior/Lucius; the producer, co-star Larry, and Suretta; women's libber Katie; pixillated Aunt Armarilla; Don Pedro, Aunt Inez, the organizer: "Everything's been arranged. There's nothing for you to say . . ." and her short husband Capucho, who has, since his marriage of thirty-five years before, almost lost the power of speech and gesture (his attempt at offering the governor a cigar hilariously reveals his sorry lifetime with his spouse); the third year American collegian who criticizes Jerry's paintings, the wealthy American, Edna Mae MacBenstrom, who cannot decide on a particular scent at the Nicole Parfumerie, and the American couple, ballsy Kay and the emasculated Jack. Kay: Jack, say good night to Milo." Jack: "Good night, Milo." Also, there are Jeffrey Cordova, that monumental talent; Jeff, the master of the put-down; the desert brigand and Wazir; Aunt Alicia, Liane, and her skating instructor, Honoré's Trouville fling; obtuse Inspector Barnes and his sidekick, J. Otto Franz and Sue, overheated Gwynne, Barton and Kitchell; and programmed Warren, and the college president and his board of trustees.

The gallery of grotesques is comprised of the spectacled, pigtailed female wallflower tooting the sour trombone, Quinton, the officious pedant who hurries Esther along, in spite of her forlorn concern over John's whereabouts, Mr. Bankoff and his wife, the inordinately lanky fellow Esther turkey-trots with, the roly-poly she polkas with at the Christmas Eve ball; the hawk-like duenna who frequently swoops down on Yolanda; the gum-

. . . Satire: The Big Apple's impersonality despite Ella (Judy Holliday) and Jeff's (Dean Martin) hellos, Bells Are Ringing.

cracking ladies on the subway in "Pay the Two Dollars"; the ruttish Oriental merchant in "Limehouse Blues"; the Irish stevedore who bruises Les on Forty-Second Street, the giant stringbean spinster in the penny arcade, the chorus-line peroxide blonde, who refines her bumps and grinds when chosen to display her choreographic talent; the habitués at the Manhattan bar, especially Tommy's fiancée and business associate; the princesses of Ababu; Gigi's mother, the bad soprano who warms up in the next room and hits teeth-rattling notes while practicing for her small roles in *opera comique*, those magnificently-clad ladies and gentlemen at Maxim's; Olga, who longs to be taken to the "rrrrr-aces," the mannequins at Hastings' soiree, the denizens of Mike's cafe; and Lord Percy Moorepark.

Setting—America is the theatrical and film musical comedy's idiom conjugated in the present and past tenses. If the situation is placed elsewhere in the present, the piece is either about Americans or their presence is strongly felt. If it is elsewhere in the past, the space and time function as a perspective on present-day America and contemporary allusions and anachronisms abound. One of the lovely inconsistencies of musical comedy, this is. The genre is almost never set in the future. Transformation, within the present, is the extent of its purview. The few futuristic forays have been disastrous. *Via Galactica* (1972), about outer space, with book by Christopher Gore and Judith Ross and music by Galt McDermot, opened the new Uris Theatre on Broadway and ran for seven performances. David Butler's *Just Imagine* (1930), an Orwellian stare at New York City by

73

Brown, DeSylva, and Henderson, was also an aesthetic and commercial bust. Can it be that the future in outer space or on this planet is no place for people? Musical comedy, its motifs, setting and characters, is a valentine to America.

A superficial glance reduces Minnelli's musicals to this pattern. Contemporary Manhattan is the backdrop of *I Dood It, Band Wagon, Bells* and *On a Clear Day. Cabin* is rooted in the American South. An American city, in the year before its World's Fair of 1904, is the setting for another. *Ziegfeld Follies* is perched on a post-terrestrial space and time, through which the American past is gleaned. American show-biz is part of the combustion of *The Pirate's* nineteenth century Caribbean isle. *An American in Paris* is just that. *Brigadoon* is a 200-year-old Scottish village materializing before contemporary New Yorkers. In *Kismet's* ancient Bagdad, the poet lives out the old American get-up-and-go philosophy. Only *Gigi's fin-de-siècle* Paris remains outside this design.

But a second glance reveals that Minnelli's settings are not chosen so much to toot America's horn (if they are chosen for that at all) as to depict points in time and space which elicit in their inhabitants a reaction to escape from, transcend, or transform their particular circumstances. Minnelli's setting is from the exterior to the interior of a person and on to the enunciation of that interior. A Minnelli film plunges one into a state of soul. It is an exploration of man's spirit. As such, Minnelli has purged the genre of its parochialism and has burst its horizons.

Spring and summer are musical comedy's seasons. These temporal intervals, like the genre, are associated with lovers. They involve the out-of-doors which connotes an expansiveness and a generosity which corresponds to the genre's disposition. Finally, these seasons denote transformation and fulfillment, respectively, which is part of the genre's personality. In this aspect of time, Minnelli concurs.

Character—The musical's protagonists can be molded along the lines of an archetype, symbol, a human figure, a type, caricature, or grotesque. "Type" character is the usual choice since, with delineations softened and motivations skirted, there is more time for music, dance, and spectacle.

The musical's protagonists are bourgeois, naively optimistic, provincial, and post-Puritan. As such, they are particularizations of the American soul.

Bourgeois—The central characters live on the functional level of existence, the level where the

. . . The setting of a Minnelli-musical–a state of soul: Esther (Judy Garland) daydreams about "The Boy Next Door," Meet Me In St. Louis.

self and other are grasped in terms of operation, purpose, or use, the level of the manipulable market; or the accidental level where the self and other are grasped in terms of shape, color, and texture, where there are appearances for appearances' sake, mannerisms, the striking of attitudes, the level of technicians. They are pragmatic people. They have socially approved goals and are capable of applying means to an end. "Wait, I got an idea" is the most frequent line in musical texts. Theirs is the penny philosophy of "get up and git." Their vivaciousness and energy, seemingly inexhaustible, make one breathe a little harder. They are security-minded and gregarious. Firm-bodied, good-looking, well coiffed and clothed, their physicality is a large part of their attraction. They are equipped with a technical skill, rarely with a rich liberal education. More emotional than intellectual, more active than contemplative, they are not profoundly religious. Creatures of immediacy and relativity, their actions are in relation to the *hic et nunc* and the *ipse*. In their morality, value or good is identified with achievement and success, the not-so-good (never evil) with inertia and failure.

Naively Optimistic—In the musical, man does live by romance, the show, or talent alone. They believe that things will be, must be, better, and in their own ability to achieve this. They are good-natured with little trace of charity. They have common sense but little wisdom. Psychological or physical suffering, fear, guilt, and death are rarely confronted. Their sentiment often spills into sentimentality.

Provincial—Their world is particular and insular. They cannot see beyond their own noses and do not want to. Chauvinists all, they wave the flag in the good old Cohan way.

Post-Puritan—They are saucy and sexy people. Being alive is a pleasure to them. Women have displaced men as the stronger and more dominant of the species. Mirth, play, and celebration come, not before, or in place of, but after, sobriety, thrift, and work. Parades and parties are constant images in musicals.

Minnelli's principals are figures with enough humanity to accept and take to one's heart. If Minnelli's people do not burst the above categorizations, they do transcend them.

. . . The imposed role of mistress which Gaston (Louis Jourdan) proposes saddens Gigi (Leslie Caron).

Minnelli's people are white revolutionaries. Disenchantment with the logic and texture of their worlds drives them beyond the functional and accidental to the essential level where the self and other are grasped as base or soul, the point at which one is simultaneously the same as and different from every other, pathetic-funny, trivial-profound, earth-sky, fire-ice, demon-clown, yesterday-tomorrow, the level of artists. This deep recess of being is where a person is most fully present to himself, and therefore, most free. From this core, Minnelli's people draw breath and sustenance. They remold their world, not according to some extrinsic, impersonal pattern, but from their own image and likeness. This new creation, with its accompanying zeal and pain, makes them loners and, at times, society's fall guy, yet Minnelli's people risk this. This ardor and vulnerability, their physiognomy being second, attracts and endears others to them.

Because of this re-creation, all Minnelli's people are artists. Many are professional artists—a status grounding their disposition and behavior. Serafin is a strolling player. Manuela is soon to be one. Jerry paints. Adam composes jazz. Henri entertains in a music hall. Tony is a screen and stage star; Gaby, a ballerina; Jeffrey, a producer-director-actor; Les and Lillie, a musical-comedy composer and librettist team; Paul, a choreographer. The beggar writes verse. Gigi is a work of art fashioned by her relatives. Entrepreneur Ella gets a dramatist to finish his play, a producer to read it, an actor to be cast in it, and a dentist to compose for a club, *Cherchez la Femme*. Ziegfeld is a creative producer. "The Lady Giv[ing] an Interview" is a movie queen. Joe Reynolds performs in *Dixie Lou* and backs a show. Johnny and the crook in "This Heart of Mine" are con artists.

They are imaginative. Active yes, but they are also contemplative. Petunia lives out a rich faith life. The people of Patria and Brigadoon are religious. The poet and Marsinah constantly beseech Allah. They are immediate and relative beings. Morality comes down to the sympathy or identification of subject and object, self and world, subconscious and conscious.

Their optimism is no house built upon sand. It springs from within; it is not imported from without. Sanguine people all, but Petunia, Joe Reynolds, the coolie, and Ella display a dash of charity. Although only Mr. Smith, Tommy, the poet, and Chabot approach wisdom, all possess more than common sense. The real or true exceeds what they see, hear, taste, smell, and touch, contrary to society's approbations and sanctions.

. . . The sympathy or identification of the subconscious and the conscious: Daisy (Barbra Streisand) talks to flowers to make them grow, On A Clear Day You Can See Forever.

Little Joe faces fear, guilt, and death even though he does not confront it. Joe Reynolds is hurt by his employer's exposure and Connie's disavowal. Johnny experiences guilt. The poet begs while his daughter steals. Psychological suffering is implicit in Manuela, Jerry, Adam, Tony, Tommy, Gigi while explicit with Ella and Daisy whose gaucheries are symptomatic of it. Their sentimentality is restrained.

They themselves are at the center of their worlds. They are not parading patriots. Except for Joe's thwarting the Nazi spies, Connie's finale involving a flag-salute and an "Anchors Aweigh" tap on a battleship, Jerry's rhythmic pantomimes hailing American inventions, and Henri's plug for America to Lise, flag-flying is absent. *Follies* is,

however, a nosegay to American showmanship, particularly Ziegfeld's and the revue form. *Paris* commemorates Gershwin. One verse of "That's Entertainment" from *The Band Wagon* lovingly acknowledges and spoofs the musical's genesis: "The gag/Maybe waving the flag/That began/With a Mister Cohan/Hip hooray!/The American Way . . ." Yet *Cabin's* folklore, *Louis'* déjà-vu, *Yolanda, Brigadoon,* and *Kismet's* fairy-tale implicitly critique contemporary America while all the other ones, barring *Gigi,* contain some satire on it.

Minnelli's women span the spectrum from softly alluring to the sensual and erotic. His men are dapper, smooth, and in control, except for the two Joes. Taken as a whole, Minnelli's work

. . . Johnny (Fred Astaire) assuages his guilt by a written confession despite Victor's (Frank Morgan) objections, Yolanda And The Thief.

balances the sexes in the seesaw of power.

Festivity enters into their lives. Every film, excluding *I Dood It,* portrays two types of festivity which hones the conflict and theme. One is formal, organized, and imposed from without, an affair that the protagonist must attend, resulting in embarrassment and hurt. The other arises extemporaneously, a creation of the protagonist, a buoyant and lively occasion. The Paradise Cafe versus the picnic and Petunia's birthday party; the Christmas dance versus "Skip to My Lou" and the cakewalk during Lon's send-off; the luncheon with the "angel" versus the wedding feast, the carnival's start is opposed to its finish; Manuela's wedding to Don Pedro counterpoints her wedding to Serafin; the Beaux Arts ball counterpoints the Montparnasse Cafe; the party introducing the cast

and crew to the backers in Jeffrey's apartment counterpoints the surprise party of the same cast and crew on the stage after the show, the caviar-and-champagne gala in the spacious marble hotel ballroom versus the pizza-and-beer haustus in the cramped but cozy hotel room; the impromptu bachelor party for Charley counters cocktails in the Manhattan bar; Marsinah's shopping spree through the markets counters the Wazir's Grand Ceremonial; the merrymaking in anticipation of Trouville in Grandmother's quarters counters Maxim's; Ella's blind date at the expensive restaurant vies with her breakfast in Jeff's apartment, the stroll along Broadway with the pedestrians' greeting-exchange and shared peanuts takes on Hastings' soiree; Warren's dinner party for his employers belies Daisy's cocktails with Chabot at

. . . Two types of festivity: the impromptu bachelor party for Charley . . .

. . . versus cocktails in the Manhattan bar, Brigadoon.

the Americana; the banquet's beginning with Melinda and Robert at opposite ends of the elongated table belies its conclusion with the two embracing in the scullery.

Mechanics of the Melodrama—Minnelli's films display a keen sense of the mechanics of the musical's melodrama. A musical makes only essential points and makes them with dispatch. In the film musical, only incidents central and important to the main plot are portrayed. *St. Louis, Pirate, Band Wagon* are models of compression.

The space is concentrated. The melodrama is an analysis of one space rather than a synthesis of many spaces—the Smith home and environs.

Time lapses are not usually great, and the action, whether on the surface or the below-the-surface levels, is continuous, or nearly so. A Minnelli musical sets itself up briskly and moves to do what it sets out to do. In every piece, the setting, the characters, and the conflict are firmly locked in the opening sequence. The characters and conflict are sustained throughout. What is more, the ending keeps the characters in focus and centers on the conflict's climax—fantasy fulfilled. At the Fair, the Smiths remain center foreground. Even the fireworks display is from a point of view which retains them in this position: their backs to the camera. The closing shots record the family's reactions. Usually the musical ends with a pyrotechnical fanfare of music, dance, and spectacle that disregards the plot and characters: Henry King's *Alexander's Ragtime Band* (1938), Irving Cummings' *Down Argentine Way* (1940), Busby Berkeley's *Strike Up the Band* (1940), *The Gang's All Here* (1943).

In a Minnelli musical, a scene is written with a foreshadowing of the subsequent scene, thus thrusting one forward to what will happen next and heightening the sense of continuity in time and action.

Incident condensation, concentrated space, continuous time and action, compact and dramatically-functional exposition and finale, and foreshadowing contribute to the cohesion of the whole and the musical's allegretto tempo.

To say that the genre is non-psychological, that is, interested more in that and how things are done rather than in why, or in Minnelli's case, semi-psychological, is not to say that it is non-subjective. The musical handles emotional states splendidly since its ingredients of music and dance can explore, penetrate, and present emotion more compellingly than dialogue.

Affectivity is mercurial in musicals, especially Minnelli's, since his sequences are strung together also by the principle of contrast which adds a further dramatic dimension to the piece. Petunia rests content in the back pew and in the twinkling of an eye is lunging toward the cafe. The high angle long shot of her in the corner rocker, crying and grasping Joe's shirt to her solar plexus fades out into the cafe's flashing marquee against a dizzy boogie-woogie rhythm. Esther lets the white muslin window curtain swing before her pink countenance at the close of "The Boy Next Door" reinforcing the image's picturesqueness, her pose, as well as the ethereality of her level of being. The dissolve to the contrasting pedestrian image and earth color—a copper kettle of ketchup on a gingham tablecloth in the kitchen—is another reinforcement. Yolanda's sultry bubble bath at her luxurious estate counterpoints her chaste shower at the convent school. Manuela's bedroom dissolves to the flamboyant port-of-call. Hot pink drowns out a cool blue; an orchestra revving up for Henri's performance, the lovers' silence by the Seine. Central Park swallows up Tony's rage and Gaby's frustration in the hotel suite. Gigi leaves for Maxim's self-possessed; she returns in shambles. In Sutton Park, Ella is fulfilled, forlorn, and fulfilled again. This kaleidoscope of moods heightens the musical's swift pace which invests the proceedings with more tension, piquancy (on the principle that black is not black unless seen against white), and fascination.

Love at first sight, luck, chance, coincidence, serendipity (the phenomenon of finding agreeable and valuable things not sought for), apocatastasis (the phenomenon of every seed of seeming defeat blossoming into the flower of glory, happiness, or reward), magic or seeing the impossible happen,

. . . The intimate finale: Esther (Judy Garland) and John (Tom Drake) at the fair, Meet Me In St. Louis.

colossal derring-do, divine providence, miracle—all are part of the nuts-and-bolts of musical comedy's melodrama and also contribute to its spirit of high bounding energy.

Side by side with cause and effect, Minnelli uses these techniques, neither indulging in them nor patronizing them. Bound up as they are with the protagonists' subliminal life where they are quite natural and matters of fact, these phenomena never appear inconsistent and therefore disruptive of the fabric.

One cheers Fleetfoot's gospel of Little Joe's six-month reprieve, the understated, miraculous relinquishing of Joe's crutches at the picnic, the specially sent tornado, and Georgia's conversion which puts Joe's account in the black. In spite of Reynolds' employer's ironic summary, "My

pants-presser borrows a suit, meets a stage star, they exchange three words and then get married. It happens every day," one accepts it all, plus Joe's suicide when the gas jets happened to be turned off and his discovery of the spy plot. Merely from gazing at John across the way, Esther falls in love. John catches the trolley. At the Christmas ball, Gramps waltzes Esther behind the gigantic fir. With nary a missed beat, she waltzes out from behind the tree with properly attired John in her arms. His fancy clothes were retrieved in time. Yolanda's doting with her "angel" on the telephone turns to love. The timely materialization and evaporations of Mr. Candle, his photograph of the newlyweds five years hence (the technological equivalent of "and they lived happily ever after") are part of Patria's logic. A first glance and the

. . . The miracle: Little Joe (Eddie 'Rochester' Anderson) disposes of his cane, Cabin In The Sky.

. . . Divine providence: Yolanda (Lucille Bremer) converses with her guardian angel (Leon Ames) as Johnny (Fred Astaire) wonders about the photograph of their future family, Yolanda And The Thief.

thief gives his heart to the lady; the coolie to the Eurasian. Serafin is a master of tricks, magic, and derring-do—the cigarette in his mouth, the smoke from his nose, the hypnotism, walking the garland-tightrope, slipping from the iron and chains, the lickety-split change from funeral black to bright motley. Serafin, passing Manuela in the marketplace, is smitten then and there. The troupe's music floods Manuela's ears as she wistfully recalls Port Sebastian. Her engagement ring matches the bracelet on top of the chest of stolen jewels. Crayon and pen materialize in Ziggy's hands, the show before his inner eye. In a crowded cafe, Jerry bumps into—and is enamored with—Lise who happens to be the object of Henri's affections also. Henri is on the balcony as

the lovers say goodbye. All the cans at the arcade display collapse even before Tony throws the ball, and the "?" machine explodes. Jeff is at the cast get-together to overhear Tony's suggestions and demands. *Brigadoon's* existence, its appearance before Tommy, Tommy and Fiona's love at first sight; the poet's every trick, the Wazir turning out to be the desert brigand's lost son, Marsinah's transformation at the bazaar, the Caliph's meeting of Marsinah and their immediate infatuation; Honoré in Trouville along with Madame Alvarez who catches him in all his indelicate maneuvers, Gigi's transformation; Ella falling in love with Jeff on the phone, Jeff, the dentist, and Blake turning up at the Pyramid Bar; Melinda and Robert's love at first sight, Daisy's extrasensory perception,

Chabot's transforming Daisy into Melinda, Daisy pressing the tape-recorder button are cherished Minnelli moments.

Dialogue—Since the genre possesses other elements, more elaborate than dialogue, yet not as swift, succinct, and as matter-of-fact as words (nor are they meant to be) with functions of plot advancement, character delineation, and mood establishment, the dialogue is as brief and as on-target as possible, with no set speeches or rhetorical flourishes. Musical-comedy dialogue is not realism but real speech distilled and intensified. A swiftness emerges from this distillation. Elliptical and apt dialogue, however, can be carried to an extreme, resembling a series of one-liners and/or aphorisms as in some of Berkeley's musicals at Warners and some musical biographies.

Dialogue in a Minnelli musical is always bright, compact, urbane, witty. *Cabin* displays a knowledge and respect of Negro mannerisms and superstitions. Pidgin English—in which "th's" are pronounced as "d's" and singular verbs follow plural subjects—is eschewed. In *St. Louis,* the talk is ingenuous and effortless, as full of sentiment as the people and the period. *Yolanda's* dialogue contributes to the over-all conception of a modern fairy tale: Aunt Armarilla referring to Gaston, the cook, "He knows there's a servant shortage. He has me over a barrel"; and the operator's "You spoke overtime . . . five cents please." *The Pirate's* lines are as clever and robust as the characters. *The Band Wagon's* lines have the bite, sophistication, and shameless extravagance of theatre folk.

Dialogue in Minnelli musicals has, as that of all musical comedy should, a tempo and rhythm of its own achieved through the architecture of the line, the pacing of them, and the manner of delivery which aids the technical transition between dialogue (when delivered at rest) and song, and between dialogue (when delivered in motion) and dance, thereby reinforcing the unity of the piece.

Minnelli's Melodrama—Where there's life, there's fire, jubilates the melodrama of musical comedy, certainly Minnelli's. This type of melodrama deals with man's luminous side, man getting it all together, his self-transcendence. It is a magnificat to man's achievement of his potential. Its reaction to the above side of man is to clap its hands and kick up its heels. Its point of view is from the low (what man is) to the higher than high (what man supposes, hopes for, imagines in his heart of hearts). Comedy and tragedy are realistic views of conscious man. Musical comedy is a realistic view of unconscious man.

4
ENACTMENT

Before Minnelli, the acting in film musicals was negligible. The first commandment of musical casting was that the player be singer and/or dancer. If the player could act, so much the better. (In the sixties this trend was reversed.) That no one went to a musical, let alone a film musical, to behold the peaks or even the middle ranges of the thespian art, was an unconscious and universal assumption.

Lubitsch, in all his musicals, and Mamoulian, in his early ones, directed the players broadly. Their players took neither the plots nor the characters seriously. Of course, this constituted part of their films' charm. The acting highlights in Berkeley's backstagers came down to the staccato (Cagney), sassy (Blondell), and sweet (Powell and Keeler) delivery of one-liners. The Astaire-Rogers cycle, the Fox and Universal products projected personalities. The MacDonald-Eddy series tried to. Some of the musical biogs, however, did elicit performances—Luise Rainer on the telephone *(The Great Ziegfeld)*. On the whole the early musicals' plots and characters did not warrant any care, precision, or nuance in playing.

MINNELLI'S METHODOLOGY

Although Minnelli insists on the players' singing and/or dancing skills, he is equally insistent on their acting ability, or at least in eliciting and directing a performance from them. In answer to the question, "Is acting in your musicals as important as in your dramatic features and comedies?", Minnelli was emphatically affirmative.

A sense of reality . . . and identification with the characters, which acting helps to accomplish, are necessary in the musical. Acting also contributes to the permanence of the experience. One does not forget as easily.[1]

Ethel Waters' Petunia (musical comedy looks

83

like her smile) and Eddie 'Rochester' Anderson's Little Joe move one. The tendency of black comics to overact is nowhere in evidence as the film's tone forbids this. The clown persona of Joe Reynolds, rooted in pathos, is one of Red Skelton's best turns in musical comedy. Judy Garland, rescued from Berkeley's moppet-musicals, comes into her own as Esther Smith. Her playing is "among the freshest to be found in the screen musical annals" while that of Margaret O'Brien's Tootie is "one of the most exceptional of all the cinema's portrayals of children."[2] Tootie perfectly captures the play-acting nature of children. Leon Ames' Mr. Smith and Mary Astor's Mrs. Smith are exquisitely chiseled. Fred Astaire's Johnny (his wearied, sallow countenance is unsettling) and Lucille Bremer's Yolanda (her ravishing ethereal smile is the only thing she registers) are flat though Mildred Natwick's Aunt Armarilla and Leon Ames' Mr. Candle are spirited. The critical reaction to *The Pirate* has undergone a *volte-face*, undoubtedly due in part to the distance from the Lunt-Fontanne original. Gene Kelly transforms Serafin into a magnificent jack-in-the-box. It is his greatest screen feat. Garland's Manuela broadens her comic ability. Both play on at least two levels, perhaps three, as that final *cinéma-vérité* shot of them attests—after rising from the debris of clubs, they deliver the last lines to the camera, glance lickety-split at each other, confront the camera again, turn to each other while guffawing, embracing, and then yowling. Leslie Caron's Lise is fetching and Oscar Levant's Adam effectively droll although Kelly's Jerry and Georges Guetary's Henri are somewhat smug. *The Band Wagon* is adroitly played—except at times by Cyd Charisse. Tony Hunter is Astaire's finest two hours on celluloid. As a composite Orson Welles, Norman Bel Geddes, and Jose Ferrer, Jack Buchanan's "rosy-ripe readings of satirical theater cant take precedence even over Astaire,"[3] opined critic Kael. Nanette Fabray's Lillie and Levant's Les are alive. Charisse redeems herself as the winsomely lithe Fiona in *Brigadoon* while Kelly's Tommy is subdued. The clown finally gets to play *Hamlet*. Van Johnson's Jeff is a surprisingly successful switch in his career from vacuous romantic lead to wryly comic sidekick. Howard Keel as the enterprising poet entrances one while Dolores Gray entices as the voracious Lalume. That *Gigi's* playing throughout is inspired is gospel. Judy Holliday's Ella, most critics comment, is even better on film than on stage. Dean Martin's Jeff survives. He suffuses the role with his personality rather than tailoring the role to it. Barbra Streisand allows

. . . Minnelli directs Howard Keel, Kismet *. . .*

Minnelli to direct her. Her doppelganger character, especially the Daisy-side, is warm and touching. To make Streisand vulnerable is no mean thing. Yves Montand's Chabot is not so much badly directed as miscast even though his physicality is quite adequate, for he can hold the screen alongside superstar Streisand. Scissors and splices have wrecked Jack Nicholson's Tad.

In a Minnelli musical, a role is created from the interplay of the text, the director's sensibility, and the player's temperament—a method that evinces an operative integration principle.

Minnelli outlined three ways of directing players for Bitsch and Domarchi. The ideal consists in being able to discuss with the actor all the subtleties of a character and then, to let him play it according to his temperament, from the depths. To indicate all, gesture by gesture, to the actor is a second but not very welcomed alternative. The last and worst resort, necessitated by the performer's insecurity, entails the actor's memorization of the director's playing of the scene.[4] With Domarchi and Douchet, Minnelli reiterated these points and adds that he will even rewrite dialogue if it is necessary in helping the player create the character from the text and his own personality.[5]

What also aids the projection of a role is Minnelli's maximum-rehearsal, minimum-take procedure whereby a cultivated precision and a jaunty freshness are held in balance.

The ensemble nature of the acting also contributes to the successful enactment. The characters in a particular situation are what is being expressed primarily, not a particular player's talent or personality (except *I Dood It* and perhaps *On A Clear*

. . . and Dean Martin, Bells Are Ringing.

. . . Minnelli discusses the character of Daisy with Barbra Streisand, On A Clear Day You Can See Forever.

Day which is one of the reasons these works fall below the Minnelli pinnacle). All the players work toward this end. In the ''You and I'' sequence from *St. Louis* while Mr. and Mrs. Smith reminisce at the piano in the right foreground of the screen, Rose, Agnes and Tootie, Esther and Gramps descend the stairs in the background. The intruders go to the dining room, retrieve the slices of cake they previously refused, sit down, and eat. The breaking of bread and rapt attention are signs of reconciliation. Tootie, mesmerized by the piano-duet, reaches for a lump of Esther's cake. Esther nudges her little sister's hand away while placing a piece of cake on a fork in her mouth. In the extreme background, Gramps prepares for a game of cribbage which he declined a few mo-

ments ago while Katie peeps from the kitchen door.

Furthermore, the ensemble nature of the acting is insured by the embodiment of the central motif by two or more characters in each film except *I Dood It*, the placing of the character always within a context, part of which comprises other people, and the prevalency of musical numbers that involve more than one person.

Business always aids actors in getting through parts—Jean Arthur fidgeting with the venetian blinds in Frank Capra's *Mr. Deeds Goes to Town* (1936), Elizabeth Taylor nibbling a chicken leg in Mike Nichols' *Who's Afraid Of Virginia Woolf?* (1966). More than just that, the business Minnelli gives his players connects them with the charac-

. . . Ensemble acting: the Smiths' reaction to the father's decision to stay in St. Louis, Meet Me In St. Louis.

86

ters' situation and the story's environment and *zeitgeist* which, in turn, assists them in the projection of their roles and the audience, in empathy.

Browsing for a chair covering to stand on to repair the ceiling, Little Joe spies the cookie jar and retrieves one. The gesture, indicating his relaxed, off-guard mood, prepares for his susceptibility to the siren song outside the screen door. During "The Boy Next Door," Esther touches the bannister and plant leaf and plays with her hair and dress. Since John is insouciant and cold, she must make some physical contact. Throughout the cakewalk before the party guests, Es dutifully protects her younger sister as she passes signals against a piano intro, whispers "now" to cue her start, guides her turns, glides, and lyrical delivery, while remaining slightly behind her and admiringly beaming down upon her. By catching the drapes upon entering the dining room, Es steadies the flight of John's first kiss. Before touching the piano keys, Mrs. Smith extends her fingers before her, wistfully peers at them, and gracefully exercises them. This momentary display betokens her awareness and sadness of time's "winged chariot" as well as her indominatable hope of not being its victim. Mr. Smith, recognizing the melody, twirls the end of his moustache, and one sees him for the Lothario he once was. The ebullition of going to the fair is heightened when Gramps and Mr. Smith check their watches as the carriage clip-clops off. Infuriated by Jerry's forward reaction to Lise, Milo nervously touches her nose and plays with her pearls. Tommy's solemn brushing aside of the ferns before his face when he spies the village below is reminiscent of scales

. . . Contextual business: Jerry (Gene Kelly) tips his hat to the cow in "Almost Like Being In Love," Brigadoon.

falling from a blind man's eyes. Zany antics enhance his exuberance in "Almost Like Being In Love"—toppling down a hillock, an on-the-ground intro, bellowing from a rock, slouching a hat over his face, twirling and tossing his jacket in the air, flinging picked heather away, tipping a hat to the cow, throwing a kiss to a sow. After bowing low in obeisance, Lalume immediately straightens her hair and shakes the dust from her garments. Pomp bores this permanently-on-call enchantress. Marsinah drifts into the Street of Vendors as a waif and exits as a rich young lady, continually looking back as if to confirm her belief. Minnelli chronicles Marsinah and the Caliph's courtship throughout "Stranger in Paradise" by a ballet of their hands. At Gaston's visit, Madame Alvarez inconspicuously removes the cat to a less comfortable chair, a hint at the class difference and her accommodating ways. Gigi's mannerisms and movements throughout "I Don't Understand The Parisians" —jerky, febrile, unfeminine—while conveying her snit, are an oblique attack on Aunt Alicia. Sipping a drink, staring at the paper and carbon recently placed in the typewriter, emptying ashtrays (anything to delay the moment of truth), confronting himself in the mirror again and again (the second time, removing a speck from his clothes which momentarily assuages his guilt since the gesture is goal-oriented), and finally ripping the paper from the roll to hurl in the circular file—all betray Jeff's neurotic insecurity during "Do It Yourself." The series of sitting at-rising from the switchboard, of entering-exiting Moss' apartment, of placing-withdrawing her left foot from the stairs to exit Susanswerphone, images Ella's schizophrenia. Melinda's touching the walls and furniture during "He Isn't You," reminiscent of Garbo in the hostelry's bedroom in Rouben Mamoulian's *Queen Christian* (1933), denotes her sensuality and helps to convince Chabot of her reality.

Minnelli's positioning of the players within a context, both personal and impersonal, enhances their imitations. A successful enactment is one of the reasons for the importance of spectacle in his work.

This person-in-context principle has spatial and temporal corollaries. It dictates an image size ranging from tight medium to extreme long shot. One or two smiles of praying Yolanda, the detail of the jewelry in "This Heart of Mine," a glimpse of Manuela's ravishing features during one of the verses of "Mack the Black," Serafin's visage as he introduces the new act, and Jerry's face and the rose that frame his dream are the only close-ups in Minnelli's corpus. A performance in a Minnelli film is not a matter of a series of visual isolation

. . . Contextual business: Gigi's *(Leslie Caron) mannerisms in "I Don't Understand the Parisians."*

shots being thrust upon one but a matter of observing in rhythm with the rest of the picture.

If the image is dense, or if it is a question of two or more simultaneous planes, a shot must be held sufficiently for the player to react to the context and for the *nachlange* that arises from person-in-context to assert itself as well as for the audience to grasp the meaning. Therefore, Minnelli employs the long take, which abets the enactment immeasurably.

That actors act better in long sequences, Minnelli assured Domarchi and Douchet. They have more liveliness and energy. If you isolate a detail, you must retake the whole thing cold, and make the emotion be born again. It is a little like the theatre. You play a scene in continuity and the emotion springs up naturally. The actors are much more natural than in close-ups which you film to cover yourself. Most of the times, these close-ups for cover, serve no purpose at all because the actors act a hundred times better in long takes.[6] Minnelli reiterated this point with Diehl: "I think if a scene can play in full, it's much more important; you lose so much in close-ups. It's better not to break it, you're weaving a spell."[7]

Lastly, Minnelli embellishes the enactment by having his players act with their entire bodies. Esther's figure assumes a great air of dignified nonchalance as she enters the porch opposite her crush. It is all gusto and exuberance at the party to impress John. Most of Minnelli's players are dancers versed in the idiom of positioning themselves and moving within a context. This, along with the image size and duration of the shot, encourage body semaphore.

5
SPECTACLE

Spectacle constitutes sets and props, a cast that is considerable, costumes, color, sound, and titles or credits-design. The theatrical musical comedy inherited spectacle from the operetta, Viennese and American, and the revue forms. The spectacle in primitive musical comedy, functioning more or less as in the operetta and revue, was a potent and soothing eyewash, overwhelming the audience, perhaps in an attempt to keep their minds off the agglutinative plot and their hearts from the *papier-mâché* characters and to sprinkle glitter on the drab and threadbare spots.

The film musical took after this trait of its ancestor (one of the reasons most of them are camp today) until Minnelli introduced a permutation into the form. As McVay aptly put it, with Minnelli, "art direction begins to count."[1] The sets and props are directed as are the spectacle's other elements. Besides contributing to the enactment, spectacle functions dramatically. Spectacle also strengthens the technical positioning and handling of song and dance within the whole. And the spectacle is expressed through the plasticity and sound of the image and the resources of editing.

DECOR

With Higham and Greenberg, Minnelli spoke of revolutionizing the MGM art department: "I worked very closely in with the art directors:"[2] Cedric Gibbons, Leonid Vasian, Merrill Pye, Jack Martin Smith, Lemuel Ayres, Preston Ames, William A. Horning, George W. Davis, and John De Cuir (at Paramount), and set decorators Edwin B. Willis, Hugh Hunt, Helen Conway, Keogh Gleason, Paul Holdchinsky, Richard Pefferle, Mac Alper, Arthur Krams, Henry Grace, George Hopkins, and Ralph Bretton (at Paramount). An art director designs the film's visual look, mainly the scenery while indicating props. This film architect is responsible to the director. A set decorator works for the art director. This builder takes the art director's concepts and makes them happen three-dimensionally; for example, he selects properties, materials, fabrics, colors, etc. "I save clippings," Minnelli explained.

I have boxes and boxes of them. I guess I got that from my designing days you know . . . that I used for a short cut for the art department because I

90

would give them . . . piles and piles of clippings at all times, things, suggestions, and I found it a great time saver.[3]

Not a single Minnelli interview desists from the topic of the decor's importance and integration in his work: "The decors are enormously important to me."[4]

> [Decor] flows from the subject. It renders in dramatic terms the time and space where the people live . . . Ideally, it is the projection of the characters . . . You are not able to separate the character from his milieu, to arbitrarily isolate the character by a close-up. The character's surroundings, his way of life, the chairs on which he sits, the house where he lives, all is a part of his personality. It is the history of this man. It is as others see him . . .[5]
>
> The characters are so much more real when they're surrounded by an environment that helps to dramatize them. You don't see people isolated, you see them in their surroundings.[6]
>
> I do a great deal of research and try to find the style and color sense for that particular film. Then it's a matter of the way you compose with the camera or the movement of the camera, trying to make something that fits that particular film.[7] The characters are much better when they're surrounded by their own things. You don't see people isolated. You see all around them their effects. The objects that surround them are important.[8]

Minnelli's hypersensitivity to decor's value makes two measly mistakes quite glaring. When Tony exits the arcade, the background consists of the Olympic Theatre marquee advertising *The Proud Land*. This same background occurs in a different space (at the end of a stage alley) months later. As Honoré boasts of the "power of the magic Eiffel Tower," one of its legs appears in the background. The cut to the reverse angle should have the carriage under the tower but, alas, the opposite leg appears after the shot has begun. *Etiam Homerus dormitatque*.

From these quotes, the director's methodology with regard to decor, which applies to spectacle's other elements as well, emerges as a process of researching the story's subject and its spatial-temporal context, using the dramatic elements as the criterion for the decor's selection, which is then worked out with collaborators, and lastly, translating it filmically.

Painting is one of the primary sources of research for Minnelli, a Sunday painter himself and an habitué of the gallery. "The look of [*St. Louis*] was based squarely on period shots of the town"[9] . . . and American Gothic painters. "Of course, the fair had a look of its own. There was plenty of material on that."[10] Ludwig Bemelmans' illustrations accompanying his own story

. . . The American Gothic of Meet Me In St. Louis.

influenced *Yolanda*'s design. Spanish-Baroque art affected the design of the heroine's home. "It was very spectacular but in the best baroque sense. Since her family possessed a fortune as well as culture."[11] Patches of Bernard, Miró, Tanguy and others of the French surrealist school drift through Johnny's dream.

> The style of the prologue and epilogue [of "Limehouse Blues"] was based on English mezzotints: very dim and foggy. The central Chinese [section] was done not so much in the Chinese manner as in the style of French *Chinoiserie* furniture designs, panels and so on, of the time of Louis XVI. The French of that period had their own strange conception of China as they had of an America populated by Indians with feathers. Quite absurd, but beautiful in its own way.[12]

Limehouse's prologue and epilogue also flirt with Griffith's *Broken Blossoms* (1919). Illustrations of the West Indies in the period when it was the gateway of the world enlivened *The Pirate's* look.[13] The "American In Paris Ballet" was inspired by Dufy (Place de la Concorde alive with Parisians—shop girls, elegant couples from Maxim's, gendarmes, pompiers, sailors), Renoir (the impressionistic pastel flower market of the Madeleine), Utrillo (the somber, elongated alley),

. . . *Yolanda's Spanish Baroque home*, Yolanda
And The Thief.

. . . *The movements and inspirations of "The American
In Paris Ballet"; the first and last movements: Dufy's
Place de la Concorde* . . .

*. . . the second movement: Renoir's flower market of
the Madeleine . . .*

. . . the third movement: Utrillo's alley . . .

. . . the fourth movement: Rousseau's Place de la Bastille . . .

...the fifth movement: Van Gogh's Place de l'Opera ...

. . . the sixth movement: Lautrec's cafe.

Rousseau (Place de la Bastille, all red, white, and blue), Van Gogh (Place de l'Opera against bright yellows and oranges), and Lautrec (the cafe with Du Chocolat, can-can dancers, and Jane Avril). The decor, costumes, and color are painterly, stylized to the point that they seem paintings. Appropriately so, since the ballet is a memory-daydream of a painter in Paris. *Brigadoon*'s interiors echoed Dutch painting, the exteriors, English Romantic painting. "I studied photographs of Scotland—misty monotones, yellows and greens, and based the film on those subdued colors throughout its length."[14] *Kismet* was modeled after

the place in the Orient where whole exterior buildings were cut out of brown marble rock. There was one place high up in the mountains . . . beautiful renaissance buildings that were carved out of the rock . . . inside they were just caves. I used that. I made a color drawing quickly of that kind of thing . . . so that you had the jagged

rock like inside the caves and renaissance columns and metal grills. It made it . . . look barbaric, you know as those things might be[15] . . . The garden sequence was prototypic of two dimensional Persian miniatures, they went down terraces and there were peacocks . . . [16]

Gigi was created in the manner of Sem's drawings since Sem actually did caricatures in Maxim's of the people Colette wrote about. Another exemplar was Becaud who also painted at that time.[17] New York inspired *Band Wagon* and *Bells*.

I remember when we were in New York looking for locations for *Bells*. We had been looking for a squalid-looking basement brownstone that had seen better days. We looked all day and couldn't find one. When I got to the hotel, this copy of *Life* was there with this building that had been a holdout on an entire square that had been sold for an enormous skyscraper. So they cleared everything all around it but this building with the jagged edges still standing, still being licked by the wallpaper of

. . . The Caliph's Ceremonial Hall, Kismet.

. . . Maxim's from the inspiration of Sem, Gigi.

... On A Clear Day's *Regency Period*.

the formerly adjacent building . . . so I immediately called the production manager and he immediately called these people and we got to use it.[18]

For *On a Clear Day*, "the Regency Period was chosen because the eighteenth century with its white wigs and fustian threads which hide the people never seem to work and because I could use the actual pavilion at Brighton."[19]

Decor's most obvious function is, of course, as a carrier of context, as a shaper of the story's spatial-temporal dimension. Everyone lives in a world of a certain shape. Minnelli shows that shape. This is true of all his musicals except *I Dood It* where the decor, barring the scenes backstage—the dressing rooms, the wings, the back wall and rafters of the stage, the prop room—is perfunctory and unexpressive.

But Minnellian decor usually goes beyond this function by creating a spatial-temporal atmosphere which has something to do with the olfactory, tactile, kinesthetic sensations as well as the visual and aural ones and a spatial-temporal mood which has something to do with sentiment or emotion. Dusk, the gate through which Joe departed still swinging, and the wind rustling the items spilled on the ground eloquently speak of Petunia's chilling forlornness. *St. Louis'* summer is rich, indolent, carefree with possibility; autumn—spare, chilly, ominous; winter—still, expecting, velvet; spring—fluid, sweet, joyful. One feels rigid at Yolanda's convent school. At the carnival, one's senses are assaulted and one reels from the excess which one is unable to elude. Ziggy's pink and white rococo apartment unan-

chored in a blue starry sky sets the context while conveying a tedious serenity. Port Sebastian with its bustling wharf, friendly barber shop, girl-strewn tavern, *alfresco* market stall of crabs, shrimp, and fruit, flower carts, bandshell, and sea-damp fortification wall conveys density, saltiness, and robustness. Manuela's seaport bedroom is sweltering, musty, confining. The Cafe Huguette is warm, gregarious, and exuberant. The Beaux Arts Ball is jet-propelled New Year's Eve. Forty-Second Street and the penny arcade is thick, tawdry, noisome, summery-hot but engaging in an off-beat way. Central Park, with the moon-kissed gray-green trees, the mild breeze, the horse's clip-clop rhythm, the steady rocking back and forth of the carriage, the driver enjoying his pipe while giving his horse a drink at the mushroom-shaped trough, is a place to breathe and relax. The strangers and Fiona traipse to the pinnacle of a hill overlooking the village to hear Brigadoon's etiology. A numinous feeling occurs. It is hard to breathe because of the myth, the air at this high altitude, and the scene's physicality, since high places are associated with God's epiphany. Susanswerphone is drab, depressing, and stiflingly humid. Existential boredom and *angst* cling to the boozy and bluesy walls of Barton's hangout. Hastings' vertical-dominated penthouse is brittle, sleek, and icy. The Pavilion's soiree is aromatic and erotic.

Decor delineates character. Georgia's bedroom, cluttered with clothes, cosmetics, souvenirs like a carnival doll on the trunk, and a dressing table dead center introduces her even before she enters the frame. Gramps' dresser

... *Esther (Judy Garland) and Rose (Lucille Bremer) pose like the bust of the couple atop the piano,* Meet Me In St. Louis.

98

glutted with outlandish hats discloses old age's eccentricity. During the elder sisters' ode to the fair in barbershop harmony, Esther, standing behind Rose seated at the piano, places her hands on her sister's shoulders. A bust of a couple positioned exactly as the two sisters embellishes the piano top. This pithy detail clues one in on the girls' pose while deepening the story's context—people of this period, especially impressionable maidens, copied the art of the times. Jerry's postage stamp garret reiterates his narrow straights. To place the expression of Jerry's extravagant outburst of love ("Tra-la-la-la") in such a circumscribed space as Adam's flat that when the emotion invades, and must invade his limbs, he is sent dancing atop the piano and sofa, is a witty irony on Minnelli's part. The Wazir's throne

room is enormous, and overpowering, fierce rather than splendid. Alicia's grand, formal, crystal-and-brocade quarters connotes her inflexibility, aloofness, and coldness. Gaston's lodgings are in this mold. They contrast with Madame Alvarez's unassuming, lived-in, cozy crimson apartment, connoting her malleability, warmth, and forgiveness. Honoré's bachelor billet emphasizes his youthfulness and daring.

Decor projects states of soul. Autumn and the swirling leaves and dust, the wiry branches of the black trees, the raging bonfire, the horrific masks, the imposing columns of Bankoff's porch express Tootie's wild and sinister imaginings. At the carnival, Johnny draws Yolanda back into the relative privacy of a candle shop. Dozens of candles burn luminously. An old artisan sits

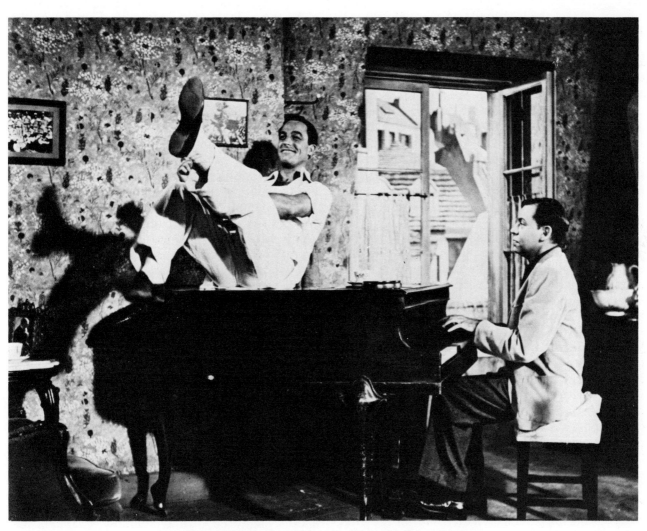

. . . The ironic placing of Jerry's (Gene Kelly) outburst of love in Adam's (Oscar Levant) cramped flat, An American In Paris.

99

carving a candle whose shavings fall into a copper pot of boiling tallow which sits on a charcoal fire. Yolanda wears a gamboge dress. The scene is suffused with a glow and ardency indicating how the pair feel toward each other. The flickering footlights and blazing cauldrons of fire during the hypnotic session typify the interior passion Manuela emanates and consequently instills within the spectators. Minnelli plays a love scene in a demolished room by placing his couple before a painting of Golden Renaissance arches, all perfection and order, that has been toppled by Manuela's hurled dagger. The backdrop lifts the romantics to another realm. In the limousine's back seat, Milo is upset with Jerry and vice versa. Her wheedling up against him rejected, she slides away and burrows into the corner as if it would swallow up and hide her abashment. Tony's first appearance, in a corner with a large magazine propped before his face, connotes retreating and pain. It is significant that as the train pulls into Grand Central, Tony is in his compartment. The cramped, claustrophobic area is made even more so by the baggage, the porter, and some of the opposite seat which appears in the foreground of the frame. The mechanical camels and bears' performance in a toy shop's window reflects Alvarez's nonplussed, distraught soul as she phones her sister within the shop concerning Gigi's refusal of Gaston. Jeff surfaces from the subway steps onto a deserted Brooklyn street late at night. A monotonous row of brownstones sport gray trash cans. The decor imparts Jeff's feeling of abandonment and uselessness.

Sometimes the decor images the plot's conflict and visually encapsulates the theme. The unadorned wooden framed Baptist church with its open vestibule contrasts with the darkly ornate Paradise Cafe with its flashing marquee and swinging doors. The hope to be at the fair is full in summer. This hope is threatened in autumn. This hope runs down during winter. But lo and behold, it is renewed and fulfilled in the spring. Cordova's suite has an entry opening onto three distinct rooms where he rewrites the play before his backers in one, co-authors grieve and the male star contemplates bowing out in another, and the primadonna dredges up her insecurities in the third. *Brigadoon,* where almost all of the action is set out-of-doors upon expansive, rambling highlands with vistas defies the confined, smoky, mobbed, flat Manhattan bar. In the village, the stress is on horizontals which relax; in the city, verticals which keeps one upright, on the defense. Generally, in *Gigi,* the interiors—Aunt Alicia's place, Gaston's estate, Maxim's, the Ice Palace,

the Bonfleur—contrast with the exteriors—the Bois de Boulogne, the parks, Trouville. Susanswerphone stands alone in a block that has been razed with rubble all around, suggestive of the one, remaining, rooted individual, Ella. Daisy's digs with its rooftop garden and hothouse, a bedroom with flower-print wallpaper, bedspread, bureau scarves, and potted plants (the natural), assails Chabot's book-lined, technologically-equipped study (the synthetic).

One piece of decor continually crops up in a Minnelli musical—the window frame and its extension, the balcony ledge. Besides providing a frame to the composition, in which case it functions purely aesthetically, this image crystallizes plot, conflict, and theme. The window frame and balcony ledge, situated yet opening onto a view, prospective, or horizon like some wharf on the infinite, contains the dialectic of immanence-transcendence, present-future, reality-fantasy.

To the right of Little Joe's head resting on the pillow, wind blows through the curtains on the opened window and wafts Joe into a dream. The funnel-shaped tornado, destroying the Paradise Cafe and Joe's dream which inspires him to achieve it in reality, is glimpsed through a window frame. Esther's two daydreams, "The Boy Next Door" and "Have Yourself A Merry Little Christmas," are delivered at window ledges. John is on the other side both times. Through the trolley's window, Esther pines for her beau. From the bedroom window, Mr. Smith gazes below at Tootie pummeling the snowmen. This incident triggers his decision to remain in the Midwest. Also, the border of the photographs that open each section of the film is a metaphorical equivalent of the window frame. Johnny, quite apprehensive, keeps peering from the train's window as it enters Patria. Leaning against the balcony frame which superintends the village below, Johnny smokes, then goes to bed and dreams. The beginning of the dream, setting the wheels of his fantasy in motion, finds him at the same balcony ledge. Yolanda first sees Johnny at the carnival from a balcony ledge. Ziegfeld's realization of a new follies is done from his balcony ledge. The thief's first gesture in "This Heart of Mine" is to scrutinize the ballroom from outside the French windows. Inside, his fantasy will begin. Through these same windows, the camera pokes its nose to discover his change of heart. In "Limehouse Blues," the movement from reality to fantasy happens in front of the curio shop's shattered display window. Manuela addresses the legendary Macoco from her balcony in the opening sequence. She paces before the balcony ledge of her second-floor bedroom in Port

. . . The window frame crystallizes plot, conflict, and theme: Jerry (Gene Kelly) waves to the children below, An American In Paris.

in "This Is My Beloved." The stranger on his tower responds in kind. Lalume, on the parapet, peers through a telescope for the poet. Although Gigi delivers most of "Say A Prayer For Me Tonight" before a mirror, she does stand before her opened balcony during some of it. Her debut is the point when her fantasy is resumed. At the basement window, Ella imagines, "It's A Perfect Relationship." Jeff ends his self-remonstrance at the window in "Do It Yourself." Jeff's soul-searching dissolves to Ella by the window. On his balcony terrace, she confesses that he is "Better Than A Dream." On Larry Hastings' penthouse ledge, she concludes "Drop That Name" and receives Jeff's proposal. Daisy's first regression begins: "I see it . . . a window." On a window seat, before curtains billowing from the opened window, Chabot's elixir transforms Daisy into Melinda. Chabot converses with Melinda, "He Isn't You," before a window. Daisy asks "What Did I Have That I Don't Have Now" by Chabot's balcony window. Chabot hypnotizes Daisy by telepathy from his window and atop the Pan Am building overlooking Manhattan, imploring "Come Back To Me." When Daisy departs, Chabot walks on his balcony ledge and waves goodbye. Outlines of square boxes that suggest window ledges, emanating one from another, comprise the film's credits.

The stage, of course, and its metaphorical extensions—the Kensington Avenue porch and staircase, the lobby tier in the Patria Hotel, Port Sebastian's bandshell, the arcade's bootblack stand, the mosque's steps, and Sutton Park—especially when seen as a platform elevated above the audience, is a piece of decor also crystallizing plot, conflict, and theme.

Minnelli often uses a single prop to score a dramatic point. The hammock, an item of furniture connoting laziness, sensuality, even sin, occupies center frame during Georgia's seduction of Little Joe. Katie admonishing Rose and Esther with frozen bloomers intimates her authoritarian, no-nonsense, and earthy ways. As the mother superior explains to Yolanda about guardian angels, a puppet box framing a guardian angel over a girl is in the background. Yolanda makes her devotion to her "angel," in the hotel lobby through the stair's iron grillwork, suggestive of a cloister, thereby suffusing the ambiance with a sacred feeling. The rail that separates Jerry from Lise at the Beaux Arts Ball encapsulates their relationship.

The decor is always in keeping with the film's overriding dramatic method or procedure. *Cabin* is folklore and most of the decor has a folkloric

Sebastian, through which seep the music, hubbub, and excitement of the show below. By going below, literally and metaphorically, she begins to create her fantasy. From her balcony ledge at home, she witnesses Serafin's arrival and daydreams of him as Macoco. Serafin enters Manuela's apartments through the balcony and delivers his marriage ultimatum to the townfolk from a balcony. Jerry ends his waking and breakfasting at the window ledge, where he waves to the children below. This day will see the start of his career and romance. From his window, Adam looks below at Henri who will take care of his depression momentarily. Jerry ruminates about his life which vitalizes his fantasy from the Moulin de la Galette's balcony ledge overlooking Paris from the top of Montmartre. Tony gazes from the Twentieth Century's window as it pulls into Manhattan which will eventually keep alive the once and future star. Fiona delivers her daydream, "Waitin' For My Dearie," by a window ledge. After she meets the stranger, she is imaged twice more by the window that opens upon the countryside beyond. The muezzins are seen on minarets overlooking the city. Marsinah on a graded terrace ledge awaits the stranger. On the turret, she reminisces about him

. . . Prop as a dramatic point: Katie's bloomers, Meet Me In St. Louis.

quality about it—the backyard, always used for comings, goings, and gatherings with its ironing board and washing machine on the rickety back porch, the clothes lines, the white picket fence, the axe in the tree stump with shavings lying around, a hammock, chickens dawdling here and there, the chapel, the town with its cafe, the picnic area. The idea department of hell is conceived with pipes on the ceiling and a vault for a door, suggestive of "down below." When the vault opens, smoke seeps through. The dwelling is a modern conference room, with glass windows in the background through which nothing but swirling smoke can be gleaned, the air-conditioning indicated by the icicles on the pipes, the sleepy devil at the switchboard, the enormous desk, the intercom system, the box of Havanas, the swivel

chair. The decor works so far since it expatiates and evaluates the film's implicit but prevailing dialectic—present day technological "reality" versus the almost mythic pastoral "fantasy." (The use of folklore inherently involves such a contrast.) Moreover, this image of hell can possibly emanate from Little Joe's subconscious. The dialogue and action, however, are directed along lines of an idea session at a Hollywood studio and the scene misfires. This is foreign to the protagonist and exists only on the level of an in-joke. Suggestive of "up there," heaven is a series of steps, starting with the cafe's staircase. Smoke has taken the place of the structure's second floor, ripped away by the tornado.

St. Louis is not a realistic representation but a memory. Memory, whether pleasant or painful, is

. . . The folkloric depiction of hell, Cabin In The Sky.

always exaggerated. It has the power to make the ordinary extraordinary. If pleasant, then the memory is permeated with a yearning for "the splendour in the grass, of glory in the flower" that nothing can bring back. A happy reflection, the film's decor is idealized and tinged with pathos and consequently, psychologically and dramatically accurate. *On A Clear Day*'s breathtaking Regency sequences are rose-colored also.

The modern fairy tale, *Yolanda*, is set in the Acquaviva estate,

> a sort of legendary castle inspired by traditional colonial Spanish baroque, in which is incorporated Catholic motifs and a host of extravagant modern gadgets: a bathroom . . . complete with fountains, a waterfall, steam jets, the toilette table that is a shrine reserved for worship of beauty and romantic meditation . . .[20]

a sunken garden with fountains, does, trees, and a marble angel's presiding presence, a door with four peepholes to warn against intruders like salesmen. A taxi somewhere between an American sedan gone to rot and a surrey with a fringe on top, billboards scattered along the train's route, and a town square paved with coruscating zebra-striped swirls are part of the locale.

The decor's filmic translation is an artifact, studio designed and shot. The few inserts of the real world (the clouds at the picnic, the ocean, train exteriors, the establishing shots of Paris, the credits-design of New York), the rear projections, and some location shooting in *Gigi* and *On A Clear Day,* are not significant enough to discredit this thesis. Moreover, the rear projections are lit and shot in a studio and the locations are rearranged quite extensively by the director.

Although all of Minnelli's musicals, except the last, were done during the height of the hothouse studio system or at least at the periphery of its

*. . . Minnelli's attention to detail is stunning as in this
section of the Halloween sequence,* Meet Me In St.
Louis.

decline when location shooting was eschewed, aesthetic and semantic considerations prevail here. The genre is essentially expressionistic. Minnelli makes it more so by his central concern, setting, and characters. Minnelli is considerably abetted in the expression of this world by a decor that can be molded and controlled by his personal vision, built to his own specifications as only studio decor can be. Reality can never yield the plethora of details, a necessity for art and artists, that Minnellian decor contains.

Neither naturalistic nor realistic, the decor is expressionistic, the creation of a spatial-temporal continuum, albeit researched and dramatically related, filtered through the director's spirit. As such, one gets the distillation or the essence of a place and period imbibing attitudes and feelings. "Essential Oils—are wrung—/The Attar from the Rose/Be not expressed by Suns—alone—/It is the gift of Screws—" Minnelli holds no mirror up to nature but places a lamp next to it. His is the recreative rather than mimetic tradition of art.

The decor is peopled. The decor frames or surrounds the characters and cast at all times, and often Minnelli's people interact with it. His work contains no strictly spatial descriptive passages. The opening of *Paris* has Jerry's voice over. A chorus puts one *in medias res* as the camera roves over the highlands. The camera follows a mailman to the Susanswerphone establishment. Barring three or four exceptions, passages in which a character is divorced from the background are

. . . Minnelli arranges the French children on the sidewalk for "I Got Rhythm," An American In Paris."

non-existent. Minnelli is a *metteur-en-scène*, a practitioner of the art of *mise-en-scène*.

In its cinematic appropriation, this term, although still very much the chameleon, has more or less solidified along the lines set by André Bazin in his essays in the first translated volume of *What Is Cinema?*: "The Evolution of the Language of Cinema" and "The Virtues and Limitations of Montage."[21]

Aesthetician Brian Henderson offered a definition expatiating on Bazin:

> It is, baldly, the art of the image itself—the actors, sets and backgrounds, lighting and camera movements considered in relation to themselves and to each other . . . as opposed to the relation between images, which is the central expressive category of montage. [It] requires the duration of the long take (a single piece of unedited film, which may or may not constitute an entire sequence) . . . It is the long take alone which permits the director to vary and develop the image without switching to another image . . .[22]

Murnau, according to Henderson, is the purest example of this style (and perhaps the only one) while Ophuls and Welles use this method but not exclusively. Minnelli has avowed his great admiration for Ophuls and considered Welles "one of the two or three greatest movie makers in the world."[23]

Henderson's definition must be qualified when discussing Minnelli's *mise-en-scène* which first of all involves a reciprocal relation of characters and/or cast to decor as already exemplified.

Sometimes the relation issues into an interac-

tion of character and decor. Minnelli's protagonists are all creators of fantasy, artists of one sort or another, *metteurs-en-scène* in their own right, who, through the abracadabra of themselves and a particular context, transfigure fact into fancy—Esther's "The Boy Next Door" with a half dozen rearrangements by the window seat, her "Over The Bannister Leaning" with its dimmed lamps (again, Esther apes the art of the period—here the lyrics of a Victorian ballad); Johnny's angelic epiphany on an elevated lobby corner before a Biblical-inspired mural, with an impressive throne-like chair, back lighting to create a nimbus, and no extras (he shoos away a guest); Jerry's set along the Seine to romance Lise; and Tony's in Central Park to placate Gaby.

The character's positioning in relation to decor or another person has dramatic value. After Manuela's declaration of love to Serafin that twists the knife in Don Pedro's heart, Minnelli's direction lifts the players to melodramatic archetypes, accentuating the proceeding's high histrionics: the villain's dash for the couple, the heroine taking refuge behind hero, the villain seizing her arm and swinging her between them while flaunting a revolver. "By Strauss" ends with Jerry on his knees in the foreground, the flower lady atop the piano, Adam standing on the piano stool, the cafe owners embracing in the center, and Henri propped on the bar, all raising one arm with the index finger extended and looking screen right toward the audience—an emblem of the finale of Viennese valse-opera. "Almost Like Being In Love's" finale finds Tommy with arms spread on a

. . . Minnelli arranges Ann Blyth and Vic Damone within the decor, Kismet.

105

*. . . Johnny (Fred Astaire) and Victor (Frank Morgan)
as* metteurs-en-scène, Yolanda And The Thief.

middleground, and the garden paraphernalia in the background. Jerry and Lise's meeting at the Flodair affords an exquisite example—in the background, dancers and tables; in the rear medium plane toward the left, Lise with her party; in the front medium plane toward the right, Jerry with Milo, Tom, and the American couple; and in the foreground, more dancers. As Tony emerges from the train in middleground, reporters semicircle around him filling the foreground while, in the background, the expected star detrains. Cordova's vestibule is transformed into a three-ring circus where Les and Lillie try to prevent Tony from storming out in the foreground while Gaby, followed by Paul, bolts from the red room in the middleground. At the same time, Jeffrey and backers erupt from the living room in the background. While the poet soothes his daughter in their makeshift abode, the Caliph's procession in the background is seen through the shelter's broken bricks and patches.

Mirror shots are frequent in Minnelli's films, adding depth to the composition but more often than not contributing a semantic value. A doppelganger image, a mirror suggests the two worlds the protagonist straddles. Also, the mirror connotes identity, a corollary of Minnelli's dominant motif.

Little Joe first appears straightening his tie before a bureau mirror with the sweepstake ticket pinned by its wooden frame and dice before it. Petunia and Little Joe, peering through the cafe's bar mirror, descry heaven's entry. In front of the cheval glass, Esther arranges herself while musing about John. Prior to Lon's party, to which John is invited, Esther pinches her cheeks in dismay before the dressing mirror: "Personally, I think I have too much bloom." Yolanda, preoccupied with her angelic meeting, primps before her pier glass. Serafin dons strolling clothes before a mirror. A revolving mirror liberates Manuela and Don Pedro's inner self. The image of Henri's head in the cafe's wall mirror dissolves to his projection of Lise. A fun house's crazy mirror sends Tony's drearies out of town. They play a return engagement, however, before his dressing room mirror after the opening. Mirrors grow from the huckster's palms as Marsinah is transformed. A pool of water reflects the Caliph's bridal procession. A park lake traces Gaston's awakening. Preceding her Maxim-debut, Gigi meditates before a wall mirror. Jeff castigates himself before a mirror. Brighton Pavilion is wall-papered with mirrors. "He Isn't You," Melinda's colloquy with Chabot, is delivered for the most part before a mirror.

hillock in the top right background, and Jeff with hands by his side below in the bottom left foreground. The placement is psychologically accurate—Tommy, dynamic and high, Jeff, static and low while the interim space is indicative of the difference between them. As the poet formulates his plan of attack, he mounts the mosque's ledges until he is above his fellow beggars and the populace in the congested square below on the left, typifying his control and power. In the background, Marsinah must rest on a table for support while her father straddles the foreground like some Colossus of Rhodes during his *apologia pro vita sua,* "The Olive Tree." In "Say A Prayer For Me Tonight," the camera makes a prolonged pan to find Gigi, bathrobed and holding a cat for support. It is as if she were hiding and wanted to be left alone.

Two or more planes within the frame are utilized simultaneously in every composition—the Smiths' mid-summer dinner, the garden scene where Johnny in the bushy tree occupies the lower left foreground, the statue of the angel in the left middleground, kneeling Yolanda in the right

. . . The poet's (Howard Keel) edge on his fellow beggars and populace indicated by his relationship to decor and the other characters within the frame, Kismet.

. . . The use of planes: Classroom decor in background, hypnotized student in rear median plane, Dr. Chabot (Yves Montand) and students in front medium plane, Daisy (Barbra Streisand) in foreground, On A Clear Day You Can See Forever.

As much as possible, the playing of the action is continuous since this method enhances enactment, with an image size (EMS to ELS) that frames the proceedings with a camera positioning, angle, and movement that follows the action when dynamic (Lon's bicycling home) or underlines its essentials when static (Jerry's first encountering Lise at the Flodair) and in a fairly lengthy duration. Minnelli works primarily within the frame. This architecture is, in no small way, due to men like Sidney Wagner, George J. Folsey, Charles Rosher, Harry Stradling, John Alton, Alfred Gilks, Harry Jackson, Joseph Ruttenberg, and Milton Krasner behind the lens.

With *Brigadoon* in 1954, Minnelli initiates his association with the wide screen process of Cinemascope, two-and-a-half times wide as it is long, introduced the previous year by Twentieth Century Fox. (His last musical is shot in Panavi-sion, an improved version of scope.) Of course, 'scope was trendy. Although disesteeming it—''I never did like Cinemascope very much. It's not so much that it's wider as that there's less on the top and bottom. I don't think it's the right composition for pictures''[24]—Minnelli achieves quite a rapport with the screen's new dimensions. 'Scope intensifies the limitlessness of space and the freedom of movement that is part of *Brigadoon*'s atmosphere and mood. By cluttering the immense frame in the Manhattan bar, the atmosphere is more suffocating. Parts of *On A Clear Day* work this same way. The Pavilion is sensual and entrancing; and the study, academic and distancing. *Kismet's* Bagdad is even more fabulous. Minnelli's topography invariably helps his use of 'scope.

The cutting is extremely minimal in the musical numbers. The dramatic scenes, on the other hand, are built from a relationship of parts, each held

. . . Minnelli's rapport with Cinemascope: Brigadoon's *reaction to Harry's departure which will break the spell.*

rather long. No part, however, is a close-up of a detail of that scene. (Details, if used, are carved against a background.) Reaction shots and inserts are rare and symbolic shots, even rarer. The parts continue the action, whether verbal or visual. The content of some sequences prescribe rapid cutting. "Gesticulate's" cutting establishes the appropriate theater-in-the-round metaphor. The poet has turned his prosecutors, hemming him in on all sides, into an audience enthralled by his performance. In each cut, however, the camera scrupulously holds on the entertainer's right hand, pantomiming the story of Sinbad, in the frame's center. The use of visual and verbal rhymes in "And This Is My Beloved"—moon, balcony, her poet-father, the Caliph's fatherly poet-laureate, her face with his voice over, his face with hers—makes the lovers one and their rapture more intense. The cutting of "It's A Bore" is structured along lines of a debate as the song is. "Go To Sleep" is built from confession and reprimand, passing back and forth between ego and superego.

Minnelli's procedure in the start and finish of a scene or sequence alternates between induction and deduction. At the start, he either opens from a detail in medium shot which scores a dramatic point or he begins with an over-all shot of the proceedings and then concentrates on the central action. From the two bottles of champagne in the magnum encircled by longstemmed glasses, the camera pulls back to Tony and his valet in the dressing room, disclosing the tradition of drinks after opening night and Tony's loneness. As the scene unfolds, the detail, a celebrative image, intensifies Tony's dejection. Most of the starts of the scenes and sequences of *Bells* are designed this way. *St. Louis'* sequences and *Gigi*'s scenes and sequences begin deductively. At the finish of scenes and sequences, both methods are used. The St. Louis fair ends on the family, the Patria carnival zeroes in on the lovers, thus preserving an intimacy. Most of *Brigadoon*'s scenes and sequences end with a god-like shot of the proceedings to emphasize space and the protagonist's awesome altitude.

What is constant, however, about the starts and finishes of scenes and sequences is movement, either camera movement (if the subject is static), or more commonly, the combined movement of the camera and the subject—the opening of the summer sequence, Johnny and Victor's entry into the marketplace, Jerry's arrival at the Flodair and Beaux Arts Ball. Minnelli guides one's eye through visual movement.

On the whole, Minnelli employs the single camera on the set.

In dramatic and musical sequences, I very seldom use more than one camera. And I end up usually using the first camera because it follows the action.[25]

The editing, therefore, is practically done in the camera. The snipping and pasting by Minnelli and editors Harold F. Kress, Albert Akst, Blanche Sewell, Adrienne Fazan, David Bretherton, and Flo Williamson comes down to a tightening or refining rather than selecting, arranging, and rearranging.

Minnelli's camera point of view is essentially objective. Subjective point-of-view shots are infrequent in Minnelli's work. The camera is almost Esther catching a glimpse of John across the lawn or watching him enter his bedroom. It is almost Tootie looking at Mr. Bankoff or Mr. Smith gazing down on his daughters in the backyard. The camera is almost Yolanda riding in the back of the automobile that carts her from the convent.

Although eschewing subjective shots, Minnelli's camera, by its angle and movement, is expressive of his characters' states of soul. In this sense, it is subjective. Petunia scurries along the town's sidewalk in search of Little Joe. The camera scurries also and rises little by little from low to high angle. As the distraught lady nears the corner, a gun shot sends people scrambling every which way. By the time Petunia turns the corner, the camera has reeled back to a high-angle long shot to include the cafe's flashing marquee, its front, and its swinging doors, all of which dwarf Petunia. Camera angle, movement, and composition make one throb with astonishment and desperation, thereby exposing Petunia's innards as her pursuit for her almost repentant husband ends at the cafe's swinging doors and the crack of a gun. The camera has stopped, so has Petunia and her heart. The camera is relentless, ferreting Jerry out as he tries to escape the furies. Pinning him against the fountain, the camera rocks from side to side, approximating his hysteria. At the conclusion of "Gesticulate," the camera reels back to reveal performer and audience, then swirls around to the poet throwing himself at the Wazir's feet. The camera's extravagance matches and underlines the performer's bombastic bow, thus intimating his satisfaction over his bravura performance.

CAST

Being democratic, musical comedy is full of people. This is partly due to the convention of the chorus, a large assembly of singers and/or dancers ushered in for the production numbers, partly to people the scenes of festivity prevalent in the form, and partly to intensify the form's energetic spirit, for energy has something to do with mass. This characteristic was only heightened in film where space was unlimited—Cecil B. DeMille's *Madame Satan* (1930), Berkley's extravaganzas, most of the Astaire-Rogers' finales.

The cast, although considerable in Minnelli musicals, has less to do with the genre's conventions or the medium's possibilities of imaging multitude and magnitude than it does with the story's context.

Minnelli employs cast, whether in the dramatic or musical sequences, production or otherwise, to enrich the drama. (Recall the use of caricature and grotesque.)

> I also cast all the extras . . . I always pay a lot of attention to extras because usually they just go down the street and pick their noses or do anything, and the action is in front of them. But I think it's terribly important to have extras in relation to the people they surround.[26]

Almost the same care in enactment is lavished upon the leads as upon the cast. Sergeant Fleetfoot, before zooming off to heaven to get a first-hand report, bends his knees, folds his arms back, rests his hands on his chest, and begins to flap his elbows.

Production numbers do not predominate, except in *I Dood It*. The musical numbers usually express the protagonists' underside and, as such, are private, intimate happenings. The production numbers that are part of a show are controlled—"The Lady Gives An Interview," "New Sun In The Sky," "Louisiana Hayride," the Dem-Bones sequence of the jazz ballet. The tableaux, "Bring On The Beautiful Girls" and "I'll Build A Stairway to Paradise," are appropriate since they are presented as part of a revue, a form synonymous with grandeur.

When not part of the show, the chorus is controlled as well as contextual, thereby strengthening the dramatic motivation of the musical sequences and aiding integration—worshippers in "Li'l Black Sheep," the neighborhood guests in "Skip To My Lou," the junketeers in "The Trolley Song," the second graders in "This Is A Day For Love," carnival revelers in "Coffee Time," the port's inhabitants in "Niña," the spectators in "Mack The Knife," the people of Paris in the ballet, the show's cast in "I Love Louisa" and the reprise of "That's Entertainment," the villagers in "Down on MacConnachy Square," "I'll Go Home with Bonnie Jean," Jean's female bridal party in "Waitin' For My Dearie," the whirling dervishes of the marketplace in "Fate" who, with arms extended beneath their caftans, resemble spinning wheels, thus connoting the subject of the poet's meditation, the hucksters in "Baubles, Bangles And Beads," the Caliph's entourage in "Night Of My Nights," the "seven ages" of females in the park in "Thank Heaven For Little Girls," the toffs at Maxim's in "Gossip," betters and backers in "A Simple Little System," spectators in "Just In Time," guests in "Drop That Name."

Minnelli also employs the cast as part of the technical handling of a number which tightens integration. Often during a song and dance, a crowd of spectators gathers—as usually happens

. . . *The controlled and contextual chorus of worshippers for "Li'l Black,"* Cabin In The Sky.

. . . *Johnny (Fred Astaire) and Yolanda's (Lucille Bremer) pas de deux, "Coffee Time," amid spectators,* Yolanda And The Thief.

when people perform spontaneously—and applauds at the end which caps the number instead of letting it fall off, provides a bridge to the subsequent proceedings, and suspends one's disbelief, as in "Going Up," "Shine," "Honeycomb," "Skip To My Lou," "Coffee Time," "Niña," "Mack The Knife," "Be A Clown," "By Strauss," "'S Wonderful," "Shine On Your Shoes," "I Love Louisa," "Gesticulate," and "Just In Time."

Another effect of having an audience surround the musical performers and framing them in the composition is formulated very well by Béla Balázs.

> It is interesting to observe that in a film in which we see onlookers watching dancers dancing [or singers singing], the motionless public appears more realistic to us than the dancers [and singers] who are in rapid movement. The reason for this is that the immobility of the audience is the familiar everyday behaviour of all onlookers, while the movements of the dancers [and singers] express a distant, exotic experience outside our workaday usage.[27]

Thus, this image embodies the reality-fantasy dialectic.

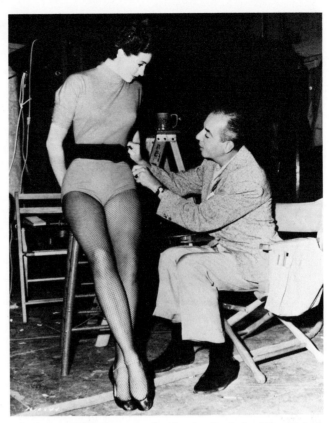

. . . *Minnelli fixes Cyd Charisse's belt,* The Band Wagon.

COSTUME

"The style of the costumes is enormously important to me. I was a designer of costumes at the beginning of my career . . ."[28] Besides outlining the characters to direct one's focus on them (clothes bring out the characters and not vice versa), costumes make dramatic points. The film world's most pretigious couturiers assist Minnelli in this achievement—Irene, Irene Sharaff, Helen Rose, Tom Keogh, Karinska, Orry-Kelly, Walter Plunkett, Mary Ann Nyberg, Tony Duquette, Cecil Beaton, and Arnold Scassi.

To distinguish anxious Esther from the carefree junketeers enroute to the fairgrounds, she is hatless while the others sport quaint bonnets and boaters. She also wears black and white while the others don pastels. Lise's black-and-white outfit in the Flodair differentiates her from the crowd. In the park, Gigi's plaid jumper offsets her playmates' solid dresses. Melinda's beaded ivory sheath glistens amid the rainbow habiliments of the Brighton gathering.

Kelly's rolled-up cuffs, white socks, and penny loafers throughout *Paris,* his red socks in *Brigadoon,* Astaire's purple socks, and the bootblack's pink ones in "Shine On Your Shoes," from *The*

Band Wagon, enable one to concentrate on their feet during the dance.

Little Joe's tie indicates his reverence toward church. Lucifer Junior and his cohorts' hair on both sides of their heads is twirled to resemble horns. Georgia, in a polka-dot blouse whose ends are tied in a knot on her abdomen, is a lady on the make. Before entering the backyard, she plucks a magnolia from the tree and places it in her hair. The resonance to the Adam and Eve Myth (backyard/garden, bare abdomen/nakedness, magnolia/apple), which also contributes to the film's folkloric texture, highlights its seductive mood. Georgia's feathered boa, swirling and slithering throughout "Honeycomb," insists on her sinuous, luring femininity. Petunia, resplendent in all the glamorous panoply she could beg, borrow, and buy, invades the cafe. Due to the particular modesty prevailing at the convent school, Yolanda and her fellow students wear a gray gown in the shower which completely covers their bodies. Nothing but their feet and their heads are seen. Even their arms are underneath and they scrub in complete secrecy. As far as is known, their bodies have never been seen by any living

111

. . . Georgia's (Lena Horne) clothes turn her into the seductress Eve as she tempts Little Joe (Eddie 'Rochester' Anderson) under the gazes of the good and bad angels, Cabin In The Sky.

thing—only a cake of soap. The meeting with her angel extracts from Yolanda a backless midnight lace gown, indicative of her respectful yet flirtatious attitude. Ziggy's robe imparts the feeling of laziness and boredom. It is dramatically salient that when Manuela hears the show's fanfare in her seaport bedroom, she wears a petticoat. Intrigued, she puts on a skirt and cape, preserving modesty but also cloaking her deep-seated feelings. During the hypnosis, the cape falls away, revealing the petticoat's top. While resisting a sailor's clutches, her auburn hair, once tied primly in a bun with a black band, splashes onto her shoulders. Coiffure, too, is dramatic in portraying the surfacing of Manuela's id. (Yolanda's tresses fall in "Angel," Marsinah's in "Baubles, Bangles and Beads," indicating that their defenses are

down.) Her histrionic bent, as incorrigible as Serafin's, is transparent in her choice of the black lace veil and mahogany taffeta dress to meet Serafin/Macoco's demands. The funeral colors will elicit more sympathy from the village audience. Jerry's harlequin outfit catches his ambiguous plight. The poet is rigged out in clothes that pretend a lot but are badly in need of repair. Jaunty but desperate is he. At the posh reception, clothing reduces Ella to a fish out of water. The white, black, grey, slinky, sleeveless sheaths of the females assail Ella's tomato-red, puffy, crinoline tent. Daisy's high necks and covered fronts counterpoint Melinda's decolletage. Daisy is sexually repressed; Melinda, flagrantly sensual. Daisy resembles the fragile flowers she makes grow. Her hair style, fluffy angel wings with bangs, approximates a flower pot (this surely dictated the film's logograph—Streisand's countenance on a flower pot with a bunch of brightly-colored posies blooming above). A nightie and blouse are flower-print. Her white coat and stockings, her bandana and dungarees have flowers on them. The tartan skirt with matching suspenders over a white blouse crowned by a tartan tam and her tangerine coat with layered epaulets and up-turned white bonnet with tangerine ribbon belong in a garden or hothouse. Melinda is regal and impressive, her hair upswept with a headdress of ringlets, bejewelled and magnificently-draped in floor-length raiment.

Brigadoon's *soft colors and their dramatic value: Fiona's (Cyd Charisse) cream dress and yellow shawl connotes youth and newness. The dress' orange underside picks up Tommy's (Gene Kelly) undershirt and socks, designating their mutual attraction and his rekindled spirit. Lundie's (Barry Jones) black-and-white underscores his god-like presence while Jeff's (Van Johnson) gray-blue represents his coolness to fantasy.*

COLOR

Decor, costumes, and lighting are the carriers of color in Minnelli's work. Color is important and essential because it not only records, but reveals as well. It builds a scene in terms of spatial-temporal dimensions, atmosphere, mood, and character. Color renders the excess of Port Sebastian at a time when every nationality in the world was represented. A harsh white light is thrown on Jerry's face, flattening relief and softening modeling. His face takes on an abstract quality, thereby smoothing the transition from reality to reverie. The black and bronze color pattern of Adam's "Concerto in F," along with the static camera, the frequent cuts on musical beats rendering them clean and sharp, endow the daydream with a cold formality and stiff elegence that totally contrasts with the reality-frame. The ethereal quality of

"Waitin' For My Dearie" is reinforced by the cream and beige color scheme. Black and gold are the dominant colors for the malicious, avaricious Wazir; blue and green for the young, naive Caliph; yellow, amber, rose, and white for the maiden; fuchsia for the vibrant poet; gold for calculating Lalume. That wisp of gray smoke from a gentleman's pipe adds another note of unreality to Ella and Jeff's love-making in the park.

Color is also an integral part of the film's structure. It flows throughout a Minnelli musical like visual music, affecting one's emotions precisely as music affects them. This use of color is an emotional expression of the plot, conflict, characters, and theme.

Good and evil fight for the soul of Little Joe, a struggle expressed throughout in terms of light and darkness. When good is in the ascendancy, the compositions are high-key. When evil is dominant, they are low-key. The semidarkness engulfing Little Joe when Lucius Junior and his comrades appear is dispersed by the luminosity spread by the General and his host. The entire film is immersed in a warm solution of pink-brown sepia tones. This attractive rotogravure effect heightens the folkloric quality, thus solidifying theme.

St. Louis' four seasons are designated by specific colors—summer's reds and roses, autumn's oranges, yellows, browns, winter's deep blues and fuscous, and spring's white. The darkening of the values parallels the dimming of the family's hope of attending the fair. When all seems lost, the color is drained from the frame. Mr. Smith, in an ebony smoking jacket, leaves the window from which he witnessed Tootie's destruction of the snowmen in the black night. He rambles through Agnes' bedroom in darkness, descends the steps to the parlor, and comes to rest in an indigo chair. Brown barrels of paper-wrapped objects sling jagged shadows across the room. Even the walls have square areas, lighter than the rest, where colorful pictures used to hang. He strikes a match to light a cigar and keeps the orange flame burning, suggestive of the light in his head or idea (the use of the prop as dramatic point). The camera dollies in and the scene suddenly is suffused with light and warmth. The flame burns his finger. He shouts "Anna," rises, and turns up the desk lamp. The family in variously-hued frocks resembles a crazy quilt on the steps. Gramps turns up the gas jets. The climax comes when the Smith family is assured of being in St. Louis for the fair and color rushes through the house like blood through a once-frozen body. The dazzling white of the next sequence, denotes newness and renovation.

. . . Daisy's (Barbra Streisand) high necks and angel wings . . .

. . . counterpoint Melinda's (Barbra Streisand) decolletage and upswept ringlets, On A Clear Day You Can See Forever.

Brigadoon's greens, russets, yellows are warm colors that bring one closer to the milieu. They are contrasted with the distancing steely grays, blacks, and glaring whites of the Manhattan bar.

Cinemascope had been developed for brilliant colors like candy-boxes: bright reds, bright greens, bright blues, and so forth. So it was completely wrong for *Brigadoon* . . . So we set up a laboratory at Ansco because they were able to handle the Cinemascope size. So we had an ansco positive and a technicolor negative which made the colors softer.[29]

The fairy tale of *Yolanda* is painted in the colors of a child's crayon box. The uniforms of the schoolgirls are bright red, those of the nuns, sky-blue and white, and the rooms of the estate, pink and green, while the carnival is rainbow hued.

The pastels of a Parisian springtime run down to black and white as Lise dances with her fiancé and Jerry with Milo at the ball. In Jerry's memory, the colors revive.

Kismet's splashy color design resembles illustrations from an Arabian Night book for children. *Gigi* is an impressionistic mood piece, a style endemic to the story's context. As Jeff searches for Ella, the color evaporates. In *On A Clear Day*, the colors of the memory sequences are richer than those of the present, thus contrasting Melinda's personality with Daisy's.

Color helps in changes of mood. Petunia's desperate "Happiness Is Just A Thing Called Joe" becomes jubilant as two black faces dissolve into white sheets. Frequently, Minnelli has pastels followed by brighter colors and low colors followed by scenes in high.

At the other end of the spectrum from the then fashionable 100 per cent color musicals, Minnelli employs a system of color coordinates—a method of disciplining or controlling the color to rivet the attention of the audience on the important features within each frame (color has a diffusive effect on the viewer, causing his eye to wander). As well, this method serves to augment the emotions. Using contrasting colors, in combinations, is Minnelli's most frequent approach.

Any scene in Minnelli's work illustrates this technique. For example, the scene in the older girls' bedroom just prior to Lon's party from *St. Louis*. Soft blue—the ribboned border around the dressing mirror, the pad on the chair before it, the early evening sky outside the window, Esther's dress. Beige and auburn—Esther's hair, the lampshade, the tie on Esther's dress, Rose's dress, a wicker chair. Pink—the window-curtains, the chair covering on the left edge of the screen, the wallpaper with blue-grey stripes, the girls' peaches-and-cream complexions. This soft blue-beige-auburn-pink arrangement outlines the two girls, their femininity, their youthful bloom, as well as the evening and era's mellowness.

SOUND

The rich diversity of effects, the alternation of

114

effects and silences, the sound close-ups and long shots, and the expressionistic use of sound are the most characteristic traits of Minnelli and company's (Douglas Shearer, Wesley C. Miller, Benjamin Winkler, Elden Ruberg) tracks.

The bonfire crackling, a cat's meow, the neigh of a horse, the wind's whir, and dead brittle branches splintering under footfalls contribute to the eeriness of the Halloween night that Tootie faces alone as she wends her way to the Bankoff's. This mosaic of effects is also a projection of her self-induced hysteria.

A heavy silence at the dinner table conveys the family's discomfiture after Warren's call, except for the head of the house whose crunch from the celery stalk meets with disapproval and further silence which relaxes finally into overlapping conversation-starters and nervous laughter. Reality-sounds—people chattering, motors racing—are blotted from Jerry and Lise's encounter by the Seine, intimating a world apart.

As the bedroom dissolves to the backyard in "Happiness Is Just A Thing Called Joe," the track emits a sound close-up. In other words, the volume is intensified, representing the quickening of Petunia's high spirits. A sound close-up of the fair song as the camera dollies into Mr. Smith with a cigar in one hand and lit match in another indicates his change of heart. Warren's strident "I love you" followed by his timid seasonal greeting christen him as a gauche, self-conscious individual. Sound close-ups characterize Port Sebastian as feverish while counterpointing it with the previous scene in Manuela's home.

God's voice booms like a distant drum, and appropriately so, since the Southern black folks' hearts are engraved with the fear of the Lord. A horn substitutes for the announcer's voice at the ball in "This Heart Of Mine," typifying his pomposity and authority. During "That's Entertainment," a celebration of the power of entertainment to transport one to another realm, effects approximating gangsters' lingo spill from Tony and Jeffrey's mouths. To designate the show's fate, a chorus utters birth pangs, a bell tolls, the pangs dwindle down to ululations against lugubrious music, a clarinet sourly and mockingly plays the first four notes of "You and the Night and the Music," more bells toll, the clarinet encores. This melange becomes a dirge that accompanies the cortege of first-nighters as they leave the viewing. The deafening, metallic cacophony accompanying one's plummet into Manhattan dissolves into overlapping conversations, shouting, and noise, which contrasts with the previous dulcet and lilting Scottish air and Fiona's ever-softer repeti-

tions of "I love you." In the Manhattan bar sequence, the babble of voices and effects seems a few frames out of synchronization, making everyone and everything sound even madder and more irritating. Gigi's mother is never seen but her character is precisely defined by the sound of a bad soprano practicing scales off in the next room. When Gigi, Gaston, and Grandmother put the index finger of their right hand in the cheek of their mouth and pop it out, the sound of a cork being released from a champagne bottle is heard, adding more élan to their merrymaking. To register Jeff's revelation as to Ella's identity and whereabouts and his concomitant shock, his jaw sinks and the sound of a subway screeching to a halt comes out of it.

CREDITS

Part of the theatrical musical comedy's spectacle is the drop curtain, unveiled during the overture, which performs the functions of providing context and sometimes mood. Breaking with the film musical's precedent of throwaway titles, Minnelli uses the titles or credits at the beginning of his musicals as a drop curtain in all save two musicals, *Paris* and *Brigadoon*. There, the design comes down to a white invitation embossed with black letters against a cyan background with a miniature French flag in the upper right corner for *Paris* and embossed with red letters against a tartan cloth for *Brigadoon*.

A warm-up, *Cabin* has a billboard surrounded by trees and flowers on which a cabin floats on clouds and then flies about amidst musical notes and instruments. *I Dood It*'s titles are superimposed over Jimmy Dorsey's orchestra in a rendition of "One O'Clock Jump." The golden titles of *St. Louis* are printed inside a gilt-edged American Gothic frame against a cerulean background. The frame is hung against a pink and white wall. Each seasonal sequence sports its own drop curtain. The Smith home is framed by gold leaf intertwined with flowers and a pink ribbon for summer, by leaves and purple grapes for autumn, by a red satin bow interlaced with holly against a blue background for winter, and by gold leaf intertwined by pink roses against a cream background for spring. *Yolanda*'s design is dawn's arrival on a lush Patrian hillside where a teacher with a llama enters to conduct *alfresco* lessons. A scrapbook's cover, divided into myriad miniature squares of gorgeous girls, is the *Follies'* pattern. Credits for *The Pirate* are superimposed upon an ancient map of the Caribbean drawn about 1810. A museum-like display encasing Tony Hunter's black top hat, silver-tipped cane, and ivory gloves prefaces *The Band Wagon*. Gold letters over a pink background flecked with ancient Near Eastern grill work in rose introduce *Kismet*; Sem's drawings of *fin-de-siècle* Paris, *Gigi*. Top to bottom, quite impersonal location shots of Manhattan—aerial views of the Hudson River, skyscrapers, the East River and then ground shots of empty lots, a building being razed, the stock exchange—provide *Bells'* drop curtain. *On A Clear Day* employs square outlines, representative of window ledges.

SURREALISM

The conclusion of this chapter is an appropriate place to deal with the surrealism in Minnelli's work since this topic concerns the visual look of his films.

Burgeoning in France between the world wars, surrealism was neither an art movement nor doctrine, but a state of mind among artists that was supposed to do nothing less than change both the world and man's belief in himself. In 1924 psychologist André Breton, the pope of surrealism, published its creed. *Manifeste du surréalisme*. "The basic idea," according to Hornstein, Percy, and Brown

> is derived from a combination of Dadaism and Freud: the automatic, illogical, uncontrolled fantasies and associations of the mind represent a higher reality than the realistic, deliberately manipulated world of practical life and ordinary literature. Essentially, the surrealist strives to present a dream world, leaving the interpretation to his audience. He cultivates free association and the automatic . . . decries any concept of art or talent (since these terms imply a deliberate control on the part of the artist), and . . . delights in the illogical and inexplicable . . . As a concerted effort, surrealism broke up at the beginning of the second world war, largely as a result of political dissension among its adherents. Although it produced no masterpieces of its own [nor did it seek to], it exerted considerable influence on a good deal of modern and contemporary thought, literature, and painting, [and film].[30]

Surrealism's heyday in America was the thirties, the decade when Minnelli was a fixture on the New York theatrical scene. He acquainted himself with works of the surrealists and collected many of Max Ernst's pieces. A friend to Man Ray and Hans Richter, he financed a few of their short films. And in the *Ziegfeld Follies of 1936*, Minnelli, along with George Balanchine, brought surrealism to the Great White Way.

The principal subject of a Minnelli musical immediately sparks an association with surrealism. A considerable portion of his musicals happens on the subliminal level of his characters' being. In some instances, the entire film unfolds on this level. This underside, for Minnelli and his people as for the surrealists, is more real and true, and must be tapped if reality is to be improved.

In the expression of these inner realms, surrealistic technique is present—the vastly incongruous juxtapositions of objects and relations, the seeming illogic, the contextual way of imagining, the aura of strangeness and in the dreams, even madness, the great interest in the "object," and especially the second and third states of the object outlined by Salvador Dali—"the object [assuming] the immovable shape of desire and [acting] upon our contemplation . . . dream-state articles . . . the object [as] movable . . . such that it can be acted upon . . . articles operating symbolically . . ."[31]

Minnelli, however, is not as audacious and abandoned in the use of these techniques as most of the surrealists. But then, he is not an official member of the group and he is working in a mass medium that continually popularizes, if not vulgarizes, movements, trends, and styles.

> I think the fantasies that are in people's minds are all important, but they have to have a certain kind of discipline. I think they do in Buñuel, illustrated so beautifully in *Belle De Jour* because he used fantasies in the right way. You can't just use them any way and then break off in the middle of them and start a new style."[32]

An example of this control is that his characters' spiritflights are psychologically motivated and have reality counterparts within them. Little Joe is delirious with fever. Lucifer Junior is Lucius, his wining and dicing partner. The good angel is Reverend Green. Fleetfoot is the deacon. The temptress is Georgia. Fear and guilt induce Johnny's nightmare which contains details and actions of the previous afternoon and early evening. The Chinaman is stunned into his paradisiacal vision with his beloved by the fatal wound and approaching death. The incidents of Manuela's daydream, elicited by repression, correspond to Serafin's bravado in the courtyard and the illustrations from the book on Macoco. Anxiety over Lise's departure, spilling over into hysteria, triggers Jerry's memory of his personal and professional life in Paris. Melinda's peach chiffon gown rhymes with Daisy's peach chiffon scarf. Floor-length white sheer curtains, flowing through the entrance of the music room, rhyme with the wafted curtain in Chabot's study. *Angst* and

Jane's words ignite Tommy's memory.

Examples of surrealism and surrealistic resonances are scattered through Minnelli's work. They usually occur at the transitions into or out of interior states and during the depiction of these states.

An extinguished lamp on the bedside table lights itself. The camera warily pans right. A large shadow approaches the bed. (Shadow is an image connoting some on-the-verge threatening, promising, or curiosity-arousing incident.) A half-opened window comes into frame with curtains blowing incessantly. This heralds Little Joe's dream. Hades as a modern organizational office has a surreal touch about it. A lamp on a gingham tablecloth shakes, as does Georgia in the screen's left frame, both before a curtain-flapping window through which a funnel-shaped tornado is seen at the tip of a converging perspective. Georgia walks toward the camera in a dazzling white gown as the cafe topples all around her and fires break out here and there—a Venus rising from the debris. Pickaninnies dot the snow-white road to heaven.

Tootie's trick-or-treat sequence has small children costumed in absurd remnants of adult clothing, grotesque masks against a black night, a raging bonfire, gnarled trees casting elongated, weird shadows, and the babe relishing the group's chant: ''Tootie is the most horrible of them all.''

Ziegfeld Follies continues the surrealistic strain in the entrepreneur's home of pink structures floating in royal blue space; the props and frames against colored cycloramas of the nightmare, ''Pay the Two Dollars;'' the blue and white fairy garden; the Oriental paradise; and ''Beauty'' with its clouds, caves, rocks, foam, girls clad like vestal virgins, and converging perspectives.

The mixture of the baroque and modern, the spiritual and sensual throughout *Yolanda* is bizarre and uncanny, especially the ''Angel'' sequence in which the song's spiritual lyrics, its hymn-like melody, the girl's reverent (or is it glazed?) delivery are juxtaposed with alluringly sensual, often erotic, actions—the bubble bath, the adornment. So is Armarilla's sliding down the bannister with her gratified eyes staring into the camera (the second state of the object) and Johnny's dream with a five-handed man, the shower of gold coins, the wrapped maiden, the gambler's former world materializing on the crags, the gliding terrain and the mad veil (the third state of the object).

Surrealistic overtones permeate ''The Pirate's Ballet''—Manuela substituting for the white horse (second and third states of the object), Macoco's machete lopping off her rabbit ears, the scalloped spotlight, and elongated shadows against the fiery horizon.

Henri's projection of Lise as superwoman, especially the simultaneous conglomeration of poses, Adam's illusion of grandeur, the rose and the harried escape from the preying camera during Jerry's memory are surrealistic touches in *Paris*.

The nightmarish rehearsals—the ornery sets and props that seem to take out their revenge on Jeffrey, ''You and the Night and the Music'' with Tony and Gaby coughing in a scalloped spotlight amid flash fires, smoke clouds, and an ominous rendition of the song by the chorus, ''Triplets'' with adults Tony, Lillie, and Jeffrey enacting the dark side of babies in a playroom with black wallpaper, ''The Girl Hunt Ballet''—all have a surrealistic quality about them. ''Girl Hunt'' is not intended as a surrealistic piece as Johnny's ''Will You Marry Me?'' The number gives the impression of being that to the degree that the director was ''making a parody of a somewhat surreal literary genre [that is, Mickey Spillane].''[33]

The sights and sounds in the Manhattan bar sequence have a touch of the surreal as does the stop-motion effect that changes the habitués of Maxim's into droll mannequins.

Chabot's projection of Melinda's night waltz before the Pavilion and on the banquet table, Daisy's bedroom where two heads seem to pop from the beds of a hothouse, Chabot's voice emerging from a cooking instructress, a cop, a wizened couple, a saleslady, a little boy, a French poodle, and Daisy being swallowed by the dawn are surreal.

The end of Duke Ellington's musical interlude, ''Going Up,'' with a frame full of jumping bodies and waving hands; the chorus' hand-slapping and leg-kicking in ''Coffee Time''; the countless quavering palms that frame Manuela at the end of ''Mack the Black''; Gaby against a razzle-dazzle sunburst at the finish of ''New Sun in the Sky''; the Wazir's court turned corybantic by the poet; the conclusion of ''A Simple Little System'' with choristers in a broiler room flinging their programs, shaking their hands, and raising their arms and of ''Drop That Name'' with the guests racing to the penthouse ledge and wringing their arms above their heads like revivalists embody this sensibility, as well.

. . . Surrealism: Johnny's (Fred Astaire) former world materializes on the crags during his nightmare, "Will You Marry Me?", Yolanda And The Thief.

. . . Surrealism: Tony (Fred Astaire) as the private eye and Gaby (Cyd Charisse) as the mysterious woman in "The Girl Hunt Ballet," The Band Wagon.

6
MUSIC

DRAMATIC MOTIVATION AND RELATION, TECHNICAL POSITIONING AND HANDLING

Except for a few numbers in *Cabin* and the entire *I Dood It*, the integration of music, vocal and instrumental, is a matter of dramatic motivation and relation, technical positioning and handling. What Lubitsch and Mamoulian attempted, Minnelli achieved.

Rehearsal and performance are the usual motivations for the song in a musical film. Party or some other form of festivity—fair, carnival, embarkation or return, procession, wedding, birthday, parade, picnic, liturgy—is also frequently employed. And these occur in Minnelli musicals. But more often than not, the motivation has something to do with the subliminal life the protagonists visit, straddle, or inhabit, from which they derive their own naive grace.

Minnelli uses song as an expression of this state and very appropriately for, as man has known since the dawn of creation, song is elevated speech, a heightening or deepening of the everyday. Its expression demands more from man than mere talking—more concentration, energy, emo-

tion, physicality and so, draws man out of himself more than mere words. To sing, they say, is to possess one's soul. Thus, song constitutes a time apart from the ordinary, a special sphere, the sacred. That is one of the reasons why it has been for every people a necessary element in worship, as well as in celebration and theatre.

The subliminal life is also extraordinary, more intense than the everyday, an explosion of instincts unveneered by civilization. It is the level where one tastes wholeness, unity, where "Between the idea/ And the reality/ Between the motion/ And the act/ Between the conception/ And the creation/ Between the emotion/ And the response . . ." falls very little shadow. It is another country. They do things differently there. Song, therefore, is the perfect medium for this experience as it is for festivity and performance with its elements of extravagance and whimsy that also contrast with the everyday.

The problem of relation is resolved by the number having something to do with the dramatic elements—setting up the plot (the narrative), advancing it (the love ballad), bridging plot's incidents (the interlude), delineating character (the soliloquy, the character ballad, the patter song, the address), revealing a subjective state or feeling (the personal lyric, the interior monologue), establishing context (the charm song, a popular or period air), creating atmosphere and mood (the tone poem, the rhythm song), crystallizing conflict and theme (the debate or argument), or any combination of these.

The instrumental music, whether overture, interlude, leitmotif, reprise, song-introduction, or dance accompaniment must function dramatically also. It must put the audience *in medias res,* making plot or character points, heightening atmosphere and mood, and bridging talk and song, walk and dance.

Title music, a rule of thumb for all film genres, intimates the setting, tone, and sometimes the conflict that follows. Whereas an overture in the theatrical musical is usually a collage of the show's music, the film's overture usually involves only one or two songs that are the outstanding numbers of the piece.

As for the technical positioning, the number grows from the dialogue and action and smoothly passes into the rest of the scene (which makes for a tighter integration) or constitutes the upbeat on which the scene ends.

Dialogue just prior to the song is at its most paced, rhythmic, and compact, thereby aiding the transition to verse. Frequently, the dialogue contains words and phrases that appear in the song's lyrics. Background music steals underneath the dialogue and segues into the melody or snatches of it. A kind of melo-declamation results when the tempo and rhythm of the dialogue is coincident with the tempo and rhythm of the music. During the song, the singer often hums, de-das, delivers some of the lyrics recitative, or engages in dialogue. A number continues, but never interrupts, the preceding action. Most often the number is the climax of a scene.

Exiting from a number, when the scene runs on, involves the foreshadowing of the rest of the scene within the number, the continued action, ever-diminishing background music unless interruption or applause occurs, and dialogue which refers either to the fact of the song or its content. When the scene ends with the number, the transition device to the next scene is built into the number itself by virtue of its culminating the scene.

The technical handling includes, first of all, the structuring of the number. Besides being prepared for, each number has a beginning, middle, and end. Within each, an incident or emotion is established, developed or analyzed, and pointed to. There is suspense here, not merely ignorance on one's part as to what will eventuate, but a desire to know

what will result. Minnelli favors two different types of structure, the first being an additive approach where details are piled, one on top of the other, until they reach a climax. The other structural type is circular in that it ends as it began, but involves an exploration in between. Each Minnelli number is a mini-drama.

The sensitivity and care taken in the enactment of the dramatic sequences is insisted upon by Minnelli in the musical sequences. Each number is endowed with an excess of business that is related to the song's content. If the business entails sound effects, they become part of the musical whole and have the effect of various instruments. The same carefully crafted *mise-en-scène*, casting, costuming, coloring, and track, as in the dramatic sequences, are used to bring out the song's dramatic values which, in turn, establish and/or reinforce the story's dramatic points. The singer and/or dancer often interacts with the decor to such an extent that it seems animated. The movement within the frame and the camera movement during a number are dictated by the music's distinct tempo and rhythm, often in harmony with them (the camera "merrily rolls along" Patria on the sing-song anthem and glides through the Street of Vendors on the silvery, gossamer "Baubles, Bangles and Beads"), but otherwise, in counterpoint (sections of the "Girl Hunt Ballet"). The cutting is minimal, always on a beat occuring at the end of the song's lines, at the caesura within the line, or between the introduction, verse, or refrain of a song. When the number spills into a dance or a ballet, there is a cut on movement (a turn, a jump, etc.) so as to seem invisible. Cutaways from the central action are avoided, so as not to disturb the flow or trance that is in keeping with the special reality that the musical sequences express. It also helps the dramatic tension inherent in a number to cohere.

In general, the score for a theatrical musical contains about a dozen numbers. The secondary characters of the subplot are given songs. A film musical score, original or adapted, contains about one-half to two-thirds of that amount. In both cases, the score must be a thing of contrasting tempos and rhythms.

EXEGESIS OF SELECTED MUSICAL NUMBERS

Li'l Black Sheep

Cabin's first number is an auspicious omen. In the backyard, Reverend Green encourages Little

. . . The enactment of Barbra Streisand in the musical sequence, "What Did I Have That I Don't Have," in which she discovers Chabot's attention has to do with science not romance . . .

. . . the reaction—she was supposedly cured of cigarettes . . .

. . . the calm before the storm . . .

121

Joe to the service and the scene dissolves to the congregation hymning "Li'l Black Sheep," a robust Negro spiritual in the revivalist tradition, inspired by Jesus' parable of the shepherd and the lost sheep. Besides providing setting, atmosphere, and mood, the liturgical song thrusts the plot forward to Joe's scheduled and highly anticipated conversion while filling one in on Joe's backsliding background. The camera, framing the worshippers in a high-angle medium shot, pans from left to right, right to left, repeating the cycle while advancing steadily to the back of the chapel where Petunia and Joe sit. The advance is halted several times by soloists who chant a verse and inaugurate a concatenation of whispers and nudges among the gathering. Some of the congregation even have the audacity to twist their necks toward the rear. There is something there they

should know about. The song's lyrics only remind them of this. The camera's restless movement and the cast's rumormonger business vividly declaim their anticipation. The camera assumes a high-angle long shot position, framing the entire tossing to the melody's feverish rhythm that describes their anxiety.

Then, it cuts to Petunia, chanting the last two lines as she rises. She puts the lid on their steam. The mood change is established by her languid, majestic pacing of the lines, the size of the image: an extreme long shot to an extreme medium one, the change of the camera angle from high to slightly lower and of the composition from the entire congregation to Petunia from the shoulders up. All this is expressive of her resoluteness. At the very end, the camera pulls back to reveal the assembly somewhat calmed by Petunia's

. . . The carefully-crafted mise-en-scène *for "Li'l Black Sheep,"* Cabin In The Sky.

123

dominant intervention. The number dissolves into the sermon.

Meet Me in St. Louis

St. Louis's opening musical sequence, one of the most fluent in all film musicals, touches almost every dramatic base. It advances the plot by introducing and delineating the house and its members, establishes the conflict, and provides context and mood. A framed, faded photograph of an old suburban neighborhood with white filigreed mansions and wide lawns turns into color, growing larger and larger until it bursts its edges and begins to breathe, move a bit, and, finally, come to life. A horse-drawn beer wagon with two boys fighting atop the yellow barrels creaks up the street while a shiny red motor car hoots in the opposite direction (America is on the verge of the scientific age). Passersby saunter beneath emerald trees and bicyclists pedal every which way, among whom is Lon turning into a red-roofed Victorian residence with barbershop-striped awnings.

Cut to Lon depositing groceries on the kitchen table where his mother and the maid are absorbed in making ketchup. While thumbing through the latest Sears and Roebuck catalogue, he off-handedly hums the fair song. Enter Agnes, dripping wet from a late afternoon swim, who is warned by mother: "Don't track up the floor now." Putting on clodhoppers, she replies: "I won't," and begins the lyrics of "Meet Me in St. Louis" in the kitchen, continues through the parlor where she sneezes on the word "fair" (quite a natural piece of business), up the staircase, along the upstairs corridor, all against the clump-clump rhythm of the shoes. At the bathroom door, which is locked, she jumps back as Gramps starts the song over her feeble, shaky

. . . Agnes (Joan Carroll) is about to begin the fair song,
Meet Me In St. Louis.

124

rendering of the second "Louie" near the song's close due to her fright.

Cut to Gramps concluding a shave in the bathroom where he extends the natural pause after the first line of the song with: "I'll be out in a minute, Agnes." Overlapping her, "All right, Gramps," he continues the song: "Meet me at the fair."

Cut to Gramps prancing out of the bathroom which Agnes enters, down the corridor, and into his room where he tries on different hats before his dressing mirror, while improvising some lyrics: ". . . we coochie coochie coochie/ We'll be a tootsie-wootsie/ Meet me in the fair," and substituting others with la-las and de-das. From below his open window, the correct lyrics are heard, faintly at first but quickening in volume. Glancing below, Gramps watches a tennis party, among whom is Esther, approaching in a horse and buggy. Amid cheers, laughter, and adieus, they chant the song's last lines before depositing Esther on the curb stone.

Not one of the myriad imitations of this type of musical opener has approached the perfection displayed here and in *Yolanda, Brigadoon, Gigi, Bells,* and *On a Clear Day.* Stale and dreary is Walter Lang's "Our State Fair" from *State Fair* (1945) as is his "It Might As Well Be Spring" which apes "The Boy Next Door," window-frame and all. Mamoulian comes off better than Lang in "It's Our Home Town" from *Summer Holiday* (1947) while Gene Kelly raises all the ingredients to the tenth power for "Just Leave Everything to Me" from *Hello, Dolly!* (1969) with inversely proportional effect.

The Trolley Song

"The Trolley Song" in *St. Louis* best exemplifies the dramatization of a musical number. It fades in on a yellow sign being changed by a trolley conductor. "Skinner Road" becomes "Special to Fair Grounds." The camera dollies back and pans over the trolley, the excited people boarding, and several men grabbing the track and taking it from left to right. The camera's change of image and its movement impart additional gusto and energy to the proceedings.

Cut to a medium shot of Esther among the group. Unlike the others who give their undivided attention to Quinton reeling off the fair's economic details, Esther looks anxiously about. An even tighter shot of her gesture unhinges her from the reality. And one knows the reason why from the previous scene. At the party's end, Esther's query to John: "You'll be joining the crowd Friday as we go to the fairgrounds?" was greeted by a condi-

. . . *Esther (Judy Garland) spies her beau in "The Trolley Song,"* Meet Me In St. Louis.

tional promise: "If basketball practice isn't too late." All rush aboard and the conductor urges Esther to "Hurry up, miss. We haven't got all day." She reluctantly steps on: "Are we all here?" Quinton, the officious, self-appointed cicerone puns: "It's just too bad for those who aren't. Time, tide and trolley wait for no man. Let her go, motorman," With a hiss of steam and a clang of the engine, the vehicle moves off screen left as Esther peeps out from the landing steps.

Cut to the motorman ringing the bell in the front, the trolley rattles and keeps rattling throughout, the scenery passes through the open window, and the passengers gather round and sing as people usually do at the start of a junket. "The Trolley Song's" brisk, driving tempo and rhythm suggest that everyone get out of the way.

Cut to a girl's gingham dress ascending the circular stairs to reveal Esther's face behind grill work. She feels like a prisoner behind bars. Deciding against the stairs, she goes dazedly through the aisle, oblivious to the offered peanuts, seat, and song-fest, retraces her steps, climbs to the second story, goes to the front, leans over the rail and looks around. The camera has tossed with Esther from right to left, left to right, and right to

125

left, registering her state of distress. At the song's conclusion, someone shouts, "Hey look," and all run toward the back.

Cut to two girls' dresses parting like a curtain on stage, to reveal an extreme medium shot of Esther in sheer delight.

Cut to rushing Johnny with a hand clasped to his boater. Esther spins around and gathers the girls to regale them about her romance in the introduction and verse of the song. She becomes a choral conductor during her entertainment, leading the group to fill in the details about the trolley, while she holds the narrative line. In the distance, someone yells "Hi ya, Johnny," which overlaps Esther's "Stop, stop, stop, went my heartbeat." The camera dollies out somewhat and relaxes as Johnny enters screen right. Minnelli's direction of Esther between the Scylla of propriety and the Charybdis of uninhibitedness is stunning from this point on. Her outstretched left hand, accidentally touching his, is quickly retrieved. She catches him out of the corner of her eye, and keeps him there. Her right hand is tremulously unsure. It touches her hair and attempts to grab the overhead strap to steady her rapturous flight. She misses, then succeeds. She positions herself on the seat's edge, seizes the rail in front and gazes fixedly before her. Finally, resting back in the seat, her arms folded, she looks at Johnny, nods a faint hello, and finger waves with her left hand wrapped around her upper right arm. Then, she turns away abruptly, and stares straight ahead as before. The song enriches the context not only because of the setting on the trolley but also because invention songs were very much in vogue around the turn of the century, the period of the film. It also develops a relationship, expresses a mood by ingenuously equating the tizzy of a trolley ride with the thrill of budding romance, and crystallizes the theme—the group's excitement about the fair six months away and Esther's emerging fantasy of John. The receding rear of the trolley dissolves to an autumnal picture, with a waning clang, clang, clang giving way to ominous chords, which foreshadows complication.

This Is a Day For Love (reprise) and Other Bits and Pieces

Musical numbers powerfully register emotional highs and lows. The reprise of "This Is a Day for Love," underlining Yolanda's arrival home, for example, contains a moment of sheer exhilaration. Cut to a peasant atop a sun-drenched garden arch waving a forsythia sprig and releasing a host of doves against a cerulean heaven. Wafted by the music, the camera glides in and down (from top left to bottom right), catching the maidens scurrying across the foreground from left to right to make room for Yolanda and her entourage passing forward under the arch in the median plane. The elemental sing-song anthem-waltz, the equally elemental garden setting, the yellow and olive color combination, the peon's undulating arms, the burst of birds, the dashing maidens, and most of all, the tilting camera that departs from the natural lines of movement make one's heart leap for joy.

A similar moment occurs during the ballad, "Happiness Is Just a Thing Called Joe," from *Cabin* as two black faces dissolve to white sheets in the backyard over a melody that quickens in volume and tempo. Petunia de-das and fills in the lyrics only with the proper noun. Besides the color and sound change, the camera, previously static, is expansive, flowing, and animated—a fast pan left to right across white sheets to locate Petunia, quick tracking before her as she walks to Joe in the wheelchair, stares at the sun, pushes him under the shade of the house, and returns to the clothes line. The song's last line corresponds to Petunia taking the last item from the nearest clothes line. Throwing the shirt's arms around her neck, clutching its body to her breast, she whispers "Little Joe" twice, laughs at her own silliness, and repeats the name again.

At the finale of *Paris'* " 'S Wonderful," Henri and Jerry shake hands and kid each other's exuberance as well as their own by shouting superlatives and rhymed retorts as they move from each other: " 'S wonderful/ 'S wonderful/ 'S exceptional/ That's why I feel/ 'S magnifique/ It's what I seek . . ." Unable to contain itself also, the camera tracks out to an extreme overhead long shot with Jerry in the right background and Henri in the left foreground, separated by a street. The people within the environs clap. Cars stop.

Dissolve to a long shot of a taxi pulling up before the Bel Ami Cafe. Jerry bursts forth. After paying the driver, he hastens on the wings of the smooth melody toward the camera with a face seemingly transfigured by some beatific vision.

Cut and track with him descending the steps. During the flight, he twirls his cap away. The camera pans right to include Lise whom he enfolds within his arms, whirls around, and lowers to the ground. The camera soars to a long shot. The business and movement within the frame along with the camera's attitudes, accented by the music, pitch Jerry and the audience, to the Everest of euphoria.

The second time through "The Night They Invented Champagne," from *Gigi*, Gaston is con-

. . . Madame Alvarez (Hermione Gingold), Gaston (Louis Jourdan), and Gigi *(Leslie Caron) celebrate the forthcoming trip to Trouville, "The Night They Invented Champagne."*

verted and sings while Gigi hands Grandmother the yellow rose and polkas with her. The chaperone has come around too. The camera tracks before the ladies, around the table, tilts down and holds on their raised, swishing skirts and kicking heels, and then tilts up. The glissando camera movement, the particular images selected, the bubbly lyrics and polka rhythm make one heady.

At the opposite pole, pathos and *weltschmerz* mount in *St. Louis'* "Have Yourself a Merry Little Christmas." "By Myself" from *Band Wagon* and "The Party's Over" from *Bells* are threnodies.

Niña

"Niña," an exquisite character sketch from *The Pirate*, is Kelly at his dazzling best. Serafin leaves his troupe with the dirty work of erecting the stage. Breezily, he strolls through the marketplace of Port Sebastian to take in the feminine sights and also to advertise, which really amount to the same thing for him. As a damsel passes, he tips his hat and utters: "Niña." While still cruising the passing maidens, he stops to converse with a man getting a haircut in an alcove: "Beautiful town you have here, sir, beautiful." Customer: "You're one of the actors, aren't you?" People gather and Serafin is aware of them. "Then you know," he teases. The impromptu audience laughs. Another girl passes before him and then another. Both are greeted with the word "Niña." A melody steals underneath. Customer: "Say, why do you call all the girls 'Niña?'" Serafin: "My friend, there are so many beautiful girls in the world with so many

127

. . . Serafin (Gene Kelly) begins to gather an audience to advertise his craft and show: "Beautiful town you have here, sir, beautiful . . ."

dollies in. He follows the girl on the flower cart and the camera tracks with him. He is stunned by two coquettes under parasols out for an afternoon stroll and walks backwards with them. The camera halts and tracks out.

Cut to him flirting with the brazen tavern tarts. One even pulls her dress further off her shoulders. Lyrics terminated, he runs across the courtyard, scales a wall to a dark damsel waiting on the second story balcony, follows her inside, and makes love to her through a circular opening of the pink wall. The camera pans right, cranes, and pans left. Then, on the upper crosswalk between the homes, he lies with a girl. The camera pans and cranes. He swings on a bar onto the balcony across the way and pins a girl against a wall as the camera pans. Here, his flirtation is interrupted by the duenna who goes for his head with her fan. He ducks, plummets down the pole while throwing the damsel a kiss (after being hit on the shoulder by the duenna's fan), and lands with the tavern girls. The camera tilts down and dollies out. With one of the girls, he eats fire. He puts her cigarette inside his mouth, kisses her, takes the cigarette out, and blows smoke in her face. He sidles up to still another local inhabitant who draws him in the

names. I find it very confusing, so I simplify things, I use one." Barber: "But why, why did you pick 'Niña?'" Serafin: "Why not?" Of course, the Niña ploy is a conversation starter and attention-getter so characteristic of this ham. He has hooked an audience and he performs. He strolls through the narrative introduction: "When I arrive in any town/ I look the ladies up and down . . ." The camera, throughout the number, duplicates his acrobatic movement informed by the song's bolero tempo and rhythm. In the pause between the introduction and verse, the rascal taps a girl on her butt with his cane and calls her "Niña." "My name is Aretha," she corrects indignantly. "But you could be Niña for me, couldn't you?" he pleads, then sinuously eases into the verse's first line which happens to be "Niña, Niña, Niña, Niña." At each occurrence of the word "Niña" in the song's lyrics, Serafin flirts with another girl. All find his charm irresistible.

Cut to a long shot of him racing across a lane to the tobacco girl by the column. The camera races too. He reaches round the shoulders of the fruiterer and purloins one of her apples as the camera

. . . he renders the tobacco girl benevolent . . .

128

. . . shows off before the damsel on the second floor . . .

. . . *makes love to her through the circular window* . . .

. . . escapes the duenna by means of the pole . . .

. . . adds females to the act . . .

. . . uses the bandshell for a·stage . . .

. . . conveniently ends this show before a poster of himself, "Niña," The Pirate.

open square to dance while the previous girl grabs back her cigarette. The camera pulls back to give Serafin room. To his delight, the audience increases. He uses the pin-striped bandshell in the square's center as a stage, on which to display his terpsichorean wares. He swings around the poles, performs dance tricks on the steps, and then flamencoes. He adds females to the act. The audience is mesmerized. For the finale, he jumps onto the stage, recently erected by the troupe. His hat is thrown to him and he shakes it before a poster of himself with flames coming out of his mouth (reminiscent of the cigarette trick) underlined by the legend "The Great Serafin and His Famous Artists". The camera dollies in. The scene has come full circle. Besides intoxicating the viewer with Port Sebastian, the song and dance delineate Serafin's bombastic yet ingratiating persona. He is an actor first, last, and always. Spontaneous though it may be, his musicale is a performance and an advertisement for himself and his show. The number also demonstrates the power and magic of his talent, and, by extension, the art of acting, singing, and dancing. It just makes people stop in their tracks and forget their routine for a little while. The number thus mirrors the film's central motif. Finally, the entire scene contrasts with the next in which Serafin encounters still another girl, Manuela, to whom he never once utters "Niña."

Our Love Is Here to Stay

Paris contains Minnelli's most haunting love ballad and *pas de deux*, "Our Love Is Here to Stay." Henri and Lise at a dinner table dissolves to Jerry pacing back and forth outside the Bel Ami Cafe, awaiting Lise. People are seated at tables in the background.

Cut to Lise entering from screen left. The couple takes a table. An old gentleman stares at her. Lise abruptly asks to leave: "Would you mind if we didn't sit here?" Cut to a long shot of her coming forward in the lead, Jerry running behind. Lise stops so Jerry can catch up. "Let's walk along the river," Jerry suggests. All Minnelli's *pas de deux* ("Coffee Time," "This Heart of Mine," "Limehouse Blues," "Dancing in the Dark," "Heather on the Hill," "Just in Time") occur out of doors where there is more room to express emotion.

Cut to an overhead long shot as they turn a corner and descend the steps to the riverside. The camera tracks alongside of them. The sound effects around the cafe have disappeared. Their small talk and laughter have a resonance, due to the slight echo caused by their sublevel surroundings. He offers her candy, a typical American-to-foreigner gesture. At the bottom, she leans against the wall as he places his right arm against it. He reaches for her hand and the camera pulls out, as if shocked at this familiarity, to reveal them engulfed by this extraordinary decor and color—the bridge's gas lamps in the background reflected in the indigo water, an equally blue heaven sprinkled with stars, elegant ash trees in bloom along the breakwater, all softened by a wispy fog, all soulless, save for them. The intimate gesture, the liquid camera, the *mise-en-scène*, the soundtrack, and the subsequent song and dance lift the action to another plane.

Dissolve to the tree tops to indicate the passage of time and tilt down to find the couple below. The romantic interlude is still all thrusts and parries until Lise, atop the breakwater, leans against a tree with hands cuffing her knees. Jerry leans against the breakwater some distance from her and hums the unassuming, almost conversational strains of "Our Love Is Here to Stay," snatches of which he sang to her while dancing at the Flodair, and to himself as he waited for her to answer the phone. His coat is flung on the wall. She interrupts by asking about America. He obliges but slips in the fact that she is beautiful.

Cut to a long shot, slightly overhead, as Jerry sits on the parapet to get closer. The camera dollies in. She hums a few bars of the song. One of her hands falls. Jerry plays with her fingers. She retrieves her hand and places it around her knees as before. He touches her left leg while continuing on about her loveliness. Lise vacates her seat and walks away, but as Jerry begins quite definitively: "It's very clear/ Our love is here to stay/ Not for a year/ But ever and a day," she stops, smiles back, and exits screen left. The camera holds on Jerry.

Separate cuts to her beside the wall, and he at the breakwater indicate their initial hesitation, or mistrust, before the commitment. Then the camera pans with Jerry over to Lise. Her hands are behind her back, indicating fear. His thumbs are in his pants pockets, suggesting that he respects her feelings and somewhat shares them. During the last stanza, his right arm leans against the wall as if to keep it or anything from crashing upon their relationship, a contrast to the crumbling Rockies and tumbling Gibraltar which after all are "only made of clay." He looks into her eyes and takes her to him.

Cut to a long shot with the camera panning right to record Lise's resistance and perturbation. He calms her down.

Cut to a medium shot in which they dance in each other's arms or float off the ground. Still

. . . Jerry (Gene Kelly) and Lise (Leslie Caron) are uncertain in "Our Love Is Here To Stay," An American In Paris.

unsure, they kiss with hands behind their backs. Finally, he places his arm around her waist and she reciprocates. They tread lightly on the soft music toward the background.

Cut to a medium shot as she turns to him at the bottom of the steps and asks, "What time is it?" She darts up the steps. He grabs her to arrange another meeting. They kiss. She continues the flight. The noise of traffic and passersby invades the soundtrack. The decor is practically gray stone. The number develops their relationship and expresses their inner level of being (the materialization dependent upon their descent below), which nourishes their fantasy.

By Myself

In *Band Wagon's* "By Myself," Minnelli captures, suspends, and bores into Tony's melan-

cholia. After being put down by the two businessmen in the club car, the frame dissolves to the train going under the tunnel at 110th and Park Avenue and then to the inside of Tony's compartment where he locks his case and gives instructions to the porter about his luggage. Through the window, the platform of Grand Central comes slowly into view. New York is Tony's last chance. He tries to make contact and ease his apprehension with a feeble joke to the porter, "You couldn't make up my berth for the night here, could you?" The porter, unaware of Tony's depression, ignores the remark. This is another slight. Tony de-das "By Myself." Another put down awaits him as he steps from the train. The press gathers not for him but for screen goddess Ava Gardner. Star, reporters, and crowd exit screen right. The holding-back-yet-thrusting-

133

. . . One of a series of put downs—press gathering for screen star Ava Gardner and not Tony Hunter (Fred Astaire)—that sets the mood for "By Myself," The Band Wagon.

forward strain of "By Myself" insinuates itself.

Cut to Tony watching the party depart. He is left alone on the platform except for the lowly porter who ironically comments, "Movie stars, people just won't let them alone, will they?" Tony: "No. I don't know how they stand it." Tony rests his elbow on a case, suggestive of the support he needs. He lights a cigarette to calm himself. It puts him in a reflective mood. Memory of his former star status collides with present reality. His loneliness and rejection border on self-pity: "I'll go my way by myself/Like walking under a cloud/I'll go my way by myself/All alone in a crowd . . ." The porter reenters with a dolly to take up the trunk that Tony leans on.

Tony is denied even this support, and it becomes still another affront. No matter. He dons his summer straw in a way that seems to shoo all the hurts away. He walks forward on the carpet, his pace dictated by the melody. The camera follows slightly to the side. At last, there is movement and direction. Porters pass the other way. At a kiosk, he stops to finger a huge hard-cover novel, the resort of the lonely, but decides against it. He switches the cigarette to his right hand while he puts his left hand into his pants pocket, still nervous and on the defensive. He stops on the song's last line to extinguish the cigarette, grinding it into the pavement as if he were stamping out his fear. The metallic and cold color and sound scheme of Tony's gray suit, cream luggage, straw hat, maroon pocket handkerchief, hat band, and carpet on the cement pavement, the porter's white uniform and noisy bustling, the steely gray Santa Fe Express in the background, the white smoke pouring from its belly, and the gray steam hissing and sizzling between cars where two workers clang their wrenches do nothing but compound Tony's despondency.

As he passes out of the frame, cut to him walking into the waiting room at Grand Central. The camera pulls back to a throng of people, each and every one of whom are oblivious to him. Refusing to react to this slight, Tony ya-das while mixing with the crowd. Faint, but ever-quickening, shouts of his name and a jangle of bells deter him. He looks around, but sees nothing. He moves forward again, as the melody segues into a melange of raucous and tinny sounds. He stops. Cut to Les and Lillie Marton, a fan club of two, running into the frame.

Shine on Your Shoes

This number, from *The Band Wagon,* dramatizes and motivates the transition between insecurity and assurance. The stroll down Forty-Second Street with Les and Lilly disheartens Tony further. A long shot records Tony, hands on hips, looking in the direction of the departing taxi in which he packs his guides. He turns to head toward the penny arcade in the background. The crowd jostles him. The colors, like the inside of a jukebox, are bright, garish, heavy; they tend to come forward and grab Tony and the viewer.

Cut to Tony, straining above the noise of the *hoi polloi,* the games, and the honky-tonk piano, to ask the man at the food counter: "Excuse me, I'm a little fuzzy. Wasn't this formerly the Elgin Theatre?" The short-order cook retorts by slamming a hot dog in Tony's palm. The camera follows Tony further inside, as does a hungry lad. Tony bumps into a grotesque, the spinsterish giantess, peering into the nickelodeon. He spins around to see a display labelled "The Gorilla Bride." He turns and notices the hot dog in his hand, searches for a trash basket, sees one, and heads for it, the boy hot on his trail.

Cut to Tony at the basket turning to confront the boy. He hands the lad the frank and pats him on his head. This lightens his spirit. In the left background, a man is getting a shine on a bootblack's stoop. Tony steps on a vibrator and his body becomes charged. This is also an upper. All the while, the grateful boy watches in the extreme right foreground. The grotesque at the "?" machine in the left foreground feverishly spins the handles and bangs the machine to no avail. Tony then tries the machine. He too is unsuccessful. He turns around, arms akimbo, and

spies something. He exits. The kid, munching the frank, follows.

Cut to Tony heading toward Madame Olga's fortune-teller machine. The first card makes Tony shudder, while the second brings on a smile. Little by little, his blues are subsiding. At pokerino, he shakes the machine and five aces light. The arcade's honky-tonk rhythm gets into his bones and he begins to strut. At a "test-your-love-appeal" machine, "gorgeous" flashes. Tony is almost smug. He fixes his tie and cocks his head back. A crazy mirror causes him to laugh at himself and, by extension, his former meanies. He even caps the gag by returning to the "test-your-love-appeal" machine and puts his hand on his hip in wonderment. The colors and sounds, especially the rinky-tink piano and clarinet that shout and exhilarate, the good luck and fortune of the amusements, the bit of kindness to the lad, all have hemmed Tony's tattered soul. Buoyant Tony, sauntering rhythmically with his head in the sky, trips over the extended legs of the bootblack, who, with head hung low, rests on his stand's lower step, an echo of Tony's former state.

Cut to a low angle medium shot of the bootblack looking up at Tony, who now has learned his lesson and can offer help:

. . . Tony (Fred Astaire) receives a lift: a shoeshine, a bootblack stand that is a kind of a stage, and an audience in "Shine on Your Shoes," The Band Wagon.

When you feel as low as the bottom of a well/And can't get out of the mood/Do something to perk yourself up/And change your attitude/[the next three lines are spoken] Give a tug to your tie/Put a crease in your pants/And if you really want to feel fine/Give your shoes a shine . . .

The camera pulls back to a long shot to include the bootblack stand and Tony's tap twirl while underscoring the lyrics, ''Give your shoes a shine . . .'' Tony delivers the verse on top of the stand while receiving a shoeshine. The vigorous, slap-happy, toe-tapping rhythm is accented by sound effects filled in by the bootblack knocking the two brushes together, his brushing Tony's shoes, Tony's stamping on the shoe-horses, and his clapping. The exhilaration is enough to take one's breath away. People passing in the foreground and background stop and look. Dolly in to the central action.

Cut to a long shot when the bootblack struts around the stand, snapping his rag to the song's beat. Here, too, the sound effects accentuate the rhythm. Dolly in as Tony jumps down and takes off his hat.

Cut to Tony handing his hat to the bootblack. He is off and so is the camera. Elation takes the form of a frenzied movement that coalesces into short dance spasms in double then triple time. He feverishly repeats ''got a shine on my shoes'' to himself in the crazy mirror, at the rifle range where Tony's steps scare a customer into firing, before the two-bits photomat booth from which the screaming grotesque ejects herself as if the mad Tony planned to rape her, to the camera

. . . Prop as a dramatic point in ''Shine On Your Shoes:'' Tony (Fred Astaire) simulates vibrator's charge which ironically does not come from the machine but from himself, **The Band Wagon.**

inside the booth, and to the man before the display of beer cans where Tony takes a ball to throw at the cans which collapse during his aim.

Cut to a long shot of Tony spinning away from the display, pretending motion on the vibrator (he does not need that support anymore), and then turning the handle, slamming his hand, and briskly kicking the "?" machine repeatedly. A butt with his rear, and the machine erupts, just as Tony has, into American flags, fireworks, and hurdy-gurdy music. People congratulate him, even the grotesque. Tony has an audience, an appreciative one.

Cut to a long shot of the bootblack handing Tony his hat, brushing his pants and coat, shaking his hand, and waving goodbye. The audience joins in the adieu and Tony goes his way, this time not "by himself." The jubilant music dissolves to a strident, ominous chord as the image of Tony among an audience dissolves to the billboard of the Stratton Theatre, where "Jeffrey Cordova presents *Oedipus Rex*/ adapted from the original Greek by Jeffrey Cordova/starring Jeffrey Cordova/directed by Jeffrey Cordova." "Shine On Your Shoes" expresses a state of soul and advances the plot. It gives Tony the needed confidence to meet the new theatre genius, Jeffrey Cordova. This newfound confidence has been gained by gathering an audience and entertaining them by his old routines in a place (a penny arcade) where competition from attention getters, mechanical ones no less, is very stiff. As a performance, the number embodies the central motif of the film itself.

The Band Wagon Show

"New Sun in the Sky," "I Guess I'll Have to Change My Plan," "Louisiana Hayride," "Triplets," and the "Girl Hunt Ballet," although performed on the stage as part of the reupholstered show, are, by no means, throwaway numbers. Not merely motivated, they are dramatically functional. The show is a revue, a non-plot musical, decked out with numbers typically found in this form. "New Sun in the Sky" is the number with a girl backed by a male chorus line. "I Guess I'll Have to Change My Plan" is the male duet with top hats, tails, and canes in the soft-shoe genre with literate, civilized lyrics. "Louisiana Hayride" is the number that capitalizes upon an offbeat, but significant, musical taste of the time (every revue has at least one). In this case, it is the fifties' swinging country fiddle songs. "Triplets" is the specialty number. The modern jazz ballet is not only the balletic production number, but also a topical satire of the pulp fiction of Mickey Spillane. As such, the numbers deepen the context and delineate a type of theatrical musical fare.

Also, the numbers are done as they would be on stage. The use of limited space and lighting is theatrical. By preserving the theatrical illusion, the numbers are atmospheric.

Furthermore, the numbers, "full of laughs and entertainment," are made to Tony's specifications, informed by the old hat but sure-fire shtick, flair, and bounce. Consequently, the show is a success. Tony is reborn. Memory enables Tony to achieve his fantasy. The numbers snowball the plot to its conclusion.

The romp, "New Sun," also reveals Gaby's subjective state. The backdrop's amber sunburst, her gold spangled dress and red muff, the line's yellow shirts, their waving arms indicate her "new high" due to the revamped show, but more especially to Tony. Their mutual love renews the ballerina. Tony and Jeff's "I Guess" recapitulates the plot thus far (Tony must give way to Jeff; Jeff to Tony) and foreshadows its conclusion (they exit arm in arm).

In each formula number, lovely, unexpected things happen. "New Sun" opens with black silhouettes against a bronze, blazing sun. Minnelli breaks the clichéd male duet of "I Guess" in several ways—opening the number with their backs toward the audience, having Jeff wear a red carnation and Tony a white one (usually the partners are dressed identically), using pastel green, pink, and violet stripes for the floor and backdrop (usually the duet plays against a solid curtain), and hits cliché on its head when the swells flip their hats back with their canes, bounce the canes on the floor but *failing* to retrieve them, allow them to fall. "Hayride" begins with the rear of Lillie's red hair flecked with daisies. The camera dollies back to reveal the cartoon scenery matching the broad hillbilly manner of playing. At the end, the cast boards the wagon and lighting creates the sense of movement, as it would on the stage. The camera pans across the backdrop of "Triplets"—black wallpaper with brightly colored trains, planes, boats, flowers, trees, yard, plots of grass, kites, and a school on fire (a prelude to what is to transpire) and then pans down to reveal Tony, Lillie, and Jeffrey in white bonnets from which peeps a red curl (suggestive of their hellion spirits), white dresses, and white booties huffing and puffing with their entire bodies in high chairs. They detest their triplicity. Their positioning side by side reminds them that their state is inevitable and makes them even more intolerant of each other. Even their detestation is in triplicate, underscored by the clever lyrics and quick cutting to each in turn: "A-E-I . . . If one of us gets

*. . . Tony (Fred Astaire) and Jeffrey's (Jack Buchanan)
"I Guess I'll Have To Change My Plan . . ."*

. . . The Band Wagon *Show: Gaby's (Cyd Charisse)*
"New Sun In The Sky . . ."

. . . Lillie's (Nanette Fabray) "Louisiana Hayride . . ."

. . . Tony (Fred Astaire), Lillie (Nanette Fabray), and
Jeffrey's (Jack Buchanan) surreal "Triplets . . ."

. . . Tony (Fred Astaire) as the Spillane-like private
eye and Gaby (Cyd Charisse) as the mysterious woman
in "The Girl Hunt Ballet."

140

measles/ The other one gets the measles/ Then all of us gets the measles . . .'' Each in turn fiercely lifts the table of the ''high chair, high chair, high chair'' and jumps to the floor where these *enfants terribles* stump and stamp, and then kick each other.

Once in the Highlands, Brigadoon, Down on Mac-Connachy Square

Brigadoon's opening sequence uses languid movement within the frame, a peripatetic camera with protractive movements to build tension, color liquescency, images melting into one another through the slow dissolves, mellifluous melodies, and a lilting pace, all of which thoroughly entrances. The camera pans down the russet and olive wooded slopes, licked by an indecisive mist.

Dissolve to two hunters rambling cautiously within the woods.

Dissolve to birds flying into a tree while a pale yellow pushes the gray toward the left bottom of the frame. A babbling brook resonates and the camera pans left to a stone bridge with water trickling beneath. The yellow grows richer. The stream glistens with sun starts. A male chorus softly chants the narrative, ''Once in the Highlands,'' which segues into a mixed chorus singing the charm song, ''Brigadoon.'' Both songs with a Scottish cast to them as well as the chorus-over device establish the context, put the viewer *in medias res*, set the awesome, mysterious mood and the fairy-tale tone—''Once in the highlands . . . of Scotland . . . this is what happened . . . to two weary hunters who lost their way.''

Dissolve to the top of the bridge; lemon yellow wipes the gray away. The camera tracks to an ox amid others of his species rising from the ground.

Cut to a slight breeze blowing the mist from the brambles. Through these brambles, the camera pans up while dollying into a village that seems to materialize on the spot.

Cut to the camera dollying in toward a house and then around its corner to a window while in the same direction, from left to right, amber chases away the lemon yellow. Dissolve to the interior where a woman, fully-clothed, sleeps in a rocker in the center foreground. Sunlight streams through the rear window. Smoke comes from a brazier in the left foreground. The old lady awakens, quite startled, dropping the blanket that has kept her warm.

Dissolve to the door of a bed in the wall. Light passes over it. The doors open and nightshirted Charley climbs out and smiles at the light.

Cut to light falling on Jean Campbell in bed. She rises on an elbow, takes a sprig of white heather

. . . Two hunters (Gene Kelly and Van Johnson) ramble cautiously within the woods, Brigadoon.

from under her pillow, and caresses it to her cheek. It is all very reminiscent of Genesis' account of creation's dawning, and very appropriately, since this is the story of the rebirth of the village and Tommy.

The sequence continues. Dissolve to puppies sucking the mother collie. The camera pulls back to reveal a stable boy awakening from his bed of hay. Off-screen, a voice bellows: ''Come all to the square.'' The boy rushes outside to the landing to see and hear a procession of villagers with their wares exhorting all within range to the fair ''Down on MacConnachy Square.''

Cut to a long shot of this group moving horizontally from right to left while another group with their wares moves vertically from back to front. The contrasting movement makes the frame dynamic and more alive. With each successive shot, the frame contains more clusters of people, animals, and wares, more multi-directional movement, more colors, and a fuller, more sonorous chorus. (By this accumulative procedure, Minnelli, as in ''Cabin in the Sky,'' ''Skip to My Lou,'' ''Meet Me in St. Louis,'' ''This Is a Day for

Love," "By Strauss," "Embraceable You," " 'S Wonderful," "Shine On Your Shoes," "I Love Louisa," "Louisiana Hayride," "I'll Go Home with Bonnie Jean," "Dance of the Clans," "Baubles, Bangles and Beads," "The Night They Invented Champagne," "Drop That Name," and "Hurry! It's Lovely Up Here," grabs all the viewer's senses, shaking him alive.) In every cut, however, the initial group who takes the viewer into the square is never lost. Once there, the camera pulls back as if overwhelmed by the masses, the objects, the activity, and the hues.

Cut to vegetable sellers and follow them to the cheese stalls. Pass along to maidens dying wools and follow one of them with a stick of variously-colored skeins who stops before a house where Charley, exiting, is rushed and cheered by a host of well-wishers. Off to the side, however, is Harry, holding a basket of wool, sneering in disdain. Amid the festivity, the conflict between the two men is caught. A lady publicizes her jug of cream and grabs Charley to engage him in a dance. The camera pulls back to frame the dancers in a traditional fling.

Cut to the candy maker, who advertises by giving a red taffy to a child while four lasses look on. Follow the girls bursting into dance while encouraging the ensemble's participation. Toward the end, they prance around Charley, then purchase flowers from a stall to tease him. He runs forward. They follow. He turns to wave. They reciprocate. He exits screen bottom. So do they. This tone poem sets the plot in motion, reveals the village's gladsome disposition, and enriches the context.

I Remember It Well

Kobal's *Gotta Sing Gotta Dance: A Pictorial History of Film Musicals* contained a curious rumor about *Gigi*. "Though uncredited, Chuck Walters shot several of the film's songs in Hollywood as a favor to Freed, including "The Night They Invented Champagne" and "Not For Me.""[1] Concerning "Champagne," Minnelli recalled that "Chuck Walters did the choreography . . . I asked him to rehearse that. I shot it." If Kobal's "Not For Me" referred to "She Is Not Thinking of Me," this number was shot on location by Minnelli. The other number in question ("several" according to Kobal) was the title number about which Minnelli cleared the air:

When I was in Paris doing *The Reluctant Debutante*, Lerner went into Freed's office . . . He was afraid that we weren't close enough with the camera to get the words whereas I thought that going through Paris was so much more

important and you could certainly hear them. So at great expense, Chuck Walters shot it in the backlot in close quarters but they did not use one inch of it.[2]

Gigi's "I Remember It Well" is a drama of time in which past, present, and future meet momentarily and then drift apart. Honoré, entering the cafe terrace spotted with strolling and resting vacationers, ogles his new affair mincing up the stairs. Her turnabout beckons him on but laughter stops him in his tracks.

Cut to the laughter's source—Madame Alvarez at a table overlooking the ocean. Evasive no longer, Honoré approaches.

Cut to the two at the table against a cloud-speckled sunset. Madame Alvarez informs Honoré that the girl with his nephew on the beach is her granddaughter. Cut away to the youths on mules. Gaston falls off. Cut back to the *alfresco* table as Madame Alvarez meets Honoré's surprise: "Ah yes, time doesn't stand still for all of us." Honoré: "We had good times too, didn't we? Come to think of it, those last days we spent together were by the sea, weren't they?" Cut to Madame Alvarez's side in the left foreground and Honoré's front in the right background and median plane. This shot is alternated with a reverse angle and a two shot throughout their memory.

All three variations of the tight medium image size in which no one else appears makes the past transcend the present. Honoré confesses: "I was so much in love with you, I wanted to marry you . . . so I had to do something . . . the soprano . . . I couldn't stop remembering, especially the last evening, alone . . . I can remember everything as if it were yesterday." He sings: "I Remember It Well," a memory-waltz, faltering on his part since she must correct his every detail. But she is not hurt and does not seem to mind. In fact, when he quietly asks toward the end: "Am I getting old?", she declares: "Oh no, not you/ How strong you were/ How young and gay/ A prince of love in every way" while reassuring him with a pat on his hand, the only touch between them. The song expresses their characters and sensibilities as does their positioning throughout. Her two hands poised on an umbrella handle indicates her insecurity and protectiveness (she needs the umbrella's support and shade), her discreteness in confronting him, her definiteness about the past. His gloved left hand on top of the chair next to him suggests his self-assurance, expanse, and casualness.

The song also states the film's conflict and theme. Every sixteen bars of the melody, the colors of the horizon get darker and more

. . . Honoré (Maurice Chevalier) assures Madame Alvarez (Hermione Gingold): "I Remember It Well," Gigi.

dense—pink-red, red-purple, purple-brown, imaging time's wings, the song's subject, enriching the scene's nostalgic mood, and hinting that their relationship has no future. The low camera angle throughout, besides investing these two people with great dignity, allows them to be seen against this visual correlative of the horizon. The ivory clothing, clouds, crockery, vase, and tablecloth add to the incorporeality of this Proustian set piece.

As the melody fades, they laugh and look over the balcony at Gigi and Gaston, dragging mules against waves gilded by a sunset. Their laughter at love and time's illusion, their look away from each other to the young are gestures full of wisdom. Besides igniting the memory (Madame Alvarez and Honoré's last days were spent at the sea), offering another image of time's "swift foot," providing ultra smooth transitions in and out of the number, and leavening the rueful tone, the youthframe adds more tension and suspense to the film.

The juxtaposition makes one wonder whether this generation will go the route of their ancestors. When the song is later used instrumentally over Gigi waiting for Gaston in her bedroom after his proposition to Madame Alvarez, one wonders again. The scene climaxes with a wave breaking on the shore, still another image of time running down that flavors the whole. Dissolve to Madame Alvarez answering Alicia's summons concerning the weekend in Trouville.

Gigi

Gigi's title tune is a soliloquy, a type of daydream, in which Gaston discovers that Gigi is no longer a juvenile he is fond of, but a woman he loves. The number, the quintessence of Minnelli's cyclic structure ("Happiness Is Just a Thing Called Joe," "Life's Full of Consequence," "The Boy Next Door," "Yolanda," "This Heart of Mine," "Limehouse Blues," "Niña," "Mack the Black," "Be a Clown," "The Pirate Ballet,"

143

... *The youth-frame of "I Remember It Well:"* Gigi
(Leslie Caron) and Gaston (Louis Jourdan).

"I Got Rhythm," "Our Love Is Here to Stay," "Dancing in the Dark," "The Girl Hunt Ballet," "Waitin' for My Dearie," "The Olive Tree," "I Remember It Well," "It's a Perfect Relationship," "Better Than a Dream," "What Did I Have That I Don't Have," "Come Back to Me"), is constructed along the lines of a journey, and quite appropriately, since journey implies movement, direction, and change and this is precisely the song's content. That the journey ends where it begins is also fitting since Gigi is its source and end. The number is a musical variation on Eliot's theme: "We shall not cease from exploration/ And the end of all our exploring/ Will be to arrive where we started/ And know the place for the first time." Flabbergasted by Madame Alvarez's suggestion that he provide for Gigi financially as he would for a mistress, Gaston storms out of her apartment. The camera tracks before him as he

slams the door and descends the corridor steps.

Cut to him dashing down the outside steps and crossing the courtyard. The rapid cutting during the number's first half invests the sequence with an edge.

Cut to him approaching his chauffeur outside the entrance of the courtyard: "Pierre, do I look upset?" He answers his own question by grabbing his coat, putting one arm in its sleeve, ripping it from the chauffeur, and hurling it back in the car. He exits.

Cut to him hiking across and down the street while shouting: "She's a babe/ Just a babe/ Still cavorting in her crib/ Eating breakfast with a bib/ With her baby teeth and all her baby curls . . ." He stops suddenly.

Cut to an overhead shot and a slow tilt down as he crosses before the fountains, an image evocative of cleansing and newness. Pensive and hesi-

144

tant, he rests on a bench. The camera's movement, the movement within the frame, the long take as well as the change in melody (pulsating to unassuming), and his soft ruminative patter corroborate this:

Of course that weekend in Trouville/ In spite of all her youthful zeal/ She was exceedingly polite/ And on the whole a sheer delight/ And if it wasn't joy galore/ At least not once was she a bore/ That I recall/ No not at all . . .

He rises and walks though not as militaristic as before, while exclaiming, though not as vociferously as before: "She's a child/ A silly child/ Adolescent to her toes/ And good heaven how it shows/ Sticky thumbs for all the fingers she has got . . ."

Cut to a low angle of him against the sky. He leans on a statue, saunters off, and comes to rest again between two statues, walks a bit, but stops to lean against a column. The delivery, the start-and-stop movement, the business of leaning, the melody and transposition betray his imbroglio:

Of course, I must in truth confess/ That in that brand new little dress/ She was surprisingly mature/ And had a definite allure/ It was a shock at first to me/ A most amazing shock to see/ The way it clung/ On one so young . . .

Cut to an overhead long shot as he strolls onto the park bridge, an image restating his psychological crossing over, and forcefully states: "She's a girl/ A little girl/ Getting older it is true/ Which is what they always do . . ." The lyrics record progression also—first "babe," next "child," and now "girl."

Cut to an extreme medium shot of him, hands on hips, against bushes which line the bridge. "Till that unexpected hour/ When they blossom like a flower . . ."

Cut, again, as he crosses over the bridge and slowly traipses on the green. His voice falters: "But there's sweeter music when she speaks, isn't there?/ A different bloom about her cheeks, isn't there?/ Could I be wrong?/ Could it be so?/ Oh where, oh where did Gigi go?" Dolly in on the refrain's lilting melody to Gaston at rest before a pond with white columns and swans, intimating the order and peace he is on the brink of. Finally, he sings: "Gigi, am I a fool without a mind?/ Or have I really been too blind/ To realize . . ." He sits on the white iron grill seat with elbows on his knees, rises, and begins to retrace his steps.

The subsequent shots concern this retreat: between the two statues, against a fountain, the sidewalk, the courtyard, the outside steps, the

. . . *Gaston's (Louis Jourdan) retreat: the sidewalk, "Gigi."*

interior corridor stairs, and the apartment's door whose bell he rings. The soundtrack explodes with a repetition of the last two bars of the song. Like Gaston, it cannot be still. Gaston confronts Madame Alvarez: "Are you alone? I have an important business matter to discuss with you." The door shuts and the frame dissolves to Alicia's reactions to Gaston's proposition. The number contains plot, character, and thematic values.

Love with All the Trimmings

Daisy's first trip through time details her love affair with Robert Tentrees. The extremely sensuous *mise-en-scène* and business are made even more so by the soft focus throughout. Cut and tilt down from the majestically-frescoed ceiling of nude figures to the magnificent chandeliers.

Cut to liveried servants stacking the ornate banquet table with even more succulent victuals. Dozens eat at the repast except for Melinda in the right background and Robert in the left foreground who stare at one another from across the table— among all that color, white and black, stasis among all that movement. As Melinda brings the white wine to her lips and licks the goblet's top with her tongue, she ruminates (voice over)

145

. . . Melinda (Barbra Streisand) stares at the gentleman on the other side of the table in "Love With All The Trimmings," On A Clear Day You Can See Forever.

"Love With All the Trimmings." The lyrics, a comparison of love to an edible feast, are suggestive; the melody, played on a harpsichord and recorder, subtly alluring. Pressing the tumbler to her exposed breasts (her decolletage is severe), her cheek, across her eyes, under her chin, then down her front, Melinda attempts to cool off. Cut to Robert raising the crystal to his lips, then to her sipping the wine with her tongue. Cut to a long shot of the party with the two lovers drinking in unison.

Cut to the hypnotic session with Chabot, the present ironically counterpointing the past.

Cut to Melinda consulting with her mother, the kitchen cook. Robert enters the scullery. The song-over is reprised. Both advance toward each other as in a trance along the table. Individual cuts (separation) give way to a prolonged two shot of their kiss (union) and the camera, as dazzled as the lovers, pirouettes 180 degrees. Not since Fiona and Tommy rushed into each other's arms, on the castle's steps, has the camera been as shamelessly romantic.

7
DANCE

DRAMATIC MOTIVATION AND RELATION, TECHNICAL POSITIONING AND HANDLING

The tapestry of a Minnelli musical is completed by the threads of the dance. While Berkeley rendered ersatz-dance or musical movement filmic (that is, he expressed rather than recorded it through photography and editing), the Astaire-Rogers collaborations realized the dance's dramatic possibilities. With Minnelli and the choreographers whom he works "very closely with"[1]—Charles Walters, Eugene Loring, Robert Alton, Gene Kelly, Michael Kidd, Jack Cole, Charles O'Curran, Howard Jeffrey, and Betty Walberg—these two achievements are combined. Like music, the integration of dance comes down to dramatic motivation and relation, and technical positioning and handling for all his films save *I Dood It*.

The remarks on music's motivation are also applicable for the dance. Dance, too, is a perfect medium to represent the subliminal self, festivity, and performance since it is coalescent movement, a harmony of disparate energies, directions, and contours, a movement that is elevated and extraordinary as these spheres of being are. Whereas song constitutes a time apart, dance constitutes a space apart.

Ballroom Dancing—Four types of dancing occur in Minnelli's work, all dramatically valid. The ballroom dancing—folk, period, or contemporary—enriches the piece's landscape and time and the scene's mood. The vertiginous jitterbugging of "Going Up," in deference, of course, to the forties when the film was made, bears witness to the rhythm of black people and their abandon in celebration. Johnny's foxtrot with Connie at the Club 42 is a further instance of his bungling. "Skip To My Lou" is a hand-me-down reel. The cakewalk is the sound of ragtime in the air. The Christmas ball is a potpourri of waltzes, turkey trots, and polkas. That is how America moved at the turn of the century. In "Coffee Time," modern American swing (Johnny) encounters and marries traditional Spanish flamenco-folk (Yolanda) in keeping with the plot and its modern fairy-tale tone. The "La Traviata" sequence opens with a

. . . *Ballroom dancing: the turn-of-the-century cake-walk by Esther (Judy Garland) and Tootie (Margaret O'Brien),* Meet Me In St. Louis.

Theatrical Dance Routines—The routines of minstrelsy (the parade, the march, the strut, the shuffle, the drill, the line, the sand dance, etc.), vaudeville (the clog dance, the buck and wing, tap with its two dozen variations, dance metaphors, etc.), burlesque (the glide, the dip, the bump and grind, etc.), routines that the theatrical musical comedy adapted and refined, as well as circus acrobatics and gymnastics, comprise another type of dancing. Usually, a song spills over into these routines which, in turn, shade off into a repetition of the last verse or lines of the song. These routines heighten a character's emotion and scene's mood.

Minnelli, like Zorba, knows that there are times when only dance can say what must be said. Certain states of soul or emotions, certain moods are difficult, well-nigh impossible to articulate without bodily movement. So Minnelli enlists the protagonist's entire body—hair, head, neck, shoulders, arms, hands, chest, torso, hips, thigh, legs, toes—to express them—the helper's double and triple time tap, and Petunia's merry-go-round underneath Joe's finger atop her head in "Taking

florid waltz that situates the viewer in the romantic age. The Viennese waltz of Jerry and the elders in "By Strauss" illuminates one side of the old-new dialectic upon which the entire number is built. The foxtrot at the Flodair unites Jerry and Lise for the first time. The gaiety of the Beaux Arts Ball is caught by the dancing couples. Tony and Lillie parody an engaging Austrian folk dance and polka during the rousing *Mitteleuropa* beer song, "I Love Louisa," to get everyone's minds off the show's demise. The villagers' fling during the fair, the folk dancing at Charley's bachelor party and among the bridesmaids in the kitchen, the nuptial procession and dance are part of Brigadoon's charm. The princesses' brief, violent dance is presumably a common ceremony of greeting in the mountain vastnesses of Ababu. The dance they are encouraged into by the guards is unfortunately more Broadwayese than Bagdadese. During the presentation of the brides, each performs a ritualistic dance, native to the country she comes from. Maxim's bubbles over with the waltz, suggestive of the mad, romantic whirl of *fin-de-siècle* Paris. Gigi polkas to celebrate her victory at cards. Cha-cha, Manhattan's current dance fad, is another instance of old fashioned Ella's accommodating ways. She learns it even though she would rather romantically foxtrot which she eventually does in Sutton Park. Melinda's waltzing gracefully and furiously before the Pavilion and on its banquet table affronts Daisy's two left feet while connoting her resistance to Chabot's mental cubby holes.

. . . *Astaire and Kelly's dance metaphor as a couple of young smart alecks (note the decor in the background commenting on their routine),* "The Babbit And The Bromide," Ziegfeld Follies.

*. . . Ella (Judy Holliday) and Jeff's (Dean Martin)
vaudeville routines, "Just In Time,"* Bells Are Ringing.

A Chance On Love"; Domino's tap in "Shine";
Petunia's bumps and grinds in "Honeycomb";
Johnny's discreet syncopated hand and feet taps
in "Yolanda"—nothing too elaborate or intense to
disturb the girl's illusion, just enough to ease the
pressure of his feelings; the star, photographers,
and reporters' line in "A Great Lady Gives An
Interview"; Astaire and Kelly's dance metaphors
as a couple of young smart alecks, their subdued
soft-shoe as middle-aged brokers, and their el-
derly gentlemen's conceptions of swing in "The
Babbitt and the Bromide"; Serafin's wharf-
gymnastics; his flamenco and acrobatics in
"Niña"; his devil-may-care stunts in "Be A
Clown"; Jerry's tap and dance metaphors of the
time step, the shimmy-shammy, the Charleston, a
train, a soldier, a cowboy, and Charlot in "I Got
Rhythm," of an inebriate of love in "Tra-la-la-
la," and of camaraderie in " 'S Wonderful;"

Tony's vaudeville shtick in "Shine On Your
Shoes"; Gaby's line with the male chorus in
"New Sun In The Sky"; Tony and Jeff's sleek
soft-shoe in "I Guess I'll Have To Change My
Plan"; Tony, Lillie, and Jeff's metaphor in "Trip-
lets"; the Americans' soft-shoe, a kind of Es-
peranto, in "I'll Go Home With Bonnie Jean";
Tommy's sand dance in "Almost Like Being In
Love"; Honoré's carefree strut and buck and
wing in "I'm Glad I'm Not Young Anymore"; Ella
and Jeff's vaudeville routines in "Just In Time";
Ella's role-assuming Jolson bit in "I'm Goin'
Back."

Tableau—Strictly not a dance, the tableau is an
expression of an object, idea, emotion, or event in
terms of decor, costumes, a male and/or female
chorus, their movement and positioning accom-

. . . Tableau: J. Otto Franz (Eddie Foy Jr.) explains:
"A Simple Little System," Bells Are Ringing.

150

. . . Serafin (Gene Kelly) and troupers' (the Nicholas Bros.) devil-may-care stunts, "Be A Clown," The Pirate.

. . . The Americans' (Gene Kelly and Van Johnson) soft-shoe for the villagers, "I'll Go Home With Bonnie Jean," Brigadoon.

. . . Modern jazz ballet: Tony (Fred Astaire) and Gaby (Cyd Charisse) discover their choreographic compatibility in "Dancing In The Dark," The Band Wagon.

panied by instrumental and/or vocal music. Tableaux appear in *Ziegfeld Follies* ("Bring on the Beautiful Girls" and "Beauty") since this form was crystallized in the Ziegfeld revue. When the showman opened his Midnight Frolic in 1915 as a glorified kindergarten for his blooming American beauties and potential star personalities, Lucille (Lady Duff Gordon), the supreme couturier of the time, began draping the Ziegfeld girl. Enamored with flowing chiffons and a frosty, detached haughtiness in the models, she, along with Ben Ali Haggen, created her own type of chorus, quite different from the usual singing-and-dancing group—clothes racks sacheting across the stage.

"I'll Build a Stairway to Paradise" is a Lido-type tableau in which a boulevardier in evening clothes ascends and descends a lighted staircase festooned with dazzling chandeliers and ravishing beauties, dripping in diamonds and pink swaths.

. . . Tommy (Gene Kelly) prevents Harry (Hugh Laing) from leaving the village in "The Chase," Brigadoon.

(Ziegfeld modeled his form after the French.) The first nighters exiting the Shubert resemble a cortege. The gathering-of-the-clans tableau conveys each company's individuality, pride, and militantness. The epithalamium of singing torchbearers and gaily-attired flower girls, acrobats, tumblers, dancers, lute players, monkeys, peacocks, and of course, the Caliph in brocaded apparel mounted upon a beautifully caparisoned stallion under an ornate canopy is made endless by a camera that slowly pans in the direction vis-à-vis that of the cavalcade and, more splendid, by being reflected in the blue water and set against an ebony night. At Maxim's, a handsome young couple enter. The buzz of conversation stops, the fabulously clad denizens along the bar in the right background and at the tables in the left foreground rudely turn in unison, and put their heads together to "Gossip" in a hushed whisper and freeze. The only movement comes from the headwaiter and other arriving couples greeted with the same disdain, in the median plane. At this time, every Frenchman of means had a wife as well as a coquette. These mistresses were the era's glamour people, much like today's movie stars. They met at Maxim's where chatting about the latest affairs or scandals was as yummy as the cuisine, and as scintillating as the waltz. The tableau recounts this peculiar morality. "A Simple Little System," an explication of the booking operation, is constructed along lines of a choral recital since the code involves classical music and composers. "Drop That Name," in which the guests continuously criss-cross each other like a game of one-upmanship, suddenly descend and ascend the narrow circular stairs, forming a line behind Ella to egg her on, and finally chasing her through the penthouse to the outside balcony with hands over their heads, imparts a ratrace mood and glacial atmosphere.

Modern Jazz Ballet—Arnold Haskell in his book, *Ballet*, defined this type of dance as

> a form of theatrical entertainment that tells a story, develops a theme, or suggests an atmosphere through the orchestration of a group of costumed dancers trained according to strict rules and guided in tempo and spirit by the music, against a decorative background; music, movement, and decoration being parallel in thought.[2]

The richly dramatic possibilities inherent in this dance form, which Minnelli was very well versed in during his theatre days, makes its frequent appearance in his musicals seem inevitable.
The master himself furnished the libretto for most of these ballets. Except for *Brigadoon's* "Chase," all plumb the characters' below-the-surface states. "Will You Marry Me?" is Johnny's dream-nightmare. The *pas de deux* in "Limehouse Blues" takes place in the shadow kingdom between consciousness and death. "The Pirate Ballet" is Manuela's daydream and projection. "Embraceable You" is Henri's extravagant idealization of Lise. "An American In Paris Ballet" is Jerry's sweet-sour memory-daydream. "Girl Hunt" occurs as part of a performance on a stage, an imaginary realm, one abstracted from reality. The *pas de deux* in "Coffee Time," "This Heart of Mine," "Our Love Is Here To Stay," "Dancing In The Dark," "Heather On The Hill" and during its reprise interwoven with "There But For You Go I" are romantic reveries.

Accordingly, they crystallize the theme and characterize the protagonists. Some advance the plot. Besides establishing the romance, "Embraceable You" introduces Lise. Jerry's memory-daydream is therapeutic. "Dancing In The Dark" is the discovery of the two stars' choreographic compatibility. "Girl Hunt" is an example of the show's success. "The Chase" solves one crisis—Harry's escape and the village's subsequent evaporation—but furnishes another—the Americans' immediate leavetaking.

Gestures and movements that frame the ballet are paced and rhythmic to make the transitions into and out of the dance smooth. Pantomime is often used. Minnelli is immensely aided by performers Astaire and Kelly, Charisse and Caron in whom the line between walking and dancing is indistinct. Change of mood is constant during the number which makes the sequence more dramatic.

Concerning the *mise-en-scène* of the dance sections of the musical numbers and the ballets, Minnelli keeps the dancers fully within the frame, both horizontally and vertically. Camera tricks or special effects, as in Kelly's dancing with Jerry the mouse in George Sidney's *Anchors Aweigh* (1945), within a cartoon in his "Sinbad-the-Sailor" sequence from *Invitation to the Dance* (1956), Astaire's dancing on the walls and ceiling in Stanley Donen's *Royal Wedding* (1951) or on air in Charles Walters' *The Belle of New York* (1952) are skirted. What is seen is the actual overcoming and defiance of the physical limitations by the dancers—the law of gravity, for instance, by leaping high and easily in the air. This illuminates the suprareality that these dances and ballets express.

Decor is often used as part of the ballet and seems an extension of the dancer's energy, move-

153

. . . Decor used as part of "Heather On The Hill:" the basket, the post and rocks raising the lovers (Gene Kelly and Cyd Charisse) above the ground, and the outline of the hills in all the images rendering the dancers' movements stronger and more dynamic, Brigadoon.

ment, and form and consequently, sprinkles a little magic on this special sphere. In "Embraceable You's" cream and soft pink bedroom sequence, for example, the chair yields to the seduction of Lise's thigh and leg amply protruding from her mauve split skirt. The love seat in "This Heart Of Mine," the stone bench in "Dancing in the Dark," and the trees in "Heather On The Hill" are all players. The orange fires from the torches that each hunter carries dance against the emerald terrain and black sky, adding to the chase's frenzy and peril.

The dance's action is never interrupted by cutaways. If there is an audience, it is part of the dance's composition. This, as well as the minimal and invisible cutting, help to create a spell, an enchantment that is in keeping with the level of reality depicted. A significant difference between the ballet and dance number is the use of color. Minnelli employs theatrical lighting for the ballet (solid backdrops, greater interval between shades, a reduced color spectrum) and it works since these portions, quite stylized, contrast with the rest of the film as they should, since they express subliminal states.

Will You Marry Me?

Money/reality and love/fantasy are the twin poles around which *Yolanda*'s "Will You Marry Me?" spins. The piece's tension results from these contrasting images, the reality-counterparts with a touch of the bizarre about them, and Johnny's ambiguous attitude toward Yolanda. Pajama-clad, he smokes a cigarette by the balcony ledge before retiring. Yolanda's blown kiss that closed the previous scene disturbs him. In bed, he extinguishes the light. The camera pans across and up to the top of the armoire, across the balcony, down to the rocker, and holds on the red carnation in a glass atop the bureau. The red carnation, plucked from Yolanda's garden that evening (love), was not worn since Johnny's *boutonnière* sported a white one. This reality-counterpart also reveals his reverent attitude toward the girl. Johnny's shadow looming on the wall connotes an eeriness as does the silence on the track. Securing the flower, he lights a cigarette and leans against the balcony frame—the exact *mise-en-scène* before retiring except for the exotic splurge of red.

Dissolve to him entering the marketplace as he did that afternoon, where the same people and activities prevail. Only this time, a dull yellow filter (gold, therefore money) washes the entire scene. All sound-effects are eliminated save for a softly strummed mandolin (love). It is all quite strange. The seedy fellow in the dark alcove who bummed a cigarette from Johnny (wealth) reappears with almost half a dozen arms. The bootblacks at whom he tossed some change are now rained upon, along with him, by golden coins. The marketplace in the background evaporates in a heavy mist.

Cut to him on a gold and orange striped, pebbled (in the form of coins) pavement. The pantomime spills into modern jazz as Johnny makes his way over the stone washing boards of the Patrian women who are dressed in the native costume or what Johnny imagines the native costume—balloon skirts and elaborate headdresses. They pursue, enslave (by making him pass under), encircle, and entrap him with their gray sheets, suggestive of his fearful attitude toward domesticity and, by extension, Yolanda. Pulling down the last sheet, he finds himself before a foamy lake from which arises Venus, the goddess of love, wrapped in wind-licked cream chiffons against a red-orange sunset. This image recalls the first time Johnny saw Yolanda beside a fountain at sunset. Entranced, he follows her to a purple and beige terrain of crags, rocks, sage, and wintry trees, his projection of Patria foreshadowed by his unkind comments about the region to Victor on the train, and unwraps her by means of her gold coin belt and necklace (money). It is Yolanda who confronts him with "Will You Marry Me?" (love). Her ladies in waiting enter with a treasure chest. This fantasy is interrupted by a limegloved arm (the switch in color is startling) that clutches Johnny's shoulder and turns him to face his past/reality—the gambling milieu with its puppet-jockeys, slithering bookies, puppeteer-managers, and fast woman. Their slickness, worldliness, and wealth are underscored by their dress in the style of Lawrence Fellows' advertisements in *Esquire*. Johnny extricates himself by turning out his pockets. He has no money to play. He returns to Yolanda for the money. Unexpectedly, all goes gray save for the scalloped spotlight drenching him and the girl. The denizens of the monied subculture, frozen in silhouette, witness him romancing her. He seems to be succumbing to Yolanda's love. Victor had warned him about precisely that. All becomes bright. As Yolanda reprises the last verse, the handmaidens place a bridal veil with three long trains on Yolanda's head (at their first meeting in the hotel lobby, she wore a black mantilla). A silhouette of ringing bells appears on the cream backdrop. As Johnny leads Yolanda onto a hillock, he motions one of the bridesmaids to hurry along with the treasure chest. Money will win out. Seizing the chest, he attempts an escape while the terrain revolts (it

. . . Johnny (Fred Astaire) walks over the Patrian ladies' stone washing boards . . .

. . . then he is enslaved by them . . .

The crystallization of the love-money conflict: Yolanda (Lucille Bremer) or the treasure chest.

Johnny's former gambling milieu interrupts.

He seeks out Yolanda for the money, but finds he is succumbing to her, "Will You Marry Me?", Yolanda and the Thief.

blocks his egress) and her veil objects (it wraps around his neck), suggestive of his guilt and entrapment. Rushing from Yolanda toward the camera, Johnny gets more and more enmeshed in the material.

Cut to a medium shot of him throwing the sheets and blanket from his face—an image rhyme to return one to reality. On screen left, Victor is poised with a large pitcher of water about to douse him.

Limehouse Blues

Ziegfeld Follies' "Limehouse Blues" is a breathtaking musical rendition of the *Inferno, Purgatorio,* and *Paradiso.* The camera tilts down to a sailor resting on the railing of a gaslit bridge in a blue night mottled with mist. The camera tracks with him as he wends his way past an ancient with an opium pipe, floosies in ratty feathered boas, and strapping stevedores before a basement beer hall through whose opened door can be seen and heard a husky peroxide blonde belting the melancholic, desperate title song. Some swells in Ed-

wardian dress emerge and jostle the sailor who enters the establishment. A street vendor, wheeling a hand-cranked gramophone playing "E Pinched Me" from an old Billy Barnes movie, passes and the camera follows him and then stops to stare at an angular Chinese servant in black silk tam, outfit, and slippers, slouched against the corner of a warehouse. The camera follows the lowly man around the corner, past the raddled slum, and behind a group of frisky buskers rendering "Wot Cher" in the best music-hall fashion, making the Chinaman's loneliness even more heartrending by contrast. From the right background a Eurasian beauty in lemon appears. Her color immediately sets her apart from Limehouse's blues, blacks, browns, and grays as do her mysterious features in which the west fuses with the east, her startlingly modern yet traditional clothes, her height, and the briefcase she carries hinting that she is a career woman, and, of course, her loveliness. To the Chinaman, she is nothing less than a vision. She passes before the buskers. The Chinaman follows in the background. A lubricious Oriental sugar daddy who cuts his cigarette with a whip when balked, accosts her and offers his arm. The couple stroll and pause before a window of a curio shop.

Cut to a medium shot of an exquisite fan, the object of their intrigue, and pull back to reveal the couple before it and the Chinaman off to the side. The couple continue on.

Cut to the Chinaman inside the shop inquiring the price. Saddened by its exorbitance, he leaves the shop but remains gaping at the fan through the window. Burly robbers approach from behind, push him aside, break the window glass to steal a marble vase. A volley of gun shots stirs the thick air.

Cut to a medium shot of the pathetic little man who instinctively reaches for the fan as if to protect it and, by extension, her from the lascivious businessman. Another volley of shots, and he is felled. Pan down to his hand reaching for the fan on the pavement. The "poor, broken blossom" goes out of focus. Dissolve.

Focus is restored on him reaching for a gold fan against a black background. Pull back to reveal a host of fluttering fans continually appearing and disappearing around his sallow countenance. The frame is askew. He runs after the fan but ends up in limbo. Four grotesque masks pass before him. A spotlight in the distance circles a female figure. The trial over, yellow lights, suggesting her dress as well as triumph or reward, disperse the blackness and reveal an overhead long shot of the Chinaman and his beloved in scarlet outfits in a spacious (the yellow cyclorama conveys a boundless expanse), ornate Oriental paradise. Limehouse, by contrast, is dense, cluttered, dark, drab, and infernal. They are swept into a procession of spangled creatures with helical headdresses and writhing bejewelled arms who resemble eastern gods and are led to a bridge which they cross over, suggestive of the passage from death to life, from earth to purgatory to heaven, and from desire to fulfillment. The pantomime ceases. The chorus is frozen in silhouettes, and the lovers, whom the camera dollies in on, engage in love-play with four gold fans in a scalloped spotlight. The music track, composed of very muted stirrings during the prologue builds to subdued harps and strings during limbo and breaks out in an eloquent, unrestrained rendition of the title song. Even the sense of heavy fate or doom that the melody connotes has been shaken off. At the end, the lovers are closed in by a cordon of fluttering fans as in the dream's beginning. This orgiastic image goes out of focus. Dissolve.

Focus is restored on "nobody's child," expiring on a couch before the shattered window of the shop with the policeman, inspector, and proprietor as dubious mourners. The couple passes before the window. In the doorway, the salacious man describes the fan he wishes to buy his pickup. Spying it on the floor, she bends to retrieve it. The almost corpse opens his eyes for the last time to see her beside him, closes them, and smiles. Noticing the blood stains, she drops the fan and exits with her trick. They pass before the jagged glass. The camera dollies through the window, retraces its steps to the wharf, and holds on another sailor sitting on the bridge's rail. A policeman strolls by. Fog begins to immerse everything. The last strains of the song run down.

The Pirate's Ballet

"The Pirate's Ballet" is Serafin's swashbuckling performance raised to new heights by Manuela's imagination. From her balcony ledge, Manuela gapes at the courtyard below where Serafin/Macoco frightens away the citizenry and makes the four guards hand over their rifles.

Cut to Manuela hurriedly closing the bamboo shutters, suggestive of the repression of her id. Serafin knocks the helmet from a soldier's head. Manuela opens the shutters to peek out. Serafin continues to pick off hats and laces his whip around the ankles of a runaway soldier. Manuela is intrigued. A white horse trots through, stopping before Serafin. His power extends over the animal kingdom as well. Manuela shudders in delight. Serafin tumbles with one soldier. Manuela is excited. Serafin fisticuffs with another and finally

. . . *The Chinaman (Fred Astaire) and the Eurasian (Lucille Bremer) cross the bridge in "Limehouse Blues,"* Ziegfeld Follies.

chases them away with a club and a fierce shriek as he ascends the steps of the church. Then, he confronts the stallion sitting in the foreground with its back to the camera. The actor twirls around the animal while pointing his club and making horrid faces. Manuela is enthralled. The tension of the scene arises from the action-reaction structure, imagining the transforming power of art, Serafin's violence, but especially the pleasureable, even sexual excitement that his violence arouses in Manuela.

In the ensuing daydream and projection, violence and sex are also reciprocally related. Over Manuela's enraptured visage and hard breathing is superimposed Serafin as a pirate in black shredded buccaneer pants that leave his muscular thighs bare, an open blouse, and high boots spinning around a girl in white with large rabbit ears sprouting from her bandana. This is Manuela's representation of herself. Sensuality plays with virginity. The soundtrack explodes with a heavy, languid rendition of "Mack the Black." The cruel pirate has taken the place of the dashing performer; the virgin, the mare; the pirate's machete,

159

the player's club; enemy pirates, the four soldiers; a harbor landing with a ship at dock, the courtyard. The crimson cyclorama, the fires here and there, and the black smoke suggest carnage and passion. The ballet consists of a series of bold derring-do on the part of Macoco, each feat more dazzling than the last, all a delectation to the girl. Eventually, the pirate lops off her ears with his machete, a phallic gesture at once indicative of his machismo, her masochism, and penetration. The transition out of the daydream echoes the transition in. Manuela, with a look of post-coital satisfaction on her face, slowly closes the shutters. She is no longer agitated. Assured that his performance is an unqualified success, Serafin/Macoco announces his betrothal to Manuela.

Pantomime

Pantomime, child of the dance, is also part of Minnelli's tricks. As seen already, pantomime eases the transition in and out of ballet. *I Dood It* contains two extended pantomimic sequences—Joe's attempt to put drugged Connie to bed and his making-up before the dressing room mirror. Don Pedro and the Viceroy's proof to Manuela of Serafin's guilt by carting out the treasure chest, and her subsequent revelation is a dumb show underlined by a roll of drums.

Paris' introduction of the three male principals is totally pantomimic. Jerry's, in particular, is one of the most remarkable in all film literature. The camera dollies through his garret window and pans right to find Jerry in bed in the middle of the room. He rises on one arm, looks straight ahead as if sensing an intruder, then turns over.

Cut to a medium shot nearer Jerry. A knock on the door, he looks upward, opens his eyes, rolls over, rises on his knees, and crawls on all fours to the door (the bed's head is almost against the door). He opens the door. Through the crack, his hand receives a paper bag. He closes the door. Out of bed, he stretches, bends, and yawns while his left hand, clutching the bag, scratches his back. With his right hand, he pulls a rope which lifts the bed to the ceiling. He abets the bed's movement with both hands. Next he empties the bag's contents—croissants—onto a plate, bangs the stand of the bed back, puts one bun in his mouth, and reaches for a towel on the line above. This he places on his left shoulder. On the other side of the room, he kicks the table leaf up and places the plate of buns on this half-table. With his bare foot on the seat, he slides the chair in front of the wall-length cabinet to the side. He opens the cabinet, takes the chair on top of the round table that is inside the cabinet, and slides them into the room. He retrieves a sprig of violet in a tin can, which he places on the table, and his pants and towel, which he places on the back of the chair. He puts coffee and sugar from the top of the opposite bureau on the table and flaps the bed's tail closed. His left hand opens the bureau's top drawer to secure his cap while his right reaches into the cabinet for a sweater. Throwing the sweater on the chair, and the cap on the table, he turns to close the bureau's top drawer with his knee and then closes the cabinet behind with the heel of his right foot. He opens the window to take a deep breath and to retrieve a pitcher and bowl of fruit from the sill, both of which he places on the table. The sight of a self-portrait across the room draws him like a magnet.

Cut to a medium shot of him staring at the sketch, turning the ends of his mouth up with a crayon, and finally wiping away the entire picture with a rag. A child's voice through the open window interrupts: "Jerry!"

Toward the film's close, Adam's vaudeville with the coffee, cups, and saucers, cigarettes and lighter, and glass of brandy, brought on by his knowledge that Jerry and Henri are speaking of the same girl, is also unforgettable.

Tony's ballet of unease and nervousness as the train arrives at Grand Central, parts of *Brigadoon's* Manhattan bar sequence, "She Is Not Thinking Of Me," Gaston's mad whirl, the couple's Trouville frolics, Alicia's lessons, Ella's date with her boss' nephew, and her dress redesign are pantomines. A solid portion of Daisy's past unfolds in pantomime.

Since, in pantomime, meaning is conveyed visually, gestures and movements take on a larger-than-life perspective. Consequently, the tempo and rhythm inherent in every gesture and movement are concentrated, distinct, and do not pass unnoticed as they can, and usually do, when the visual is informed by the verbal. The pantomimist's actions are a choreography of sorts somewhere between dance and walk. As such, pantomime is an integrating factor, making transitions between dramatic and choreographic passages smoother as well as investing the straight passages with a lyricism and grace that makes the piece even more coalescent. Furthermore, tempo and rhythm is perceived as coming from deep within the pantomimist as dictated by his core, and, therefore, as expressing his or her particular state of being. Pantomime, accordingly, is an appropriate method for Minnelli, interested in man's "profounder site[s]."

. . . Manuela's projection: Serafin/Macoco's (Gene Kelly) derring-do and passion, "The Pirate's Ballet."

. . . Pantomime: Gaston (Louis Jourdan) requites Liane (Eva Gabor), "She Is Not Thinking Of Me," Gigi.

Choreography of Dramatic Sequences

Another integrating factor is the choreography of dramatic sequences, achieved through the movement within the frame, camera movement, and musical accompaniment. This type of choreography occurs usually at crises or peak points in the drama and deepens the emotional content.

Against the psalm singing, a medium shot frames Petunia hurriedly exiting the chapel (top to bottom of the plane) to search for Little Joe. Her girlfriend Lillie, following behind, enforces this movement. Both rush off screen left. Dissolve.

The camera pans with Lillie running right to left foreground and then bottom to top as she enters Petunia's backyard, while Petunia, crying Little Joe's name over and over, darts from the porch door to the yard (top to bottom of the plane). The opposing movements increase tension. As the ladies near each other, two gun shots pierce the distant psalm-singing and ever-quickening ominous music. Both run out lower left frame. Dissolve.

The camera tracks while craning up from Petunia racing down the sidewalk of the town (top right corner to bottom left corner of the frame) and losing Lillie on the way while the townsfolk run in the opposite, tension-creating direction.

The cafe's brawl and its destruction, the ascent to heaven, Rose and Esther's search for Tootie, joined by Gramps, Katie, and Mrs. Smith on Halloween night, Tootie's hysterical dash from her bedroom to pummel the snowmen, Johnny and Victor's attempt at escaping Mr. Candle at the carnival, Serafin's introduction at Port Sebastian, the second meeting of Jerry and Lise at the river bank and her adieu, the quarrel in Cordova's foyer and the subsequent reconciliation, *Brigadoon*'s appearance and disappearance, the poet's retrieval of his daughter from the garden, his escape and capture by the Caliph's guards for the attempted murder of the Wazir, Gaston and Honoré's surprise attack on Liane, Alicia's going out, Gaston's dragging Gigi home from Maxim's, and Ella's hello on Broadway—all are fashioned in this way.

Brigadoon would be an interesting study on the level of movement. In the village, the camera constantly roams; people run in and out of scenes.

. . . Ella's (Judy Holliday) calamitous date with her boss' nephew (Gerry Mulligan), Bells Are Ringing.

The camera is static; people bump into each other in New York.

Choreography of Musical Sequences Not Involving Dance

When a song does not spill into a dance, the character's business usually involves some kind of movement—Manuela swaying against Serafin's chest in "Love Of My Life" or Daisy scampering through the park in "Hurry! It's Lovely Up Here." This business and the music that underlines it lifts the parts of these numbers to a choreographic height. This is still another type of choreography and another integrating method.

PACE

The cutting principle of opening and closing on movement, the camera movement, and the business, more frequently involving movement than anything else, that Minnelli gives his people, and the observance of the mechanics of musical comedy's melodrama, all contribute to a generally energetic and spirited pace. Musical comedy, certainly Minnelli's, does not have time for such a routine and common thing as catching one's breath.

162

8
ACHIEVEMENT

CATHARSIS

A Minnelli musical witnesses an association of sensibility. It is an experience of a directly sensuous apprehension of thought. Content or semantic value is in the form of sounds, figures, textures, shapes, colors, designs, movements, tempos, and rhythms. It involves the viewer sensually, affectively, and cognitively.

Furthermore, the simultaneous coalescence or integration of these forms, one with another and with the medium of film, has a subliminal effect upon the viewer. Since it is not a matter of starts and stops and technology unforced to throw itself into the circle, but one of continuous flow and harmonious expression, a Minnelli musical casts a spell or weaves a trance, lulling the viewer into the acceptance of a universe, holding disbelief in suspension, relaxing defenses, and enlarging hearts.

Catharsis, of course, is concomitant with any artistic representation. But in the case of a Minnelli musical, the "purgation" is intense, for the maker not only uses but orchestrates all the elements that have, since the year one, constituted the full, genuine poetic effect, and what is more, orchestrates them through film's potent technology.

The motif of creation, the making of a fantasy from reality, appears once again, but this time, outside the frame. Every level of one's being bristles as it is washed over by sights and sounds, full of wonder, that block out the street and drown out the noise.

With the passion of clowns and the energy of athletes, Minnelli's people let their light shine on the mountain top to transform or transcend limiting circumstances, conventions, styles, to "damn everything that is grim, dead, suffocating, motionless, unrisking . . . that won't enjoy, that won't throw its heart into the tension, surprise, fear and delight of the circus, the round world, the full existence."

Oh yes, I am . . . I done changed already. I'm going to spread the light and preach the word. Hallelujah. I feel just like a new man . . . This is the moment I often stayed awake dreaming about . . . I can't believe it. Right here where we live . . .

163

I just made a flood, broke a bridge and had the train go back and you have the nerve to sit there and tell me that something is impossible . . . Show us your magic. Make us dream if you can. What have you got, Mister Ziegfeld . . . You can make anything come true if you wish for it . . . Lise, I love you. And everything is going to be all right, I know . . . A show that is really a show/Sends you out with a kind of a glow . . . If you love someone deeply enough, anything is possible . . . Why be content with the olive/When you could have the tree?/Why be content with being nothing/When there's nothing you couldn't be? . . . Oh what miracle has made you the way you are . . . You got to do it . . . On a clear day you can see forever.

This self-transcendence is not merely depicted but celebrated and rejoiced in since it is expressed in the most festive way known to man—community, extravagant dressing up, lavish colors, music, and dance.

This world of movement, change, transformation, transcendence, and the celebration of it is desired in one's depths, is imagined in one's "polar privacy." It is a world to which one's fancy, when allowed, takes flight, a world believed in and hope for in spite of everything. For the cynic, it is a world he at least has the desire of the desire for.

A Minnelli musical energizes this primordial spirit that one can never quite shake. It makes one dream as never before. The desire of the desire becomes more urgent. Minnelli is Serafin confronting and upbraiding the viewer, a repressed, insecure, and pusillanimous Manuela, with his largesse and pluck:

I know that underneath that prim exterior, there are depths of emotion, romantic longings, and unfulfilled dreams. I can read your mind, your

. . . The Choreography of Dramatic Sequences: the search for Tootie, **Meet Me In St. Louis.**

innermost thoughts. It's my business. I can tell you your past, present, and future and release your spirit from its earthly bonds.

Significance of the Minnelli Musical

As an expression of fantasy, or another world where transformation and transcendence rule the day, and festivity, or "genuine revelry and joyous celebration,"[1] the Minnelli musical awakens one's primal and primitive feelings and puts one in contact with them. The Minnelli musical resounds through one, touching "the dearest freshness deep down things,"where one also lives, moves, and has one's being. It stirs and plays with one's instinctual, prereflective, intuitive side, one's locked-away imagination, one's innermost hopes, one's alarming sense of awe, the child, savage, and seer within, the part that a technological, bureaucratic, scientific, secularized age forgets and ignores in fear or embarrassment. Therefore, the images and sensibilities of a Minnelli musical can be a key unlocking more of the self, affording new areas of apprehension and comprehension. The Minnelli musical expands horizons and whisks one into uncharted or lost lands. One can be made more whole, more one with oneself and other selves. This self-possession can help cure the schizophrenia of modern man, that division between intellect and instinct, Pope Paul and Pope John, appearance and feeling, Goldmund and Narcissus, surface and substance, that was one of Jung's most pressing concerns:

> Primitive man was much more governed by his instincts than are his rational modern descendants who have learned to control themselves. In this civilizing process we have increasingly divided our consciousness from the deeper instinctual strata of the human psyche.[2]

One no longer has to be embarrassed to pick flowers just for the sake of picking flowers.

These new horizons can infiltrate the practical order and can qualify and perhaps make action and decision more responsible. Theologian Sam Keen in his work, *To A Dancing God*, claimed that

> responsible organic decisions can arise only when unconscious as well as conscious, playful as well as serious, sensual as well as conceptual desires and goals are taken into account . . . Without fantasy, novelty cannot arise . . . Where nothing new can be imagined the organism is driven or inhabited by the old, by visions and possibilities which were the defining limits of a former generation. Without fantasy, the fathers possess the minds of the sons and live through them.[3]

Perhaps, too, these new horizons will allow one to breathe easier and move more freely by bringing back risk in a world where everything from fertility control to interplanetary flight has become so much a matter of precision and prediction that one is smugly self-sufficient. These new horizons might also help squelch the rampant misoneism.

Minnelli's fantasy and festivity frees one from the everyday routine. More than compensation (distraction and wish fulfillment) and more than a defense mechanism (insulation), the Minnelli musical is a liberating process without which life would be intolerable, enabling one to see and feel polycromatically rather than monochromatically, macrocosmically rather than microcosmically. The lightness that one experiences from time to time is abstracted to make a whole world in a Minnelli musical. One is brought alive inside, filled with the lilt one moves to in life only when things are very fine indeed. This experience is vital if one is to preserve a balance, a sense of humor, and get on with the task of living.

In the celebration of this fantasy with its excess, chaos, and caprice, this form insists that play, this taking time and space out (on the part of the characters inside the film as well as on one's part outside the film), is an important aspect of life and an end in itself like prayer and making love.

Contemporary forms of fantasy and festivity have dried up, burst into flames, and gone up in smoke. Industrialization with its image of man as worker, technology with its image of man as thinker, and secularization with its image of man as body fed the fire. Fantasies are cautious. As a little child born with enthusiasm, joy, and a sense of the ridiculous, one is told to sit still, fold one's hands, keep quiet, and die. With Penguin Freuds tucked in coat pockets, one always checks impulsive visions against hard scientific data. The reality principle is never to be abandoned. One disregards nightdreams if one is fortunate enough to still dream. Daydreams elicit reprimands or laughter. The worst thing that can happen is to be disappointed from expecting too much, to desire and not be satisfied, so expectations and desires are tailored to the possible. Festivities are shallow and meaningless affairs. Easter is a spring fashion show. The fourth of July is an orgy of burgers, beans, and booze which results in a throbbing gut. During Christmas, the biggest ritual remaining in America, suicide rates climb, telephone hot lines grow hotter, and psychiatrists' couches visibly show a dent. A Minnelli musical brings back fantasy and festivity to contemporary life and consequently upholds life-values, important and

165

necessary ones, which modern man has abandoned.

Significance of the Pre-Minnelli Musical

Before Minnelli, the significance of the musical comedy, both theatrical and cinematic, was slightly different. To understand this difference, some basics about the Jewish sensibility and the spirit of turn-of-the-century America must be recalled.

Musical comedy is primarily an American Jewish contribution to world theatre. As William Goldman accurately enunciated: "Without Jews, there simply would have been no musical comedy to speak of in America . . . In the last half-century, the only major Gentile composer to come along was Cole Porter."[4] And Goldman's remark applies to the major lyricists, librettists, choreographers, set and costume designers, directors, and producers as well. Of course, leprechaun George M. Cohan helped to mold the first musical comedies, albeit crude and rudimentary ones.

Although the genre's elements are endemic to every man and their amalgam, whether scat or stylized, seemingly necessary for him (no age has been without some form of musical comedy), these elements are further necessitated in the Jew because of the religiousness and suffering (and these two are related) that go hand in hand with being a Jew. The musical's elements, especially music and dance, are sacred elements and have always been used in worship. They also offer release, relief, and even hope.

David sang and danced before the ark. By the waters of Babylon, the captive people plucked on their lyres. The Christ was greeted by a palm-and-hosanna procession. A sequence from Cluzot's film *Manon* (1949) involves an illegal emigration of Parisian Jews to Palestine. Huddled among the cattle in the stalls in the ship's hold, they begin to sing and dance when the engines break down.

Irony, endemic to the race and nourished through religiousness (the discrepancy between the secular and sacred) and suffering, is the stuff from which comedy, both low and high, is made. Comedy is a large part of the musical's drama.

Jerome Singer concluded that "Anglo-Saxons daydream less than Jews and Italians."[5] And the genre has something to do with daydreaming. The Jews also had production brains to get the form together.

Musical comedy could have happened only in the space and time that it did happen in—America at the start of the twentieth century, in which there was a great belief in a country's future, progress,

democracy, moral virtue, and isolationism, where the ego of a country bulged as never before. The country was new as was the century—more than new, radical and charged with energy and emotion. The country and century were young. They could go anywhere, do anything. Possibilities were infinite. The Jews were expatriates, immigrants or first generation. They were Europe outside of itself, in Eden, melting, blending, and allowing themselves that gutsy feeling one needs to let go. They were unself-conscious. The suffering, amen, was over. This spirit of turn-of-the-century America, the Jews felt in their pith and marrow. This spirit nourished musical comedy (as a matter of fact, it was the spirit of the form) which, in turn, nourished the spirit of the country. Musical comedy grew from an historical moment—the sense of freedom, possibility, and confident dawn. Minstrelsy, variety, vaudeville, burlesque, and revue wedded operetta and democratized it.

The genre was a celebration of America, not so much as America was, but as it wanted itself to be, or believed and hoped it was becoming. The content (getting the girl, putting on the show, the climb from rags to riches) and technique of melodrama, spectacle, music, and dance were an expression of the American dream, togetherness, the functioning of all the elements, getting it all together, youth, beauty, romance, new life (even though the frontier was not endless anymore), the old get-up-and get/git (which depended solely on ability and not on class), strike-it-rich and happy-go-lucky endings, rough-and-tumble style, generosity, sentimentality, brashness and daring, putting everything on the line or out in the open, speed, energy, robustness, vigor, (who cares what the neighbors think), outrageousness even at the expense of good manners, physicality, size, and perpetual movement. Musical comedy was a new mythology; Broadway a new Olympus.

As mythology, it interpreted and defined the American psyche—its attitudes and values, its joys and hopes, and its fears and shame. It bolstered the social order through images and a sensibility that impressed and molded the young and confirmed and reinforced the not-so-young. It guided and impelled to action.

When the film medium adapted the genre or spun variations, it still essentially celebrated the American dream. That the medium was new added to the genre's excitement and fervor. So did the Depression which set off contradictory responses, a sneering pessimism and a daft optimism. The film musical comedy embodied the latter response. America had dropped her baton but the parade must go on as never before. We are going to get the girl, Mr. Limey or Mr. Frog, whether you like it or not. We are going to get the show on the road, Mr. Rich man, whether you help us or not. No matter, Mr. Trouble, you're going to hear from us. Toward the end of the thirties and the beginning of the forties, there was a weakening of this event as the economy became stable. Along came Minnelli who, refusing to travel the same road (in this decade the event was America's entry into the war), pushed the frontiers of this essentially expressionistic genre (due to its motifs, its elements of song and dance, and its effects) further and deeper in content, method, and effect. And the musical grew up. The Minnelli musical renders McVay's definition of the essentials of the genre—''showmanship, memorable tunes and that indefinable element, 'heart' ''[6] embarrassingly passé and naive.

THE FILM MUSICAL'S IDENTITY CRISIS

Since *Meet Me In St. Louis*, the Minnelli dispensation of the integrated or total musical comedy has prevailed—Stanley Donen's collab-

. . . *The Minnelli dispensation: Lucy (Alice Pearce), Claire (Ann Miller), Brunhilde (Betty Garrett), Chip (Frank Sinatra), Ozzie (Jules Munshin), and Gabey (Gene Kelly), "Count On Me," Stanley Donen and Gene Kelly's* On The Town.

. . . *Minnelli is Serafin and the viewer, the repressed Manuela,* The Pirate.

orations with Gene Kelly in *On The Town* (1949), *Singin' In The Rain* (1952), *It's Always Fair Weather* (1955) and his solo efforts in *Royal Wedding* (1951), *Give A Girl A Break* (1953), *Seven Brides For Seven Brothers* (1954), *Funny Face* (1956), *The Pajama Game* (1957), and *Damn Yankees* (1958); George Sideny's *The Harvey Girls* (1945), *Annie Get Your Gun* (1950), *Showboat* (1951), *Kiss Me Kate* (1953), *Pal Joey* (1957) and *Bye, Bye Birdie* (1963); Charles Walters' *Good News* (1947), *Easter Parade* (1948), *The Barkleys of Broadway* (1949), *Summer Stock* (1950), *Texas Carnival* (1951), *The Belle of New York* (1952), *Easy to Love, Dangerous When Wet* (1953), *High Society* (1956), *Jumbo* (1962), and *The Unsinkable Molly. Brown* (1964); Rouben Mamoulian's *Summer Holiday* (1947) and *Silk Stockings* (1957); George Cukor's *Les Girls* (1957), and on the Warner lot, David Butler's *The Time, The Place, And The Girl* (1946), *Where's Charley?* (1952), *By The Light Of The Silvery Moon* (1953), and *Calamity Jane* (1953). This dispensation was responsible for one of Hollywood's hallowed moments, the film musical comedy from 1943 to 1958. Hints come before, resonances after, of course.

Today the genre is in the throes of an identity crisis. Ironically, it comes at a time when the world is most in need of the fantasy and festivity the musical can provide. The lightning success of the MGM musical anthology, *That's Entertainment* (1974), bears witness to the fact that all feel the effect of this trauma. Critic Stanley Kauffmann said it best: "What I miss most at the moment in American films are musicals in the Donen-Minnelli vein. All we seem to get now are film versions of Broadway hit musicals. The Hollywood musical, at its best, was the most poetic and free-flying of American commercial films."[7]

The symptoms, of course, were present ten, even fifteen years ago. The monetary (is there any other?) crisis in the industry shook the studio system where musical talents were trained, led out to pasture with each other, and then showcased. The upheaval was fiercest at MGM, the epicenter of the musical's golden era, where the musical repertory from star to electrician disbanded and went off to do other things. During the sixties, Minnelli teetered between dramas and comedies.

Investments had to be safe and therefore, adaptation of a pre-sold Broadway hit show was the key as far as this genre went, even though it was the originals which came off better than the adaptations during the period of grace (for one thing, the film medium was there at the moment of conception). Minnelli sadly spoke of the MGM proxy fights that raged between the New York and Los Angeles contingents that crushed the original and inventive *Say It With Music*. Minnelli, along with producer Freed, librettists Comden and Green, and Irving Berlin spent two years in preparing a musical based roughly on the career of the famous songwriter. A trinity of stories, weaving in and out of each other, represented the three

. . . *The arrival of George Sidney's* Showboat.

. . . The muscle family from Arkansas' (William Demarest, Esther Williams, Charlotte Greenwood, Donna Corcoran, Barbara Whiting) "I Got Out Of Bed On The Right Side," Charles Walters' Dangerous When Wet.

periods and styles of Berlin's music—the sophisticated songs, the popular songs, and ragtime. A ragtime ballet ended the film. Frank Sinatra and Julie Andrews were to headline.[8]

With security and the power of the property uppermost in everyone's mind, a sacrosanct attitude crept in. The shows were translated whole. Rethinking and refeeling along film lines were too risky. If there was any kind of retouching, it was in terms of addition, with more sheen, more gloss, brighter stars, more spectacle, the widest screens, and the loudest sounds. Even the reserved seats, the policy of eight or nine performances a week, the intermission, and the souvenir booklets were

aped. The art of embalming had reached new heights. No longer an entertainment, the film musical was an event. It stunned and overwhelmed, but never moved or renewed one's heart. How the genre differed from the epic was hard to say. Marcuse might say that the musical was being desublimated.

Other types of film musicals were also eschewed. But then again, by this time, most of them had run amuck. The screen revue came to a standstill at the end of the forties, with *As Thousands Cheer, This Is The Army, Thank Your Lucky Stars,* and *Ziegfeld Follies.* In the early Eisenhower years, operetta tried to share the

. . . Calamity Jane (*Doris Day*) and Bill Hickock (*Howard Keel*), "*I Can Do Without You*," directed by *David Butler*.

spotlight with the original musical comedy. *The Student Prince* was a bright success but *Rose Marie*, *The Vagabond King*, and *The Desert Song* were dismal flops. At this same time, Warners took their Depression escape plots and characters out of the medicine cabinet, coated them a bit, and tried to sell them as something new, with *West Point Story*, *She's Working Her Way Through College*, *She's Back On Broadway*, *Painting The Clouds With Sunshine*, *Tea For Two*, *Lullaby Of Broadway*, *April In Paris*, and *About Face*. The musical biography reached its peak in the forties and early fifties and metamorphosized into dramas with musical interludes, such as *Love Me Or Leave Me*, *I'll Cry Tomorrow*, *The Eddy Duchin Story*, *The Helen Morgan Story*, and *Lady Sings The Blues*. As for the star vehicles, the likes of Rosemary Clooney, Frankie Laine, Pat Boone, Elvis Presley and Ann-Margret were not charasmatic enough to hold a film together.

Another symptom was the dark mood of the times. With the sixties' threat of the bomb, the generation gap, the plight of the cities, the black revolution, political assassinations, Vietnam, drugs, and sex, the musical (or rather these mummifications) seemed irresponsible and decadent. In this period when the American mythology began to be questioned, the musical, since it embodied this mythology, was under fire.

In an effort to accommodate to the times, Broadway turned to musicals with a message, "the modern musical morality plays with stature and meaning." Minnelli's warning in *The Band Wagon* went unheeded. And the stodginess of the Hollywood versions was compounded. Entertainment was not contradictory to intelligence, as Minnelli proved time after time. The musical form could be inherently valuable, as Minnelli has also shown, without injecting heavy doses of so-called "relevant" issues—miscegenation and garish filters (a bid for technological relevance, no doubt) and *South Pacific*, race and *The King And I*, sociology and *West Side Story*, the founding fathers and *1776* which came through watered down and glaringly superficial, and made the pieces irresolute, halfhearted and schizophrenic.

. . . *The adaptation of the pre-sold Broadway hit:* Nellie (Mitzi Gaynor) *and Emil* (Rossano Brazzi), *"Some Enchanted Evening," Joshua Logan's* South Pacific.

A musical does not mean. It is.

Sometimes Hollywood, in adapting old musicals, "modernized" them, by stuffing them with topical and éngagè issues—*Paint Your Wagon*'s menage à trois—thereby throwing the whole piece out of joint.

These "more than a musical" or "not just a musical" were put into the hands of "important" dramatic directors—the Fred Zinnemanns, the Robert Wises, the Joshua Logans, the Arthur Hillers. Whether or not they understood and cared for the genre's expressionistic qualities, its lyricism, its grace, and its expanse mattered very little, if at all.

Star actors were cast whose musical talents were dubious or negligible. Singing became pattering (Rex Harrison, Lee Marvin, Clint Eastwood, Richard Harris, Peter O' Toole, Vanessa Redgrave, Lucille Ball, Albert Finney) or pantomiming to a voice playback (Deborah Kerr, Rossano Brazzi, Audrey Hepburn, Jean Seberg) and dancing, brisk and hurried movement.

The change in popular music also had something to do with the musical's dilemma. It still has not learned to sing and dance in the new way. *Bye, Bye Birdie, Your Own Thing, Godspell, Pippin, Two Gentlemen from Verona* are halfway houses. The genre and rock united with religion for *Godspell* and *Jesus Christ Superstar* and with horror for *The Phantom of the Paradise* and *The Rocky Horror Film Show* with interesting, if not exhilarating, results. Rock, however, is too limited an expression for all that the musical can and must do. Lyrics fall by the wayside in rock. Rock does not

. . . *The revival of operetta in the fifties:* The Student Prince *(Edmund Purdom with Mario Lanza's voice) and Kathy, the barmaid (Ann Blyth).*

. . . *Musical biography metamorphosizes into dramas with musical interludes: Ruth Etting (Doris Day) and Max 'Gimp' Snyder (James Cagney),* Love Me Or Leave Me.

171

. . . Dramatic actor Peter O'Toole as the protagonist of the musical remake of Goodbye Mr. Chips.

. . . The emcee's (Joel Gray) "Wilkommen," Bob Fosse's Cabaret.

lend itself to variations within a score. Stephen Sondheim (*A Funny Thing Happened on the Way to the Forum, Anyone Can Whistle, Company, Follies, A Little Night Music* and *Pacific Overtures*), whose influence on the film musical is not felt as yet, is also trying to give the musical a voice and a leg for the seventies.

Other entertainments took up this musical slack—the television variety show, the supper club, the rock concerts, filmed documentaries (*Monterey Pop, Woodstock, Gimme Shelter, Let It Be, The Concert for Bangladesh, Wattstax, Let the Good Times Roll, Mad Dogs and Englishmen*) and dramatic films so informed, wholly or partially, with music that they seemed choreographed. This last item was not as much choreography in film as choreographed film—the right sound accompanying or supporting the right movement—Blake Edwards' *Breakfast at Tiffany's.* Francis Ford Coppola's *You're a Big Boy Now,* Gene Kelly's *A Guide for the Married Man,* Stanley Donen's *Two for the Road* or the Grand Ole Opry flivvers' fling in Arthur Penn's *Bonnie and Clyde,* the percussion car chase in Peter Yates' *Bullitt,* the Bacharach bike ride in George Roy Hill's *Butch Cassidy and the Sundance Kid,* Stanley Kubrick's Straussian space travel in *2001: A Space Odyssey,* or his outbursts of Beethovian violence in *A Clockwork Orange.*

The genre needs a genie once again to dispel its present hemming and hawing. Richard Lester's beat-conscious camera and capering protagonists in *A Hard Day's Night, Help!,* and *A Funny Thing Happened on the Way to the Forum* lifted the musical to lyrical heights, but then he abandoned the genre. Vitality and daring characterized Bob Fosse's *Cabaret* with its contextual imagination, and its elements growing from a central metaphor, that of a Berlin beer hall, and its sequences shuffled with the dramatic ones, musically enhancing each other. It is too early to tell whether this is a one-night stand or the beginning of an affair. Perhaps the genre's redefinition that will recover as well as transcend its glorious past will come from the sorcerer himself who is presently joining forces with still another Minnelli.

. . . The two Minnellis, then and now.

NOTES

PREFACE

[1] The musical sequences include Judy Garland's solo numbers in *Babes On Broadway* (Busby Berkeley, 1941), Lena Horne's sequences in *Panama Hattie* (Norman McLeod, 1942), Judy Garland's sequences in *Till the Clouds Roll By* (Richard Whorf, 1946), and the fashion show finale in *Lovely To Look At* (Mervyn LeRoy, 1952).

[2] The melodramas include *Undercurrent* (1946), *Madame Bovary* (1949), *The Bad and the Beautiful* (1952), *The Cobweb* (1955), *Lust For Life* (1956), *Tea and Sympathy* (1956), *Some Came Running* (1958), *Home From the Hill* (1960), *Four Horsemen of the Apocalypse* (1962), *Two Weeks in Another Town* (1962), and *The Sandpiper* (1965). The episode, "Mademoiselle," is from *The Story of Three Loves* (Gottfried Reinhardt directed the first and third episodes, 1953).

[3] The comedies include *The Clock* (1945), *Father of the Bride* (1950), *Father's Little Dividend* (1951), *The Long, Long Trailer* (1954), *Designing Woman* (1957), *The Reluctant Debutante* (1958), *The Courtship of Eddie's Father* (1963), and *Goodbye Charlie* (1964).

[4] *The New York Times Arts and Leisure*, May 30, 1965, pp. 1, 4.

[5] *The New York Times Magazine*, Part 2, September 11, 1966, pp. 42-43, 48-50.

CHAPTER 1

[1] "Producer," *The Enquirer Delaware Ohio*, 1937.

[2] (New York: Fleet Publishing Co., 1962), p. 159.

[3] "At Home Abroad," *The Boston Globe*, September 4, 1938.

[4] "Prodigy," *The New Yorker*, October 12, 1935.

[5] "Ziegfeld Follies of '36," *The New York Times*, January 31, 1936.

[6] Baral, *Revue*, p. 204.

[7] "Minnelli: A Big Gift to Revue," *The New York Sun*, February 4, 1936.

[8] "Ziegfeld Girls Had Their Day," *The Pittsburgh Pa. Post*, December 12, 1936.

[9] "Never Had a Lesson," *Esquire*, June, 1937, p. 138.

[10] "The Designer Sets the Stage," *Theatre Arts Monthly*, 1937, pp. 783-788.

CHAPTER 2

[1] Herman G. Weinberg, *The Lubitsch Touch: A Critical Study* (New York: E. A. Dutton and Co., 1968), p. 25.

[2] Tom Milne, *Rouben Mamoulian* (Bloomington: Indiana University Press, 1969), p. 53.

[3] (London: Hamlyn, 1970), p. 220.

[4] "The Return of Busby Berkeley," *The New York Times Magazine*, March 2, 1969, Section 6, Part I, pp. 50, 52.

[5] *Ibid.*, p. 54.

[6] *Ibid.*, p. 48.

[7] *Ibid.*, pp. 48, 50.

[8] Kobal, *Gotta Sing, Gotta Dance*, p. 220.

[9] (New York: A. S. Barnes and Co., 1967).

CHAPTER 3

[1] Kobal, *Gotta Sing, Gotta Dance*, p. 220.

[2] *Film Quarterly*, XII, No. 2 (Winter, 1958), p. 21.

[3] *Ibid.*, p. 21.

[4] Kobal, *Gotta Sing, Gotta Dance*, p. 220.

[5] *The Celluloid Muse: Hollywood Directors Speak* (New York: New American Library, 1969), p. 199.

[6] *Ibid.*, pp. 198-199.

[7] *Films and Filming*, January, 1962, p. 9.

[8] *Action: The Director's Guild of America*, September-October, 1972, p. 10.

[9] "Entretien avec Vincente Minnelli," *Cahiers du Cinéma*, No. 74 (August-September, 1959), p. 4.

[10] "Rencontre avec Vincente Minnelli," *Cahiers du Cinéma*, No. 128 (February, 1962), p. 8.

[11] "Vincente Minnelli Interviewed in Argentina," *Movie*, No. 10 (June, 1963), p. 23.

[12] Curtis Lee Hanson, "Vincente Minnelli on the Relationship of Style to Content in *The Sandpiper*," *Cinema*, 11, No. 6 (July-August, 1965), p. 7.

[13] Diehl, "Directors Go to Their Movies," p. 10.

[14] William Flint Thrall, Addison Hibbard, and C. Hugh Holman,

A Handbook to Literature, rev. and enl., (New York: Odyssey Press, 1960), p. 211.

[15](Cambridge, Mass.: Harvard University Press, 1969), p. 7.

[16]Bitsch and Domarchi, "Entretien avec Vincente Minnelli," p. 5; Hanson, "Relationship of Style to Content," p. 7.

[17]Higham and Greenberg, *The Celluloid Muse,* p. 199.

[18]Domarchi and Douchet, "Rencontre avec Vincente Minnelli," p. 10.

[19]Serebrinsky and Garaycochea, "Vincente Minnelli Interviewed in Argentina," p. 28.

[20]"Minnelli's Method," *Movie,* No. I (June, 1962), p. 17.

[21]Personal Interview, February 7, 1973.

CHAPTER 4

[1]Personal Interview, February 7, 1973.

[2]McVay, *The Musical Film,* p. 47.

[3]Pauline Kael, *Kiss Kiss Bang Bang* (New York: A Bantam Book, 1967), p. 289.

[4]Bitsch and Domarchi, "Entretien avec Vincente Minnelli," p. 6.

[5]Domarchi and Douchet, "Rencontre avec Vincente Minnelli," p. 13.

[6]*Ibid.,* p. 12.

[7]Diehl, "Directors Go to Their Movies," p. 4.

CHAPTER 5

[1]McVay, *The Musical Film,* p. 48.

[2]Higham and Greenberg, *The Celluloid Muse,* p. 199.

[3]Personal Interview, February 7, 1973.

[4]Bitsch and Domarchi, "Entretien avec Vincente Minnelli," p. 10.

[5]Domarchi and Douchet, "Rencontre avec Vincente Minnelli," p. 6.

[6]Diehl, "Directors Go to Their Movies," p. 5.

[7]Serebrinsky and Garaycochea, "Vincente Minnelli Interviewed in Argentina," p. 24.

[8]Personal Interview, February 7, 1973.

[9]Higham and Greenberg, *The Celluloid Muse,* p. 200.

[10]Personal Interview, February 7, 1973.

[11]Personal Interview, February 7, 1973.

[12]Higham and Greenberg, *The Celluloid Muse,* p. 201.

[13]Personal Interview, February 7, 1973.

[14]Higham and Greenberg, *The Celluloid Muse,* p. 205.

[15]Personal Interview, February 7, 1973.

[16]*Ibid.*

[17]Personal Interview, February 7, 1973.

[18]*Ibid.*

[19]*Ibid.*

[20]Catherine de la Roche, "Vincente Minnelli," *Premier Plan Series,* No. 40 (March, 1966), p. 58.

[21]André Bazin, "The Evolution of the Language of Cinema" and "The Virtues and Limitations of Montage," *What Is Cinema?,* essays selected and translated by Hugh Gray, Vol. I (Berkeley and Los Angeles: University of California Press, 1967), pp. 23-52.

[22]Brian Henderson, "The Long Take," *Film Comment,* VII, No. 2 (Summer, 1971), pp. 6, 8-9.

[23]Bitsch and Domarchi, "Entretien avec Vincente Minnelli," pp. 13-14.

[24]Higham and Greenberg, *The Celluloid Muse,* p. 205.

[25]Personal Interview, February 7, 1973.

[26]Diehl, "Directors Go to Their Movies," p. 4.

[27]Béla Balázs, *Theory of Film: Character and Growth of a New Art,* trans. from the Hungarian by Edith Bone (New York: Dover Publications, Inc., 1970), p. 71.

[28]Bitsch and Domarchi, "Entretien avec Vincente Minnelli," p. 10.

[29]Personal Interview, February 7, 1973.

[30]Lillian Herlands Hornstein, G. D. Percy, and Sterling A. Brown, ed., *The Reader's Companion to World Literature* (New York: The New American Library, 1964), p. 429.

[31]Salvador Dali, *The Object as Revealed in Surrealist Experiment* (Englewood Cliffs, N.J.: Prentice-Hall, 1970), p. 96.

[32]Diehl, "Directors Go to Their Movies," p. 10.

[33]Bitsch and Domarchi, "Entretien avec Vincente Minnelli," p. 11.

CHAPTER 6

[1]Kobal, *Gotta Sing, Gotta Dance,* p. 232.

[2]Personal Interview, February 7, 1973.

CHAPTER 7

[1]Higham and Greenberg, *The Celluloid Muse,* p. 199.

[2](Baltimore: Morrow, 1957), p. 36.

CHAPTER 8

[1]Cox, *Feast of Fools,* p. 16.

[2]Carl G. Jung, "Approaching the Unconscious", *Man and His Symbols,* ed. by Carl G. Jung and after his death by M-L. von Franz (New York: Dell Publishing Co., 1972), p. 34.

[3]Sam Keen, *To A Dancing God* (New York: Harper and Row, 1960), p. 68.

[4]Quoted in Pauline Kael's "A Bagel With A Bite Out Of It" in "The Current Cinema," *The New Yorker,* November 13, 1971, p. 133.

[5]Jerome Singer, "The Importance of Daydreaming," *Psychology Today,* I, No. 11 (April, 1968), p. 20.

[6]McVay, *The Musical Film,* p. 11.

[7]Stanley Kauffmann, "The Future of Film: A Symposium," *Film 67/68,* ed. by Richard Schickel and John Simon (New York: Simon and Schuster, 1968), p. 292.

[8]Personal Interview, February 7, 1973.

FILMOGRAPHY

Cabin In The Sky (1942)

Production Company: MGM. Producer: Arthur Freed. Associate Producer: Albert Lewis. Script: Joseph Schrank from the theatrical musical comedy of the same name by Lynn Root. Director of Photography: Sidney Wagner. Editor: Harold F. Kress. Art Directors: Cedric Gibbons, Leonid Vasian. Set Decorators: Edwin B. Willis, Hugh Hunt. Costumes: Irene, Howard Shoup, Giles Steele. Musical Directors: Georgie Stoll, Roger Edens (associate). Sound Recordists: Douglas Shearer, William Steinkamp.

Numbers: Cabin In The Sky, Honey In The Honeycomb, Taking A Chance On Love by Vernon Duke (composer), John La Touche, Ted Fetter (lyricists) from the original score; Happiness Is Just A Thing Called Joe, Li'l Black Sheep, Life's Full Of Consequence by Harold Arlen (composer), E. Y. Harburg (lyricist); Going Up by Duke Ellington; Shine, a very old black song.

Ethel Waters (Petunia Jackson). Eddie 'Rochester' Anderson (Little Joe Jackson). Lena Horne (Georgia Brown). Louis Armstrong (the trumpeter). Rex Ingram (Lucius and Lucifer, Jr.). Kenneth Spencer (Rev. Green and the General). John W. Bublett (Domino Johnson). Oscar Polk (the Deacon and Fleetfoot). Mantan Moreland (the first idea man). Willie Best (second idea man). Duke Ellington and his orchestra. The Hall Johnson Choir.

Running time: 99 min.

I Dood It (1943)

Production Company: MGM. Producer: Jack Cummings. Script: Sig Herzig, Fred Saidy. Director of Photography: Ray June. Editor: Robert J. Kern. Art Directors: Cedric Gibbons, Jack Martin Smith. Set Decorators: Edwin B. Willis, Helen Conway. Costumes: Irene Sharaff, Giles Steele. Choreographer: Bobby Connally. Musical Directors: Georgie Stoll, Kay Thompson (associate). Sound Recordist: Douglas Shearer.

Numbers: *Hola e pae,* a traditional Hawaiian chant, Jericho by Leo Robin (composer), Kay Thompson, Richard Meyers (lyricists). One O'Clock Jump by Jimmy Dorsey. So Long Sarah Jane, Star Eyes by Don Raye (composer), Gene Paul (lyricist). Swinging The Jinx Away by Cole Porter from Roy del Ruth's *Born to Dance* (1936). Taking A Chance On Love by Vernon Duke (composer), John La Touche, Ted Fetter (lyricists) from Minnelli's *Cabin In The Sky* (1942).

Red Skelton (Joseph Rivington Reynolds). Eleanor Powell (Constance). Richard Ainley (Larry). Patricia Dane (Suretta). Sam Levene (Eddie Jackson). Thurston Hall (Kenneth). Lena Horne and Hazel Scott (as themselves). John Hodiak (the spy). Butterfly McQueen (Constance's maid). Jimmy Dorsey and his orchestra. Helen O'Connell and Bob Eberly (singers).

Running time: 102 min.

Meet Me In St. Louis (1944)

Production Company: MGM. Producer: Arthur Freed. Script: Fred Finklehoffe, Irving Brecher from the New Yorker short stories, *"5135 Kensington Avenue"* by Sally Benson. Directors of Photography: George Folsey, Henri Jaffa, in Technicolor. Editor: Albert Akst. Art Directors: Cedric Gibbons, Lemuel Ayres, Jack Martin Smith. Set Decorators: Edwin B. Willis, Paul Holdchinsky. Costumes: Irene Sharaff. Choreographer: Charles Walters. Musical Directors: Georgie Stoll, Roger Edens (associate). Sound Recordist: Douglas Shearer.

Numbers: The Boy Next Door, Have Yourself A Merry Little Christmas, Over The Bannister Leaning, Skip To My Lou,

The Trolley Song by Hugh Martin (composer), Ralph Blane (lyricist). Meet Me In St. Louis, the fair song. Under The Bamboo Tree by Bob Cole. You And I by Harry Warren (composer), Arthur Freed (lyricist). Background Music: Auld Lang Syne, The First Noel, You Are My Turtle Dove.

Judy Garland (Esther Smith). Margaret O'Brien (Tootie Smith). Lucille Bremer (Rose Smith). Joan Carroll (Agnes Smith). Mary Astor (Mrs. Smith). Leon Ames (Mr. Smith). Tom Drake (John Truett). Marjorie Main (Katie). Harry Davenport (Grandpa). June Lockhart (Lucille Ballard). H. H. Daniels, Jr. (Lon Smith, Jr.). Hugh Marlowe (the colonel). Robert Sully (Bankoff). Chill Wills (ice man).

Running time: 113 min.

Yolanda And The Thief (1945)

Production Company: MGM. Producer: Arthur Freed. Script: Irving Brecher, from a story by Ludwig Bemelmans and Jacques Thery. Director of Photography: Charles Rosher, in Technicolor. Editor: Albert Akst. Art Directors: Cedric Gibbons, Jack Martin Smith. Set Decorators: Edwin B. Willis, Richard Pefferle. Costumes: Irene Sharaff. Choreographer: Eugene Loring. Musical Director: Lennie Hayton. Sound Recordist: Douglas Shearer.

Numbers: Angel, Coffee Time, This Is A Day For Love, Will You Marry Me? (dream ballet), Yolanda by Harry Warren (composer), Arthur Freed (lyricist).

Fred Astaire (Johnny). Lucille Bremer (Yolanda). Frank Morgan (Victor). Mildred Natwick (Aunt Armarilla). Mary Nash (Duenna). Leon Ames (Mr. Candle). Ludwig Stossel (the school teacher).

Running time: 107 min.

The Ziegfeld Follies (1945)

Production Company: MGM. Producer: Arthur Freed. Directors: Minnelli directed eight of the thirteen sequences; Lemuel Ayres directed "Love"; Robert Lewis, "Number Please"; George Sidney, "Bring On The Beautiful Girls", "When Television Comes"; and the introductory sequence is done by another. Directors of Photography: George J. Folsey, Charles Rosher, in Technicolor. Editor: Albert Akst. Art Directors: Cedric Gibbons, Merrill Pye, Jack Martin Smith. Set Decorators: Edwin B. Willis, Mac Alper. Costumes: Helen Rose, Irene Sharaff. Choreographers: Robert Alton, Eugene Loring, Charles Walters. Musical Director: Lennie Hayton, Roger Edens, Kay Thompson (associates). Sound Recordist: Douglas Shearer.

Numbers: The Babbitt And The Bromide by George Gershwin (composer), Ira Gershwin (lyricist). Beauty by Earl Brent (composer), Arthur Freed (lyricist). Bring On The Beautiful Girls by Earl Brent (composer), Roger Edens (lyricist). A Great Lady Gives An Interview by Kay Thompson (composer), Roger Edens (lyricist). La Traviata-excerpt by Verdi. Limehouse Blues by Douglas Furber (composer), Philip Braham (lyricist). Love by Hugh Martin (composer), Ralph Blane (lyricist). Water Ballet, unknown music. Sketches: Number Please, Pay The Two Dollars, A Sweepstake Ticket, When Television Comes, puppet sequence by William Ferrari.

Fred Astaire. Lucille Ball. Lucille Bremer. Judy Garland. Kathryn Grayson. Lena Horne. Gene Kelly. James Melton. Victor Moore. Red Skelton. Esther Williams. William Powell (Florenz Ziegfeld). Edward Arnold. Marion Bell. Cyd Charisse. Robert Lewis. Virginia O'Brien. Keenan Wynn.

Pamela Britton. Fanny Brice. Hume Cronyn.

Running time: 120 min.

The Pirate (1948)

Production Company: MGM. Producer: Arthur Freed. Script: Frances Goodrich, Albert Hackett from the play of the same name by S. N. Behrman. Director of Photography: Harry Stradling, in Technicolor. Editor: Blanche Sewell. Art Directors: Cedric Gibbons, Jack Martin Smith. Set Decorators: Edwin B. Willis, Arthur Krams. Costumes: Irene, Tom Keogh, Karinska. Choreographers: Gene Kelly, Robert Alton. Musical Director: Lennie Hayton. Sound Recordist: Douglas Shearer.

Numbers: Be A Clown, Love Of My Life, Mack The Black, Niña, The Pirate Ballet, You Can Do No Wrong by Cole Porter.

Judy Garland (Manuela). Gene Kelly (Serafin). Walter Slezak (Don Pedro). Gladys Cooper (Aunt Inez). Reginald Owen (the advocate). George Zucco (Viceroy). Nicholas Brothers (Serafin's troupers). Lester Allen (Uncle Capucho). Lola Deem (Isabella). Ellen Ross (Mercedes).

Running time: 102 min.

An American In Paris (1951)

Production Company: MGM. Producer: Arthur Freed. Script: Alan Jay Lerner. Directors of Photography: John Alton, Alfred Gilks (for the ballet), in Technicolor. Editor: Adrienne Fazan. Art Directors: Cedric Gibbons, Preston Ames. Set Decorators: Edwin B. Willis, Keogh Gleason. Costumes: Orry-Kelly, Irene Sharaff, Walter Plunkett (for the ball and ballet). Choreographer: Gene Kelly. Musical Directors: Johnny Green, Saul Chaplin. Sound Recordist: Douglas Shearer.

Numbers: An American In Paris Suite from *Show Girl* (1924), By Strauss from *The Show Is On* (1937), Concerto in F written for a concert performance, Embraceable You, I Got Rhythm from *Girl Crazy* (1930), I'll Build A Stairway To Paradise from *George White's Scandals of 1922*, Our Love Is Here To Stay from the film *Goldwyn Follies* (1938), 'S Wonderful from *Funny Face* (1927), Tra-la-la-la from *For Goodness Sake* (1922). Background music: But Not For Me, I'm Bidin' My Time from *Girl Crazy* (1930), Do, Do, Do, Someone To Watch Over Me from *Oh, Kay* (1922), Fascinating Rhythm from *Lady Be Good* (1922), I Don't Think I'll Fall In Love Today, I've Got A Crush On You from *Treasure Girl* (1928), Nice Work If You Can Get It from the film *A Damsel In Distress* (1937), *Strike Up The Band*, title song from the 1930 show by George Gershwin (composer), Ira Gershwin (lyricist).

Gene Kelly (Jerry). Leslie Caron (Lise). Oscar Levant (Adam). Georges Guetary (Henri). Nina Foch (Milo).

Running time: 113 min.

The Band Wagon (1953)

Production Company: MGM. Producers: Arthur Freed, Roger Edens (associate). Script: Betty Comden, Adolph Green. Director of Photography: Harry Jackson, in Technicolor. Editor: Albert Akst. Art Directors: Cedric Gibbons, Preston Ames. Set Decorators: Edwin B. Willis, Keogh Gleason. Costumes: Mary Ann Nyberg. Choreographer: Michael Kidd. Musical Director: Adolph Deutsch. Sound Recordist: Douglas Shearer.

Numbers: By Myself, Triplets from the revue *Between The Devil* (1937), Dancing In The Dark, I Love Louisa, New Sun In The Sky from the revue *The Band Wagon* (1931), The Girl Hunt Ballet (a melange of Schwartz themes arranged by Roger Edens, narration by Vincente Minnelli), I Guess I'll Have To Change My Plan from the revue *The Little Show* (1929), Louisiana Hayride, Shine On Your Shoes from the revue *Flying Colors* (1932), That's Entertainment (penned for the film), You And The Night And The Music from the musical *Revenge With Music* (1934). Background Music: High and Low from the revue *The Band Wagon* (1931), Something To Remember You By from the revue *Three's A Crowd* (1930) by Arthur Schwartz (composer) and Howard Dietz (lyricist).

Fred Astaire (Tony Hunter). Cyd Charisse (Gaby). Jack Buchanan (Jeffrey Cordova). Oscar Levant (Lester Marton). Nanette Fabray (Lillie Marton). James Mitchell (Paul Byrd). Robert Gist (Hal Benton).

Running time: 112 min.

Brigadoon (1954)

Production Company: MGM. Producer: Arthur Freed. Script: Alan Jay Lerner from his theatrical musical comedy of the same name. Director of Photography: Joseph Ruttenberg, in Anscocolor and Cinemascope. Editor: Albert Akst. Art Directors: Cedric Gibbons, Preston Ames. Set Decorators: Edwin B. Willis, Keogh Gleason. Costumes: Irene Sharaff. Choreographer: Gene Kelly. Musical Director: Johnny Green. Sound Recordist: Douglas Shearer.

Numbers: Almost Like Being In Love, Brigadoon, Dance Of The Clans, Down On MacConnachy Square, The Heather On The Hill, I'll Go Home With Bonnie Jean, Once In The Highlands/Prologue, Waitin' For My Dearie. Background Music: There But For You Go I by Frederick Loewe (composer), Alan Jay Lerner (lyricist).

Gene Kelly (Tommy Albright). Van Johnson (Jeff Douglas). Cyd Charisse (Fiona Campbell). Elaine Stewart (Jane Ashton). Barry Jones (Mr. Lundie). Hugh Laing (Harry Beaton). Albert Sharpe (Andrew Campbell). Virginia Bosler (Jean Campbell). Jimmy Thompson (Charley Chisholm Dalrymple). Tudor Owen (Archie Beaton). Owens McGiveney (Angus). Dee Turnell (Ann). Dody Heat (Meg Brockie). Eddie Quillan (Sandy).

Running time: 102 min.

Kismet (1955)

Production Company: MGM. Producer: Arthur Freed. Script: Charles Lederer, Luther Davis from their theatrical musical comedy of the same name based on the play of the same name by Edward Knoblock. Director of Photography: Joseph Ruttenberg, in Eastmancolor and Cinemascope. Editor: Adrienne Fazan. Art Directors: Cedric Gibbons, Preston Ames. Set Decorators: Edwin B. Willis, Keogh Gleason. Costumes: Tony Duquette. Choreographer: Jack Cole. Musical Directors: Andre Previn, Jeff Alexander. Sound Recordist: Douglas Shearer.

Numbers: And This Is My Beloved, Baubles, Bangles And Beads, Fate, Gesticulate, Night Of My Nights, Not Since Ninevah, The Olive Tree, Rahadlakum, The Sands Of Time, A Stranger In Paradise by Robert Wright (composer), Chet Forrest (lyricist) based on the themes by Alexander Borodin.

Howard Keel (the poet). Ann Blyth (Marsinah). Dolores Gray (Lalume). Vic Damone (the Caliph). Monty Woolley (Omar). Sebastian Cabot (the Wazir). J. C. Flippen (Jawan).

Running time: 113 min.

Gigi (1958)

Production Company: MGM. Producer: Arthur Freed. Script: Alan Jay Lerner from the novel of the same name by Colette. Director of Photography: Joseph Ruttenberg, in Metrocolor and Cinemascope. Editor: Adrienne Fazan. Art Directors: William A. Horning, Preston Ames. Set Decorators: Henry Grace, Keogh Gleason. Costumes and Production Design: Cecil Beaton. Choreographer: Charles Walters. Musical Director: Andre Previn. Sound Recordist: Wesley C. Miller.

Numbers: Gigi, Gossip, I Don't Understand The Parisians, I'm Glad I'm Not Young Anymore, I Remember It Well, It's A Bore, The Night They Invented Champagne, Say A Prayer For Me Tonight, She Is Not Thinking Of Me, Thank Heaven For Little Girls by Frederick Loewe (composer), Alan Jay Lerner (lyricist).

Leslie Caron (Gigi). Maurice Chevalier (Honoré Lachaille). Louis Jourdan, (Gaston Lachaille). Hermione Gingold (Mme. Alvarez). Eva Gabor (Liane d' Exelmans). Jacques Bergerac (the skating instructor). Isabel Jeans (Aunt Alicia). John Abbot (Manuel).

Running time: 116 min.

Bells Are Ringing (1960)

Production Company: MGM. Producer: Arthur Freed. Script: Betty Comden, Adolph Green from their theatrical musical comedy of the same name. Director of Photography: Milton Krasner, in Metrocolor and Cinemascope. Editor: Adrienne Fazan. Art Directors: George W. Davis, Preston Ames. Set Decorators: Henry Grace, Keogh Gleason. Costumes: Walter Plunkett. Choreographer: Charles O'Curran. Musical Director: Andre Previn. Sound Recordist: Wesley C. Miller.

Numbers: Bells Are Ringing, Better Than A Dream, Do It Yourself, Drop That Name, I Met A Girl, I'm Going Back, It's A Perfect Relationship, Just In Time, The Midas Touch, The Party's Over, A Simple Little System by Jules Styne (composer), Betty Comden, Adolph Green (lyricists).

Judy Holliday (Ella Peterson). Dean Martin (Jeffrey Moss). Fred Clark (Larry Hastings). Eddie Foy Jr. (J. Otto Franz). Jean Stapleton (Sue). Ruth Storey (Gwenn). Dort Clark (Inspector Barnes). Frank Gorshin (Blake Barton). Ralph Roberts (Francis). Valerie Allen (Olga). Bernie West (Dr. Joe Kitchell). Gerry Mulligan (Sue's nephew).

Running time: 125 min.

On A Clear Day You Can See Forever (1970)

Production Company: Paramount. Producers: Howard W. Koch, Alan J. Lerner. Script: Alan Jay Lerner from his theatrical musical comedy of the same name. Director of Photography: Harry Stradling, in Technicolor and Panavision. Editors: David Bretherton, Flo Williamson. Art Director: John De Cuir. Set Decorators: George Hopkins, Ralph Bretton. Costumes: Cecil Beaton (for Melinda), Arnold Scaasi (for Daisy). Choreographer: Howard Jeffrey, Betty Walberg (vocal dance arrangements). Musical Director: Nelson Riddle. Sound Recordists: Benjamin Winkler, Elden Ruberg.

Numbers: Come Back To Me, Go To Sleep, He Isn't You, Hurry! It's Lovely Up Here, Love With All The Trimmings, Melinda, On A Clear Day You Can See Forever, What Did I Have That I Don't Have by Burton Lane (composer), Alan Jay Lerner (lyricist).

Barbra Streisand (Daisy Gambol/Melinda Wainwhisle

Moorepark Tentrees). Yves Montand (Dr. Marc Chabot). Bob Newhart (Dr. Conrad Fuller). Jack Nicholson (Tad). Laurie Main (Lord Percy Moorepark). Simon Oakland (Dr. Mason Hume). John Richardson (Robert Tentrees). Mabel Albertson (Mrs. Hatch).

Running time: 129 min.

BIBLIOGRAPHY

BOOKS

Agee, James. *Agee on Film: Reviews and Comments.* Boston: Beacon Press, 1958.

Aristotle. *The Poetics.* Trans. by Preston H. Epps. Chapel Hill: University of North Carolina Press, 1942.

Baral, Robert. *Revue: The Great Broadway Period.* New York: Fleet Publishing Corp., 1962.

Bazin, André. "The Evolution of the Language of Cinema" and "The Virtues and Limitations of Montage". *What Is Cinema?* Essays selected and translated by Hugh Gray. Vol. I. Berkeley and Los Angeles: University of California Press, 1967.

Balázs, Béla. *Theory of Film: Character and Growth of a New Art.* Trans. from the Hungarian by Edith Bone. New York: Dover Publications, Inc., 1970.

Bentley, Eric. *The Life of the Drama.* New York: Atheneum, 1964.

Bluestone, George. *Novels into Film.* Berkeley and Los Angeles: University of California Press, 1961.

Cassirer, Ernst. *An Essay on Man: An Introduction to the Philosophy of Human Culture.* New Haven: Yale University Press, 1944.

Cox, Harvey. *The Feast of Fools: A Theological Essay on Festivity and Fantasy.* Cambridge, Mass.: Harvard University Press, 1969.

Croce, Arlene. *The Fred Astaire and Ginger Rogers Book.* New York: E. P. Dutton and Co., 1972.

Dali, Salvador. *The Object as Revealed in Surrealist Experiment.* Englewood Cliffs, N.J.: Prentice-Hall, 1970.

Durgnat, Raymond. *The Crazy Mirror: Hollywood Comedy and the American Image.* London: Faber and Faber Ltd., 1969.

Engel, Lehman. *The American Musical Theatre: A Consideration.* New York: Macmillan Co., 1967.

———. *Words and Music.* New York: Macmillan Co., 1972.

Ewen, David. *The Life and Death of Tin Pan Alley.* New York: Funk and Wagnalls, 1964.

———. *The Story of America's Musical Theatre.* Philadelphia: Chilton Book Co., 1961.

Farnsworth, Margerie. *The Ziegfeld Follies: A History in Text and Pictures.* New York: Bonanza Books, 1956.

Gaines, Frances Pendleton. *The Southern Plantation: A Study in the Development and the Accuracy of a Tradition.* New York: Columbia University Press, 1925.

Gilbert, Douglas. *American Vaudeville: Its Life and Times.* New York: McGraw-Hill Book Co., 1940.

Gow, Gordon. *Hollywood in the Fifties.* New York: A. S. Barnes and Co., 1971.

Green, Stanley. *The World of Musical Comedy.* Cranbury, N. J.: A. S. Barnes and Co., 1968.

Hartnoll, Phyllis. *Oxford Companion to the Theatre.* London: Oxford University Press, 1967.

Haskell, Arnold. *Ballet.* Baltimore: Morrow, 1951.

182

Higham, Charles, and Greenberg, Joel. *The Celluloid Muse: Hollywood Directors Speak.* New York: New American Library, 1969.

————. *Hollywood in the Forties.* New York: A. S. Barnes and Co., 1968.

Hornstein, Lillian Herlands, Percy, G. D., and Brown, Sterling A. *The Reader's Companion to World Literature.* New York: New American Library, 1964.

Huizinga, J. *Homo Ludens: A Study of the Play Element in Culture.* Boston: Beacon Press, 1950.

Jarvie, I.C. *Movies and Society.* New York: Basic Books Inc., 1970.

Jung, Carl J. "Approaching the Unconscious." *Man and His Symbols.* Edited by Carl C. Jung and after his death, M-L. von Franz. New York: Dell Publishing, 1972.

Kael, Pauline. *Kiss Kiss Bang Bang.* New York: A Bantam Book, 1969.

Kauffmann, Stanley. "The Future of Film: A Symposium." *Film 67/68.* New York: Simon and Schuster, 1968.

————. *A World on Film: Criticism and Comment.* New York: A Delta Book, 1967.

Keen, Sam. *To a Dancing God.* New York: Harper and Row, 1960.

Kobal, John. *Gotta Sing Gotta Dance: A Pictorial History of Film Musicals.* London: Hamlyn, 1970.

Laufe, Abe. *Broadway's Greatest Musicals.* New York: Funk and Wagnalls, 1969.

MacKinlay, Malcom Sterling. *Origin and Development of Light Opera.* London: Hutchinson and Co., Ltd., 1927.

McLean, J. Albert. *American Vaudeville As Ritual.* Lexington: University of Kentucky Press, 1965.

McSpadden, J. Walker. *Light Opera and Musical Comedy.* New York: Thomas Y. Crowell Co., 1936.

McVay, Douglas. *The Musical Film.* New York: A. S. Barnes and Co., 1967.

Milne, Tom. *Rouben Mamoulian.* Bloomington: Indiana University Press, 1969.

Minnelli, Vincente with Hector Arce. *I Remember It Well.* Garden City: Doubleday and Co., 1974.

Sarris, Andrew. *The American Cinema: Directors and Directions 1929-1968.* New York: E. P. Dutton and Co., 1968.

Simon, John. *Movies into Film.* New York: Delta, 1971.

————. *Private Screenings.* New York: Berkley Publishing Corp., 1967.

Sobel, Bernard. *A Pictorial History of Vaudeville.* New York: Citadel Press, 1961.

Springer, John. *All Talking! All Singing! All Dancing!: A Pictorial History of the Movie Musical.* New York: Citadel Press, 1970.

Taylor, John Russell, and Jackson, Arthur. *The Hollywood Musical.* Great Britain: McGraw-Hill Book Co., 1971.

Thrall, William Flint, Hibbard, Addison, and Holman, C. H. *A Handbook to Literature.* New York: Odyssey Press, 1960; revised and enlarged.

Truchaud, Francois. *Minnelli.* Paris: Classiques du Cinema, Editions Universitaires, 1966.

Weinberg, Herman G. *The Lubitsch Touch: A Critical Study.* New York: E. P. Dutton and Co., 1968.

Wilder, Alec. *American Popular Song: The Great Innovators: 1900-1950.* New York: Oxford University Press, 1972.

Wollen, Peter. *Signs and Meaning in the Cinema.* Bloomington: Indiana University Press, 1969.

Zeidman, Irving. *The American Burlesque Show.* New York: Hawthorn Books, 1967.

ARTICLES

Anderson, Lindsay. "Minnelli, Kelly, and *An American in Paris.*" *Sequence,* XIV (1952), 36-38.

"At Home Abroad." *The Boston Globe,* September 4, 1938.

Atkinson, Brooks. "Ziegfeld Follies of '36." *The New York Times,* January 31, 1936.

Bitsch, Charles, and Domarchi, Jean. "Entretien avec Vincente Minnelli." *Cahiers du cinema,* No. 74 (August-September, 1957), 4-15.

Boys, Barry. "The Courtship of Eddie's Father." *Movie,* No. 10, (June, 1963), 29-32.

Chaumeton, Etienne. "L'oeuvre de Vincente Minnelli." *Positif,* No. 12 (November-December, 1954), 36-45.

Currier, Jesse J. "Producer." *The Enquirer Delaware Ohio,* 1937.

De la Roche, Catherine. "Vincente Minnelli." *Premier Plan Series,* No. 40 (March, 1966).

Diehl, Digby. "Directors Go to Their Movies: Vincente Minnelli and *Gigi.*" *Action: Directors' Guide of America,* September-October, 1972, 2-10.

Domarchi, Jean, and Douchet, Jean. "Rencontre avec Vincente Minnelli." *Cahiers du cinema,* No. 128 (February, 1962), 3-14.

Durgnat, Raymond. "Film Favorites: *Bells Are Ringing.*" *Film Comment,* IX, No. 2 (March-April, 1973), 46-50.

Ericsson, Peter. "The Pirate." *Sequence,* VI (1948-49), 44-45.

Galling, Dennis Lee. "Vincente Minnelli." *Films in Review,* XV, No. 3 (March, 1964), 129-140.

Greene, Mabel. "Minnelli: A Big Gift to Revue." *The New York Sun,* February 4, 1936.

Grob, Jean. "Vincente Minnelli." *Image et Son,* No. 149 (March, 1962), 12-13.

Hanson, Curtis Lee. "Vincente Minnelli on the Relationship of Style to Content in *The Sandpiper.*" *Cinema,* II, No. 6 (July-August, 1965), 7-8.

Harcourt-Smith, Simon. "Vincente Minnelli." *Sight and Sound,* XXI, No. 3 (January-March, 1952), 115-199.

Henderson, Brian. "The Long Take." *Film Comment,* VII, No. 2 (Summer, 1971), 6-11.

Houghton, Norris. "The Designer Sets the Stage." *Theatre Arts Monthly,* 1937, 783-788.

Houston, Penelope. "Interview with John Houseman." *Sight and Sound,* XXXI, No. 4 (Autumn, 1962), 160-165.

Johnson, Albert. "The Films of Vincente Minnelli: Part I and Part II." *Film Quarterly,* XII, No. 2 (Winter, 1958), 21-35, and XII, No. 3 (Spring, 1959), 32-42.

Jones, Tom. "For People Who Hate Musicals." *The New York Times Arts and Leisure,* May 30, 1965.

Kael, Pauline. "A Bagel with a Bite Out of It," in "The Current Cinema." *The New Yorker,* November 13, 1971, 133-139.

Lambert, Gavin. "The Band Wagon." *Sight and Sound,* XXIII, No. 3 (1954), 142-143.

Laurents, Arthur. "Look, Girls, There's the Man with Our Tap Shoes!" *The New York Times Magazine,* Part 2, September 11, 1966, 42-43, 48-50.

McVay, Douglas. "The Magic of Minnelli." *Films and Filming,* June, 1959, 11, 31, 34.

Mayersberg, Paul. "The Testament of Vincente Minnelli." *Movie,* No. 3 (October, 1963), 10-13.

Minnelli, Vincente. "The Rise and Fall of the Musical." *Films and Filming,* January, 1962, 9.

Murray, William. "The Return of Busby Berkeley." *The New York Times Magazine,* March 2, 1969, Sec. 6, Part I, pp. 26-27, 46, 48, 50, 52, 54, 56.

"Prodigy." *The New Yorker,* October 12, 1935.

Serebrinsky, Ernesto, and Garaycochea, Oscar. "Vincente Minnelli Interviewed in Argentina." *Movie,* No. 10 (June, 1963), 23-28.

Shivas, Mark. "Minnelli's Method." *Movie,* No. 1 (June, 1962), 17-24.

Singer, Jerome. "The Importance of Daydreaming." *Psychology Today,* I, No. 11 (April, 1968).

Siegel, Joel. "The Pirate." *Film Heritage,* VII, No. 1 (Fall, 1971), 21-31.

Torok, Jean-Paul, and Quincey, Jacques. "Vincente Minnelli ou le peintre de la vie rêvée." *Positif,* Nos. 50, 51, 52 (March, 1963), 54-74.

Tranchant, Francois. "Invitation à la danse." *Image et Son,* No. 108 (1958-1959), 4-10.

Troy, Hugh. "Never Had a Lesson." *Esquire,* June, 1937, 99, 138, 141.

Vaughan, David. "Gigi." *Sight and Sound,* XXVIII, No. 2 (Spring, 1958), 90-91.

Wallace, Philip Hope. "An American in Paris." *Sight and Sound,* XXI, No. 2 (October-December, 1951), 77-78.

"Ziegfeld Girls Had Their Day." *The Pittsburgh Pa. Post,* December 12, 1936.

UNPUBLISHED MATERIAL

Personal interview with Vincente Minnelli, February 7, 1973.

INDEX

189